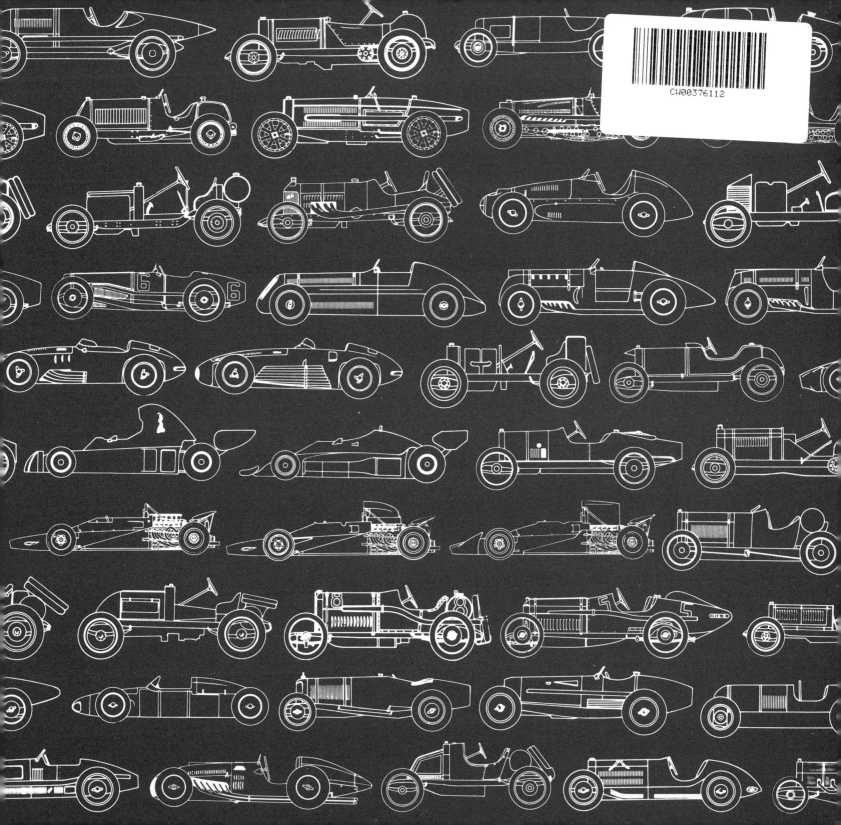

CW00376112

BLUE BLOOD

BLUE BLOOD

A History of Grand Prix Racing Cars in France

SERGE BELLU

Translated by John V. Bolster

FREDERICK WARNE

Also in Warne's Transport Library

French Cars 1920–25 by Pierre Dumont

First published in Great Britain by Frederick Warne (Publishers) Ltd London 1979

Published in the USA by Frederick Warne & Co. Inc., New York 1979

Library of Congress Catalog Number: 79-88580

Copyright © Editions E.P.A. 1978

English translation copyright © Frederick Warne (Publishers) Ltd 1979

First published in France under the title *Le Sang Bleu* by collection bibliothèque e.p.a.

ISBN 0 7232 2263 0

Printed in Great Britain by BAS Printers Limited, Over Wallop, Hampshire

0208.579

To Chantal

CONTENTS

FOREWORD

Blue blood runs in aristocratic veins.

Grand Prix cars are endowed with such veins. These cars are the highest level of development in motor racing, and indeed in the whole field of motor engineering. For the sake of these cars advanced techniques have been researched to the utmost degree, and the cars have been the catalyst for many important innovations. Here is one field of activity in which it can be claimed that men have realized perfection in both form and function: sometimes they have achieved even more – they have entered the realm of fine art.

The blue blood with which we are concerned in French racing cars is of a very special kind. It has known failure and adversity, even total catastrophe, but it is remarkable for the sheer perseverance with which its devotees worked through to triumph in the end.

Since the last war Formula 1 has supplanted the more noble title Grand Prix. To fix the boundaries of the present work, we have begun with the earliest Grand Prix, which took place in 1906 at Le Mans under the auspices of the Automobile Club de France, and which replaced the Gordon-Bennett Cup. Even at that remote date motor sport already possessed a past in the form of the town-to-town races, which had been organized since 1894.

Through its seventy years of evolution, Grand Prix racing has been affected by two great forces. One is the pursuit of perfection in all aspects of motor racing; and the other has always been the furtherance of powerful interests and ambitions – national ones up to the Second World War, commercial ones since then.

These forces found expression in the intricate handiwork of a small number of men. From the engineer to the aerodynamicist, from the mechanic to the driver, such men belong to a community of their own. Sporting men, scientists, artists and craftsmen, they share a common enthusiasm. This book is about the people who made and drove France's racing cars.

43 RACING SEASONS

N°22 E Montaut

ONE HOT SUMMER MORNING

1906

It is Tuesday 26 June 1906. Six o'clock in the morning. Fernand Gabriel has begun the history of Grand Prix racing at the wheel of his Lorraine-Dietrich. The morning is still cool, for even in summertime the countryside of the Sarthe shivers in the early hours of the day.

The engine of the winning Renault: four cylinders in two blocks of two

1906	
ACF Grand Prix Le Mans, 26/6	
1	RENAULT Szicz
2	CLÉM. BAYARD Clément
3	FIAT Nazzaro
4	HOTCHKISS Shepard
5	BRASIER Barillier

Every 45 seconds, one of the 32 competitors is released into the noise and fury. The circuit, situated close to Le Mans, forms a triangle with the points close to la Ferté-Bernard, la Fourche d'Auvours, and Saint-Calais: 103 kilometres (64 miles) of roads so straight that they go over the hills instead of round them. The layout borrows some ancient earth tracks which have been tarred specially for the race. In one area, the road has been improvised across fields with an artificial track of wooden boards.

A colossal feat of organization has been achieved by the Automobile Club de l'Ouest, at the bidding of the ACF. Grandstands and a scoreboard have been installed for the public, and for the officials a service of timekeepers and telephones is operating.

The race will be run in daylight only, on two successive days, and it is open to all manufacturers, with a limit of three cars per firm, at an entry fee of Frs 5000 per team. There is only one regulation affecting the design of the cars: the weight limited to one tonne, with an extra 7 kg for magneto ignition.

The true severity of these regulations is to become apparent during the race: all repairs, including tyre changes, must be carried out by the driver and his riding mechanic – and by them alone.

Victory for detachable rims

Early in the day the sun covers the landscape with a heat haze. The asphalt melts and trickles as the cars race over it. The men struggle to control these unstable vehicles on their large, fragile wheels. Unbalanced and out of proportion, these cars are an awkward marriage of enormous engines and light chassis. The intense heat and sharp stones rapidly destroy the rubber of the tyres. At Pont-de-Gennes, in the pits, drivers and mechanics leap from their seats: they cut off the tyres with knives, tear away pieces of rubber melted into the rims, lever on new tyres and tubes, pump them up, then restart – by hand cranking – their gigantic engines. The thermometer reads 35 C . . . With conventional wheels, this exhausting operation demands fifteen minutes of intense effort but the Renault, Fiat, and Itala teams have Michelin detachable rims, which allow a tyre change to be made in two minutes without any effort. The spare rims are already fitted with fully inflated tyres and they are simply placed on the wheels and secured with eight nuts. Thanks to this decisive advantage, Szicz on the Renault and Nazzaro on the Fiat lead the race, while the fast Brasiers, which enlivened the first hours, have lost a lot of time in the pits.

Night falls on the circuit of the Sarthe; a searchlight's spying eye travels ceaselessly around the locked parking area where the beasts sleep.

Early in the day: Ferenc Szicz preparing for the start of the 12-hour race. It was the first ever Grand Prix motor race

Fast tyre-changing using detachable rims was the key to Renault's victory in the 1906 Grand Prix of the ACF

13

Grégoire entered the smallest car in the 1906 Grand Prix. All the same, it had a capacity of 7.4 litres

Duray at the wheel of a Lorraine-Dietrich with chain drive

Monsters in the land of men

At dawn on the second day, the 17 remaining competitors again take up the chase. Thanks to his lead of 26 minutes accumulated the previous day, Szicz gains the victory at an average of 101 km/h (62.8 mph). He has covered 1240 kilometres (770.5 miles) in a little more than twelve hours. Felice Nazzaro finishes a good second after closing up on the leader during the second day.

Nobody applauds the victors: the grandstand seats are deserted under the sun and empty of their tired public.

His features heavy with fatigue, soaked with sweat, hammered by lumps of tar, Ferenc Szicz has placed his name at the head of the honours list of the history of Grands Prix. The favourite mechanic of Louis Renault, this shy Hungarian is employed both as a foreman and as first driver at Billancourt. His experience, his courage and endurance have made the Renault victory more of a human than a technical achievement.

The prestige event

The Chevalier René de Knyff, the Count de Voguë, and Quinones de Leon had succeeded in assembling a magnificent entry for this first Grand Prix, the race that took the place of the Gordon-Bennett.

Ten French firms had entered, though only nine actually started, *Vulpès* having forfeited their entry fee. From a technical point of view, uniformity was the rule; all the cars had a broadly similar architecture. The engines were of four cylinders, with capacities ranging from 7.4 litres to 18 litres. They were slow-running engines which could scarcely exceed 1300 rpm, with a specific output under 10 bhp per litre. The only area where there was no unanimity was in the transmission. Renault, Clement-Bayard, Hotchkiss, Panhard et Levassor, Darracq and Grégoire had shaft drive, while Gobron-Brillié, Brasier, Lorraine-Dietrich and Vulpès remained faithful to the chain. They were rewarded by reduced unsprung weight at the rear and consequently less tyre wear.

The victorious *Renault* did not stand out from its rivals by any advanced technical features. On the contrary, compared with the Gordon-Bennett car of 1905 from the same firm, it marked a definite step backwards in the fields of aerodynamics, chassis structure, and the position of the centre of gravity. The strength of the Renault lay in its relative stability and above all its rugged construction, a paramount quality in such a long ordeal.

Panhard et Levassor were the real monsters. Their cylinder capacity reached 18 litres which gave them a quite considerable power output of 130 bhp . . . quite considerable, that is, when compared with the 105 bhp of the Renault.

Albert Clément, the manufacturers's son, holds his 'monster' through Conerré corner. Michelin and Dunlop are already advertised side by side on the hoardings

Hotchkiss — fitted with wire wheels

Darracq — V radiator and wire wheels

At the other end of the scale in terms of horsepower, *Grégoire* entered the 'smallest' car — with a mere 7433 cc.

Most of the cars taking part in 1906 were developed from the Gordon-Bennett models of 1905. This was especially the case with the *Brasier*, which won the last Gordon-Bennett and proved to be one of the most competitive cars in the Grand Prix (it took the lap record).

Paradoxically, the most original car was three years old. The venerable *Gobron-Brillié*, with the ungainliness of a mastodon, could pride itself on having the first tubular chassis. Besides, it was driven by a strange engine with two opposed pistons per cylinder. The only other innovation of this first Grand Prix was the all-metal wheel (with wire spokes) which only *Darracq* and *Hotchkiss* used in the actual race.

And so the dice were cast

The Grand Prix of the ACF had won its first battle: both the public and the competitors had joined in wholeheartedly and in large numbers.

The French manufacturers, who enjoyed a numerical advantage, had only won by a short head and the struggle between Fiat and Renault had given this race, from its very beginnings, an international character that had not been anticipated.

However, only three foreign manufacturers had made the journey to France. They left without the cup, but full of ambition and a desire for revenge. This French Grand Prix had well and truly begun the long history of rivalry between the men and the engineering techniques of all the nations — in the name of sport.

Though it dated from 1903, the Gobron-Brillié was the only car with a multi-tubular chassis frame

10 - A   TESTÈ sur Voiture PANHARD-LEVASSOR

Panhard et Levassor produced the most powerful and most monstrous car of all, with a capacity of 18 litres!

DOWNFALL

1907

The year 1906 had been a first attempt; in the following year's race it was hoped that all the faults of inexperience would be corrected.

The epic contest, spread out over two days, was to take on more reasonable proportions, reducing excessive demands on human endurance. The race was to be completed in a single day, over ten laps of a circuit of 77 kilometres (47.8 miles) situated near Dieppe.

Motobloc's first appearance in a Grand Prix, 1907

1907		
ACF Grand Prix Dieppe, 2/7		
1	FIAT	Nazzaro
2	RENAULT	Szicz
3	BRASIER	Baras
4	LOR. DIETRICH	Gabriel
5	DARRACQ	Rigal

The Grand Prix of the Automobile Club de France, the second to bear that name, was to take place on 2 July 1907.

The biggest novelty in the regulations was for the sake of economy. In 1907 the car was a rare and costly thing. The avowed object of the competition was to popularize the motor car and the best way to interest the public was to emphasize its economy: in other words, to limit fuel consumption. The rules allowed 30 litres of petrol for 100 kilometres (9.41 mpg). Indirectly, it was hoped that this would also put a brake on the increase in the size of engines.

Certainly some of the engines did slim down a little, but the range was still between 5 and 19 litres!

Another development, and by no means the least important, concerned the cosmopolitan nature of the event. After the French domination of 1906, the Grand Prix now opened its doors to all nations: Germany with Mercedes, Italy with Fiat, Britain with Weigel, Belgium with Germain, Switzerland with Dufaux. An American had even crossed the Atlantic with his highly original Christie.

There was an innovation: the cars bore colours to identify their nationality. France was blue, Britain green, Italy red, Germany white, Switzerland red and yellow, Belgium yellow, and the USA was red and white. The nationalism demonstrated by the firms was matched by an international rivalry between the racing events themselves. The Italian Targa Florio became an internationally acclaimed event; Germany created the Kaiserpreis (Emperor's Cup). However, these two races, which were both held in the spring, were run under different formulae from that of the Grand Prix of the ACF. This lack of uniformity made it hard to compete and thus detracted from the prestige value of all three races.

The 1907 race presented Fiat with a chance for revenge. In spite of this the three most dangerous French teams did not show any great inventiveness and arrived with the same models which they had used in 1906.

Having sold their 1906 cars (or at least two of them) *Renault* built straight copies of them, except that the rear suspension was reinforced and detachable rims were fitted to all four wheels instead of only to the rear pair.

Probably underestimating the fuel economy of his vehicle, Szicz had an unnecessary refuelling stop and slowed his pace towards the end of the race. He therefore gave the victory to Felice Nazzaro's Fiat when he actually had 30 litres of petrol left in his tank, while the Italian, a better calculator, finished with only 11 litres left. The other two Renaults were eliminated, Richez overturning on the first lap and Henri Farman retiring on the seventh.

The *Lorraine-Dietrich* of Duray was the fastest car in the Grand Prix but it failed to finish. Gabriel, in fourth place, saved the honour of the firm.

Brasier entered practically the same model as in the

The 1907 Renaults scarcely differed at all from those of 1906. The wings, fitted for practising, were removed for the race

Porthos—unique with its eight-cylinder engine

The Lorraine-Dietrichs were the fastest cars in the 1907 Grand Prix

previous race, with slightly reduced wheelbase and cylinder capacity, but they remained strong competitors, both in speed (Baras was third) and in reliability. The Brasier team was, in fact, the only one to finish complete.

Clément-Bayard suffered a tragedy. During practice Albert, the young son of Adolphe Clément, the manufacturer, took a corner at Saint-Martin-en-Campagne too fast. The car left the road, struck a wood pile, somersaulted, and landed on its wheels. Gauderman, the mechanic, was thrown clear and got up unhurt. But Albert Clément was killed instantly. Three cars came under starter's orders all the same – identical to those of 1906 – driven by Alézy, Garcet, and Shepard.

Panhard et Levassor appeared with completely new cars, which had the radiator behind the engine in the manner of Renault. Their performance was disappointing and of short duration. The three cars of Heath, Leblanc, and Dutemple had all been eliminated by the fifth lap.

Darracq and *Gobron-Brillié* returned with their cars of 1906, while *Corre* and *Motobloc* made a discreet first appearance in Grand Prix racing. *Porthos*, from a Billancourt factory, distinguished themselves by entering a car with eight cylinders in line, which finished in eighth place.

Altogether the French teams put up a good show. Behind Nazzaro's Fiat, eight French cars finished in order. There was an element of chance behind the Fiat victory but it was nevertheless a warning shot. The Grand Prix of the ACF was no longer an exclusive right for French industry; and there were still the Germans, as yet shy in coming forward . . .

And it's the Gobron-Brillié again!

Panhard mounted the radiator next to the scuttle, as on a Renault

CAPITULATION

1908

The wind blew in gusts on the morning of 7 July 1908. The Grand Prix world had once more set up its tents just outside Dieppe; but nervousness prevailed among the French teams. For several weeks, Mercedes had been practising on the circuit. Benz and Opel had also been polishing their arms. As for the French, they were just not ready. They had had to adapt their cars to new regulations.

This time there was no limit on fuel consumption, but the piston area of the engines was restricted. This was brought about by limiting the size of the cylinder bores as follows: four cylinders 155 mm, six cylinders 127.6 mm, eight cylinders 110 mm. Working under those restrictions, the designers had produced new, long-stroke engines.

The minimum weight was fixed at 1100 kg.

Adolphe Clément had received permission from the State Council to change his name to include that of Bayard, so his cars were called Bayard-Clément, known later as *Clément-Bayard*. This firm entered the most modern of the French cars in 1908. Engineer Sabathié had designed a long-stroke engine with an overhead camshaft, operating valves inclined at 45°. With its 135 bhp this engine propelled the Clément-Bayard at 170 km/h (105.6 mph), which made it the only French car that was capable of worrying the Germans. Rigal finished fourth in spite of changing nineteen tyres! Gabriel, winner of the celebrated Paris–Madrid race, finished twelfth while Hautvast retired.

1908	
ACF Grand Prix Dieppe, 7/2	
1	MERCEDES Lautenschlager
2	BENZ Hemery
3	BENZ Hanriot
4	CLEM. BAYARD Rigal
5	MERCEDES Poege

Panhard et Levassor, on the other hand, were less imaginative. Their new car for 1908 reverted to chain transmission and the forward mounted radiator. As for the engine, side-valves remained the order of the day. Although out of date, this unit was reliable and quite powerful, with an output of nearly 120 bhp. The steady race of the Panhards (Heath 9th and Farman 23rd) was unfortunately overshadowed by the fatal accident to one of their drivers, the motorcycling champion Cissac.

Renault had brought along their eternal model, already seen in 1906 and 1907, but this time it was well and truly obsolete. The side-valve engine had merely been modified to come within the bore regulation and the stroke had been slightly lengthened (only to 160 mm). The combustion chambers had been reshaped to obtain better cooling and the detachable rims had a new method

For the 1908 Grand Prix Renault gave his car a new bonnet

Opposite page: *The Italian driver, Minoia, driving a Lorraine-Dietrich*

23

Baras driving a Brasier, almost unchanged since 1905

The new Clément-Bayard was the most brilliant French car in the 1908 Grand Prix

The modern look – the Clément-Bayard engine, with single overhead camshaft

of securing them rapidly from a single point, instead of the previous eight nuts. There the changes ended and Renault were among the last to stick to the cone clutch and three-speed gearbox. The performance of the team, with Caillois, Dimitri and Szicz as drivers, was about all that could be expected from their modest 105 bhp, Dimitri finishing in eighth place, behind all the Germans.

For *Brasier* the race went somewhat similarly, which was to be expected with cars which were virtually of 1905 design and had become thoroughly down-at-heel, with their three-speed gearboxes, cone clutches, and chain drive. Indeed, the three cars, driven by Théry, Baras and Bablot, made no serious impact on the event.

Beter perhaps to overlook the performance of the *Lorraine-Dietrich* team, all of whose cars failed to finish, of *Motobloc* (13th and 14th) and of Mors, still further back. Just a word for the little *Porthos* firm which, with Austin, entered the only six-cylinder cars – without success, however.

The remainder of the 48 cars which started were of French nationality, but very soon they were trailing far behind the three German firms: Benz, Mercedes, and Opel, whose immaculate white coachwork glittered as if to emphasize their superiority. Compared with 1907, the Dieppe circuit had benefited from a certain number of improvements, but only for the public.

New and more vast grandstands dominated the pits while the scoreboard was linked by wireless telegraphy to a transmitter at Mouchy, to indicate the positions at the far side of the circuit.

For the drivers, such efforts were less evident. A coating of tar had recently been poured on the road and the small cars' race, which took place the previous day,

The 1908 Panhard reverted to chain drive

had been sufficient to put the track into a pitiful state for the Grand Prix. As in 1906, the tyres and the drivers' faces suffered atrociously from the missiles that were thrown up.

After a pretty duel with Hémery on a Benz, Christian Lautenschlager, the chief mechanic at the Mercedes works, aged 31, drove to a well-calculated victory that no French firm was able to contest.

Apart from Clément-Bayard, who had been ready by the end of May, the French manufacturers had failed to realize the importance of serious and methodical preparation. However, the competitors from other countries were equally casual, and that goes for the British (Austin and Weigel – the Napier entry was turned down because detachable wheels were not permitted, although this was more an absurdity of the regulations), the Italians (Fiat and Itala), the Belgians (Germain), and the Americans (Thomas).

For the first time the Germans had given a taste of their potential: their great capacity for winning as a result of almost military-style planning and preparation was now revealed.

Garcet in one of the Motoblocs, posing at Dieppe before the race

The Porthos and its infinitely long bonnet

Mors put up a rather mediocre performance at Dieppe

DEATH OF THE TITANS

1912

By midnight of 31 December 1908, just nine competitors had signed the entry lists of the Automobile Club de France. Nine names at the closing date was too few to run a Grand Prix in 1909. It was a boycott that brought international motor racing to an abrupt halt.

Rolland-Pilain – clinging to tradition with its chain drive

The manufacturers had taken fright, and had made their escape from the rat-race of excessive horsepower and monstrosity. Furthermore, the organizers of the Grand Prix were Frenchmen, and the French had suffered two painful defeats, at the hands of Italy in 1907 and Germany in 1908.

Subsequently, during this lull (1909–11) and at various minor races for small cars, some new manufacturers had appeared and had demonstrated the charms of small-capacity engines. Peugeot, Delage, and Bugatti had come up through that school.

In 1912 the ACF once again organized their Grand Prix but, mainly as a consequence of the situation we have just described, a race within the race was also to take place. Organized by the magazine *L'Auto* (predecessor of the present Parisian daily *L'Equipe*), the Coupe de l'Auto was run simultaneously with the Grand Prix of the ACF. The Coupe was open to light cars with capacity limited to three litres. The Grand Prix itself continued to welcome the monsters of unlimited cylinder capacity (only overall width was limited, to 1.75 m or 5 ft 9 in), but it has gone down in history as the Grand Prix of the revival, marked particularly by the advent of Peugeot in top-line competition.

Segregated from its normal production, Peugeot kept a racing department, which was given life by a triumvirate consisting of Georges Boillot, Paul Zuccarelli, and above all the Swiss engineer Ernest Henry.

1912		
ACF Grand Prix 25/6		
1	PEUGEOT	Boillot
2	FIAT	Wagner
3	SUNBEAM	Rigal
4	SUNBEAM	Resta
5	SUNBEAM	Medinger

The Peugeot L-76 was still a 'titan', but it contained many modern technical features

Externally, the big Peugeot L76 was of classic appearance but its engine marked a decisive advance. It was not so much the technical solutions themselves, which had all been tried before one at a time, but the way in which they had been combined to form a coherent modern design. And this was especially the case with the valve gear, which consisted of four inclined valves per cylinder operated by twin overhead camshafts.

Claimed with a splendid optimism to develop 175 bhp, this monobloc engine gave something in the region of 130 to 148 bhp all the same, at the high crankshaft speed of 2200 rpm.

Like the other French cars – except for Grégoire and Th. Schneider – the Peugeots were fitted with Rudge-Whitworth detachable wire wheels, which were now permitted.

In the Grand Prix of the ACF, Peugeot were face to face with Fiat from Italy, of an earlier design but very formidable nevertheless, with Excelsior from Belgium, somewhat eclipsed, and two other French manufacturers.

Rolland-Pilain entered an elegant car with a well-streamlined shape but of old-fashioned mechanical design. It finished eighth behind many of the three-litre cars.

Lorraine-Dietrich, the favourites of many commentators of the epoch, produced an enormous car that was really the ultimate in antique monsters, with chain transmission (like the Rolland-Pilain) and above all a huge engine of 15 litres capacity (against 7.6 litres for the Peugeot and 6.3 litres for the Rolland-Pilain).

La Coupe de l'Auto

Run over two days and still on the Dieppe circuit (twice ten laps of 77 km), the Grand Prix saw the fierce rivalry of the Fiats driven by Bruce-Brown and Wagner and the Peugeot of Boillot. The latter driver was victorious over Wagner, the Fiat representing one of the last bastions of the old school; meanwhile the other Fiat driver, Bruce-Brown, was unfortunately disqualified for taking on petrol away from the pits.

The Lorraine-Dietrich was still a real monster with its capacity of 15 litres

The Côte had a two-stroke engine

The Grégoire had a remarkable transmission giving six speeds

Just behind the great Peugeot and Fiat, Sunbeam placed three 3-litre cars. With that performance, the end of the titans was proclaimed irrevocably.

Numerous French manufacturers were interested in this *voiturette* category, which gave them an opportunity to show their originality.

Théophile Schneider achieved a commendable start in racing, finishing first of the French cars in the Coupe de l'Auto, just behind the three Sunbeams, and in overall seventh place, after the big Excelsior.

The *Sizaire et Naudins* were full of original ideas, including the famous independent front suspension with a transverse leaf spring, a 16-valve engine designed by

29

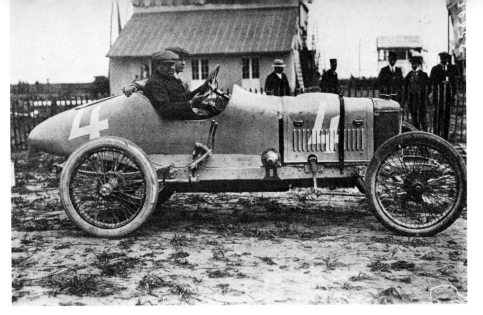

The Alcyon was endowed with a modern 16-valve engine

The Sizaire et Naudins were still original: independent front suspension and 16 valves

engineer Causan, a combined gearbox and rear axle, and a skilfully profiled body. Alas, all these things were not enough to give reliability and the Sizaires disappeared one by one from the race.

Vinot-Deguingand had also made their improvements, streamlining the body by enclosing the spare wheel in the pointed tail.

The *Grégoire* engineers, on the other hand, having tried aerodynamic shells at the Grand Prix de Boulogne in 1911, had reverted to classic lines. The transmission was more original, giving six gears of which two were direct drives, thanks to two propeller shafts.

The *Lion Peugeot* possessed, scaled down, the main characteristics of the big Peugeot (twin camshafts and four valves per cylinder) but it was outpaced by the side-valve Sunbeams and Vauxhalls. It vindicated itself by forecasting the body shape of the next year's Grand Prix Peugeots, and by winning the Grand Prix de France at Le Mans in September.

Finally, *Alcyon* with a 16-valve engine and *Côte* with a two-stroke completed the extremely colourful gallery of French voiturettes, which were fighting at close quarters with the English Sunbeams, Vauxhalls, Singers, Calthorpes, and Arrol-Johnstons and the German Mathis.

Vinot-Deguingand put the spare wheel in a shapely tail to improve the aerodynamics

Unfortunately, three *Hispano-Suizas* designed by Marc Birkigt were not ready in time, and no car of that celebrated make has ever been seen in a Grand Prix.

Distracted by a relentless search for originality, the French had lost the match against British common sense and classicism. But the modern racing car is largely derived from these 'three-litres' of the Coupe de l'Auto. It only remained for the French to put their fertile imagination into a more practical form.

Hispano-Suiza non-started in the Coupe de l'Auto

Th. Schneider recorded France's best performance in the Coupe de l'Auto

31

A SURE WINNER

1913

The Automobile Club de France again radically changed the regulations for its Grand Prix. Fuel consumption once more became the major factor and 20 litres per 100 km (14.12 mpg) was the maximum allowed; cars must weigh between 800 and 1100 kg.

The scene was changed too, the Grand Prix taking place at Amiens on 12 July 1913. The triangular circuit was shorter than those of previous years but it had interesting features, with a long straight of 13 km (8.1 miles), two difficult corners, a hairpin, and a curving road across the valleys.

The struggle was really between Peugeot, Delage, and Sunbeam, with Th. Schneider, Opel, Mathis, Excelsior, and Itala aiming no higher than to finish in a creditable position.

The victory that Peugeot achieved on the Amiens circuit was assisted by luck – both good and bad. At half-distance, Guyot's Delage was leading when a tyre burst. The mechanic leapt from the car while it was still going too fast and his leg was run over and broken, so Guyot had to change the tyre alone and drive his companion carefully back to the pits. During this time, the Peugeots of Boillot and Goux took command, followed by the Sunbeam of Lee Guinness and the Delage of Bablot. In spite of the accident, Guyot finished fifth.

The merit of the Delages was therefore greater than the results of this race would suggest. The big Delage, type Y, was developed by Arthur Michelat from the small 3-litre

1913	
	ACF Grand Prix Amiens, 12/7
1	PEUGEOT Boillot
2	PEUGEOT Goux
3	SUNBEAM Lee Guinness
4	DELAGE Bablot
5	DELAGE Guyot

The Peugeots had Rudge-Whitworth wire wheels with
'knock-on' hub caps. Georges Boillot in the winning car

A Th. Schneider in the Grand Prix de France at Le Mans

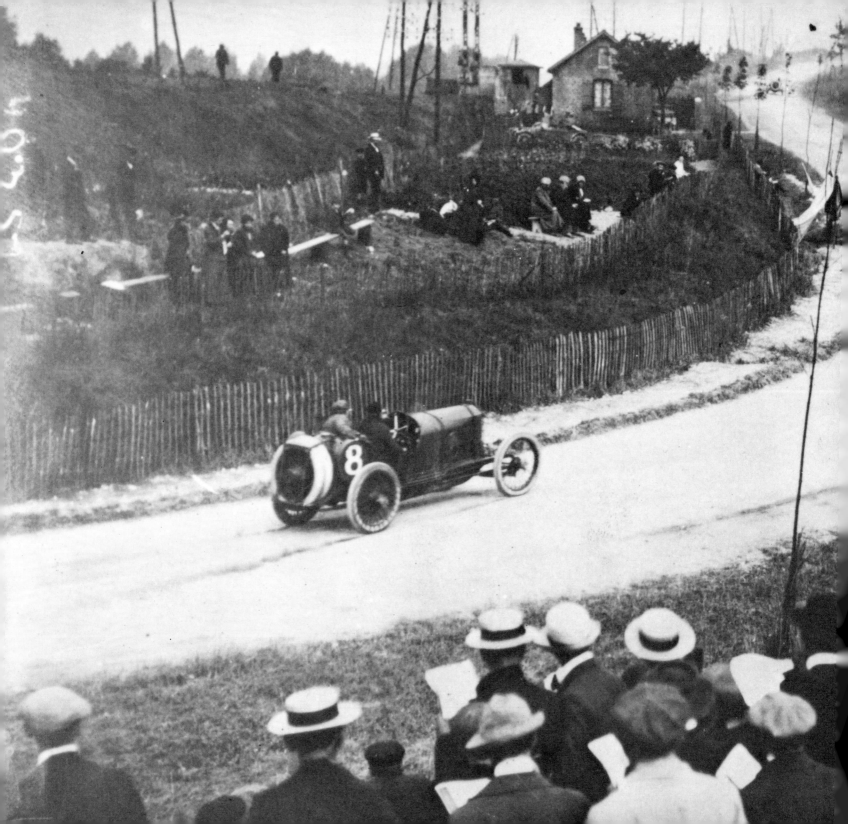

type X of 1911. It was driven by a large engine of 6.2 litres capacity, recognizable by its unusual exhaust manifold, which projected through the top of the bonnet because the valves were horizontal.

Victims of misfortune in the Grand Prix of the ACF, Delage proved their worth by winning the Grand Prix de France at Le Mans in August, and especially by René Thomas' fine victory in the 500 Miles Race at Indianapolis the following year.

For Peugeot, 1913 was a year of transition in spite of their double in the Grand Prix. The car had become slimmer but was still unstreamlined and the engine had been refined, with a capacity reduced from 7.6 litres to 5.6 litres in order to reduce consumption to the region of 18 litres per 100 km. The Peugeot had also been fitted with new 'knock-on' hub caps for more rapid wheel changing and the rear suspension had been modified.

But this Peugeot was still visibly a descendant of the monsters, and the truly modern car made its first appearance in the Coupe de l'Auto, which in 1913 was run separately from the Grand Prix. This was a more compact three-litre of 78 × 156 mm (2980 cc); it developed 90 bhp and was a forerunner of the 4.5 litre cars of 1914.

Guyot in his type Y Delage just before the start of the 1913 Grand Prix of the ACF

On the Amiens circuit, the victorious Peugeot in the Grand Prix of the ACF

35

Bablot's Delage at the French Grand Prix: always tyres to change

The last of the French manufacturers, Th. Schneider, took a somewhat quieter part, but the performance of the team in the Grand Prix of ACF was impressive nevertheless. They won the prize for regularity by taking 7th, 8th, and 10th places and finishing as a complete team. The cars of Théophile Schneider were developed from the standard productions, with side-valve engines, dashboard-located radiators, and wind-cutting bonnets reminiscent of a Renault.

The 1913 season was a tranquil one. The reduced foreign competition placed some emphasis on the performance of the French cars, among which the Delages had certainly shown their potential. This time, the era of the monsters was well and truly past; the Grand Prix story was now open to modern cars.

MODERN TIMES

1914

The summer of 1914 was a hot one . . .

The Grand Prix of the Automobile Club de France was held on 4 July. A week before – 28 June – the Archduke Franz-Ferdinand, heir to the throne of the Austro-Hungarian Empire, and his wife, were assassinated at Sarajevo.

Europe was at boiling point.

Peugeot engine with its twin overhead camshafts

1914	
ACF Grand Prix Lyons, 5/7	
1	MERCEDES Lautenschlager
2	MERCEDES Wagner
3	MERCEDES Salzer
4	PEUGEOT Goux
5	SUNBEAM Resta

In France, hatred of Germany and a fanatical patriotism burned in every citizen, right up to the Head of State. Raymond Poincaré was at the same time President of France and a son of Lorraine, and he had not forgotten 1871.

The Grand Prix took place in this impassioned and patriotic atmosphere. Five nations of Europe confronted each other, but in peace. France and Germany were engaging in a last show of prestige (and intimidation) before the fateful 2 August.

Cosmopolitan

Fourteen manufacturers from six different nations accepted the invitation of the ACF. Germany had chosen Mercedes and Opel, Italy Fiat, Nazzaro, and Aquila Italiana, Britain Sunbeam and Vauxhall, Belgium Nagant, and Switzerland Piccard et Pictet. For her part, France was represented by Peugeot, Delage, Alda, and Th. Schneider. This Grand Prix was therefore the theatre for a veritable international confrontation in which four countries had, in theory, a chance to win the victory.

Peugeot started favourites, by reason of their successes in 1912 and 1913, but Mercedes appeared to be serious rivals, with a formidable reputation and extremely thorough preparation. Mercedes also had the strongest team, with five cars on the starting line when no other firm had more than three. The Vauxhalls were impressive cars with very advanced engines, while Delage and Fiat were counting on their front brakes.

The modern racing car was born in 1914, and henceforth there would be no more monsters. The display put on by the smaller cars in the course of the last few years had sounded the death-knell of those excessively large cars. Technical refinement had taken the place of sheer size; the engine capacity was limited to 4.5 litres (a limit that came back between 1946 and 1960), the weight must not exceed 1100 kg, while the maximum width remained at 1.75 m. Notice the latitude that those few figures gave to the imagination of the engineers.

In fact, they confined themselves to very surprisingly similar solutions. All the engines had four cylinders (except Aquila Italiana), and most of them had at least one overhead camshaft. Transmission by chains had gone, while front brakes appeared on the Fiats, Peugeots, Delages, and Piccard-Pictets. Incidentally, front brakes were an item of great controversy at the time when they first appeared in public on the race track.

Peugeot

With the new regulations, it was imperative to redesign the cars of the preceding years. Engineer Ernest Henry produced a new model which was modern, shapely and 37

1914 Peugeot – sweeping lines give an impression of speed, with the spare wheel let into the tail. Victor Rigal at the wheel

The 1914 Delage was equipped with front-wheel brakes

elegant and anticipated the racing cars of the nineteen-twenties. The tapering body lines were swept into a pointed tail that housed the spare wheel. However, if the aerodynamics had gained, the roadholding was adversely affected by the overhanging weight, causing heavy tyre wear during the race.

The cylinders were cast in a monobloc, like all the cars in the race except the Mercedes (which had separate barrels) and the design again embraced twin overhead camshafts and a long stroke; the dimensions were 92 × 169 mm and only the Vauxhall of Laurance Pomeroy had a relatively short stroke of 140 mm, anticipating modern practice. The Peugeot engine developed 112 bhp at the then high speed of 2800 rpm. This unit of 4.5 litres capacity was built after the 3-litre Lion-Peugeot, and the increase in power was perhaps slightly disappointing as it was not proportional to the enlargement of the swept volume.

Peugeot was one of the four constructors opting for brakes on the front wheels. This equipment at once showed its superiority on the winding course at Lyons and made up to some extent for the roadholding deficiencies.

In a surge of nationalism Peugeot gave up their Pirelli tyres at the last moment in favour of French rubber.

Boillot's mechanic estimating his lead over his pursuers

Delage

Engineer Arthur Michelat had designed the totally new type S for 1914. If its traditional appearance resembled that of earlier Delages, it concealed some important mechanical novelties.

The engine had desmodromic valve operation, the valves being positively closed by the camshafts as well as opened. Delage chose to use Perrot-type front brakes, like their French rivals, Peugeot.

Just before the race, the Delage team showed signs of panic, changing the carburettor settings and altering the valve timing.

Alda

This little firm run by Fernand Charron had few ambitions. The three cars that were entered covered the course, but without attracting much interest. Of classic design, the Alda was the only car with splash lubrication, the others all having circulation under pressure.

Th. Schneider

Coming from the neighbouring Franche-Comté, Théophile Schneider of Besançon brought three cars, of which the sole object was to complete the race.

Confusion opposed to order

The 1914 Grand Prix took place near Lyons around Givors. The circuit was a triangle of 37.65 kilometres (23.4 miles) which concealed within its apparently gentle valleys a variety and a difficulty never before encountered.

The organization of the event could not be criticized for the display of the results or the arrangement of the grandstands. The only bad point, very important to a French public, was the insufficiency of the buffets around the circuit.

On the morning of 4 July the competitors set off to race round 20 laps of this tortuous circuit (about 752 km or 467 miles). Szicz on an Alda started first together with Joerns on a Opel. Every 30 seconds two racing cars left in this way, in front of Edouard Herriot, André Citroën (then Director of Mors), and Chevalier de Knyff, installed in the official stand. From the very first lap, the Mercedes-Peugeot duel exploded. Sailer, on the German car, played the role of hare before Boillot on the Peugeot. Among the second wave Delage, Sunbeam and Fiat were the keenest.

Under its old-fashioned bodywork the Type S Delage concealed some modern engineering features

40 *Georges Boillot driving a splendid race at the wheel of his Peugeot in the Grand Prix of the ACF at Givors*

*Refuelling and wheel changing: Duray's
Delage in the Grand Prix of the ACF*

After a few laps, Boillot was catching up and he found himself in the lead when Sailer wrecked his engine on the sixth lap. Behind Boillot three Germans were gaining ground with obstinacy, endurance, and regularity. All alone in front, Boillot was dropping back with tyre trouble. In the French pits there was some hesitation in the choice of tyres and in six consecutive stops he lost five minutes and 49 seconds.

Behind him, the Germans lapped imperturbably and Lautenschlager, the most regular of them, was looking out for the slightest faltering of the Frenchman.

On the 19th lap that faltering happened, and Boillot had engine trouble; Lautenschlager passed him. On the last lap there was high drama, for in the 'esses' Boillot knelt sobbing with discouragement and fatigue beside his blue racing car. A valve had dropped into the

The Alda, built by Fernand Charron, was conventional except for its cantilever rear springs. Ferenc Szicz is the driver of No 1

cylinder. Was this the cruel uncertainty of sport or the result of imperfect preparation?

Mercedes had won and justly so. Whatever the merits of the Peugeot team, that conclusion was recognized by all honest observers at the 1914 Grand Prix of the ACF. Military discipline, seriousness raised to an unquestionable principle, attention to detail right down to the most childish whim – these were the marks of Teutonic preparedness; they prevailed over Latin caprice, good humour and abandonment to the risks of chance. Even before the race began the disorder of the French had set the tone and betrayed their weakness.

Technically however, Peugeot appeared to be at least as advanced as Mercedes, with the exception of the quality of the tyres; for the German team this did not matter so much, as they had less weight to carry.

Charles Faroux later admitted in an article he wrote, 'we were not beaten by superiority of technique, but by the inferiority of our own preparation, organization, and discipline.'

Théophile Schneider's cars were more reliable than rapid 43

THE LEGACY OF WAR

1921

The 500 Miles Race at Indianapolis had already restarted in 1919. On the other side of the Atlantic, reconstruction in Europe was more painful. Under the Deschanel Government France ran into difficulties of all kinds. Financially, the budget deficit grew because the country was relying on the payment of war reparations by Germany. Economically and socially, strikes were spreading despite the tensions that had shattered the unity of the trades unions.

However, in the middle of 1920, the Automobile Club de France decided to hold the Grand Prix during the following year. After Lyons and Strasbourg had been investigated, the Le Mans circuit was chosen; so it fell to the Automobile Club de l'Ouest to organize the Grand Prix.

As for the regulations, these were ready made. Since 1920 the American racing cars had been subject to a three-litre limit with a minimum weight of 800 kg, and France followed their lead.

Only a few competitors accepted the invitation of the ACF. In France, Ballot were at the top of the list, fortified by experience gained at Indianapolis since 1919. The Mathis firm had become French on the annexation of Alsace, and they entered a little car of only 1500 cc, while Italy was represented by Fiat. The Franco-British combine, Sunbeam-Talbot-Darracq, promised to make a massive contribution to the number of competitors. Finally, justifying the policy of adopting the American regulations, Duesenberg agreed to cross the Atlantic.

Standardization

Without any consultation, the manufacturers had arrived at the same technical conclusions and the Grand Prix cars of 1921 had many points in common. All of them had adopted straight-eight engines with overhead camshafts. They also preferred coil ignition, only Ballot remaining faithful to the magneto. Four-wheel brakes

1921		
	ACF Le Mans, 26/7	**ITALY** Brescia, 4/9
1	DUESENBERG Murphy	BALLOT 3 l Goux
2	BALLOT 3 l de Palma	BALLOT 3 l Chassagne
3	BALLOT 2 LS Goux	FIAT Wagner
4	DUESENBERG Dubonnet	
5	TALBOT 3 l Boillot	

The French Talbot-Darracqs differed from their British Talbot and Sunbeam sisters only in having pointed tails

and Rudge Whitworth centre-locking wire wheels were also universal.

Of the two French entrants, Ernest Ballot had evidently achieved a comfortable technical advantage. This manufacturer of proprietary engines had acquired the services of Ernest Henry at the end of the war, which explains the unmistakable family resemblance of his cars to the racing Peugeots of 1914. The engine of the three-litre Ballot, built for Indianapolis in 1920, had twin overhead camshafts and four valves per cylinder. Light alloys were used extensively, and the brakes employed a mechanical servo of Hispano-Suiza type. Only the Duesenbergs had hydraulic brakes.

Opposite page: *3-litre Ballot — an unmistakable family resemblance to the Peugeot of 1914. Both originated on the drawing board of Ernest Henry*

A 2-litre type 2 LS completed the Ballot team at the 1921 Grand Prix of the ACF

The engine greatly resembled that of the Ballot, with its twin camshafts and four valves per cylinder; the imitation even went as far as the bore and stroke dimensions. The power output was also comparable at around 110 bhp, but the ignition was by coil and the mixture came from Zenith carburettors of a new type.

Unfortunately preparation of the Talbots was seriously retarded by strikes and the team had to start in the Grand Prix when far from ready, while the Sunbeams non-started.

An international season

The first international race of the season was Indianapolis. Duesenberg, Sunbeam and Ballot met for the first time, but they were all beaten by a Frontenac entered by Louis Chevrolet.

In France, a team of four Duesenbergs made a great impression when they appeared on the Le Mans circuit. After several laps, however, Chassagne's Ballot was in the lead, exciting the hopes of the French spectators. Suddenly, the blue car failed to appear – a stone had penetrated the petrol tank.

The surface of the road had got worse and worse as the race went on, with more and more of the sand being thrown off and leaving nothing to protect the cars from the sharp edges of the stones.

Murphy, relieved of the French pressure, was able to nurse his Duesenberg. He won a logical, relentless, and well-merited victory. His car was the most powerful and the lightest, and it had the best brakes.

In the month of September Italy, or more exactly the circuit of Brescia, welcomed the first Grand Prix to take place outside France. This international beginning was modest indeed, for there were only six cars on the starting grid: three Fiats and three Ballots.

The French team, more accustomed to modern racing techniques, prevailed with some ease.

One often reflects with nostalgia upon that 1921 season, when the Americans came to measure themselves against the Europeans with all their strength and sportsmanship. It is a pity that the European regulations have not encouraged their participation more often.

The Ballot firm also prepared a two-litre, four-cylinder machine, of broadly similar design to the straight-eights, to gain experience applicable to a production sports car.

Louis Coatalen had united Sunbeam, the British Talbot, and the French Talbot-Darracq under a single banner. The three-litre cars were intended to race in 1921 as three different makes, but they were virtually identical apart from some body details. The Talbot-Darracq differed from its British sister in having a streamlined tail.

FRENCH CARS AND THEIR RIVALS						
BALLOT 2 LS	4 cyl	1995 cc	(69.9 × 130 mm)	88 bhp at 5000 rpm	750 kg	160 km/h
BALLOT 3 L	8 cyl	2973 cc	(65 × 112 mm)	107 bhp at 3800 rpm	780 kg	180 km/h
TALBOT DARRACQ	8 cyl	2973 cc	(65 × 112 mm)	108 bhp at 4000 rpm	1010 kg	170 km/h
DUESENBERG	8 cyl	2964 cc	(63.5 × 117 mm)	115 bhp at 4225 rpm		170 km/h
FIAT 801	8 cyl	2973 cc	(65 × 112 mm)	120 bhp at 4400 rpm	920 kg	180 km/h
SUNBEAM	8 cyl	2973 cc	(65 × 112 mm)	108 bhp at 4000 rpm	1000 kg	170 km/h
TALBOT	8 cyl	2973 cc	(65 × 112 mm)	108 bhp at 4000 rpm	1000 kg	170 km/h

SOME AERODYNAMIC VENTURES

1922

A Grand Prix formula, both international and durable, was at last introduced in 1922, remaining in force up to 1925, which in itself was a new achievement.

Basically, these new regulations limited the cylinder capacity to two litres, with a minimum weight of 650 kg, a framework within which the engineers, in their quest for variety, found room for engines of four, six, eight, or even twelve cylinders. But a new preoccupation was exciting their imagination: aerodynamics. Research in this area had been rather modest until then, but suddenly portfolios of drawings began to appear with preposterous shapes, a response to the contemporary taste for futurism.

Ballot had thus produced a strange fuselage of circular section, wide enough at the nose to house the spare wheel, tapering to a point at the rear. This dreadful body contained some very well-known machinery, in fact exactly the same as in the type 2LS two-litre car of 1920. The Ballots driven in the Grand Prix of the ACF by Masetti, Goux, and Foresti were nominally private entries, because the Ballot firm had officially given up racing to concentrate on the production of touring cars (these incidentally were very obviously derived from the racing machines).

The Grand Prix of the ACF, run at Strasbourg for sentimental reasons that can well be imagined, saw the first appearance of Bugatti in this type of racing.

Ballot, driven by Jules Goux

1922		
	ACF Strasbourg, 18/7	**ITALY** Monza, 10/9
1	FIAT Nazzaro	FIAT Bordino
2	BUGATTI De Viscaya	FIAT Nazzaro
3	BUGATTI Marco	BUGATTI de Viscaya
4		
5		

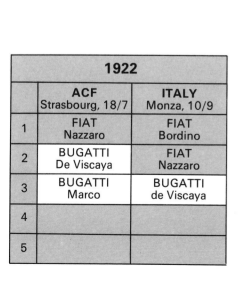

Coming from nearby Molsheim, Ettore Bugatti brought along four eight-cylinder type 30 cars. Built on a chassis derived from the type 22 Brescia, this very first Grand Prix Bugatti had several details that have continued since then in every generation of Bugattis. The rear suspension by reversed quarter-elliptic springs, the wheelbase-track ratio, the single-camshaft engine with three valves per cylinder, were all trade-marks of the thoroughbreds designed by 'le Patron'.

Among the oddities of this particular Bugatti were a double drag-link with leather joints and a mixed brake linkage, hydraulic in front and mechanical behind. For the Grand Prix of the ACF, the Bugatti had been hurriedly modified at the request of Pierre de Vizcaya, with a radiator cowl like that of the Ballot. For the Italian Grand Prix the horseshoe-shaped radiator was again exposed, but the tapering tail, with the exhaust discharging through the point, was retained for the rest of the season.

When Albert Guyot joined the Rolland-Pilain team, having once driven for Duesenberg in 1921, the design of the cars from the old Tours firm was bound to be affected. In particular, the steering was moved to the left and hydraulic front brakes were installed under Duesenberg license. The engine, designed by Grillot, was a good-looking monobloc straight-eight, with five main bearings and magnesium-alloy pistons. The body showed no

The type 30 Bugatti had a cowl fitted over its radiator for the Grand Prix of the ACF

Then, for the Italian Grand Prix, the Bugatti lost its streamlined cowl. It arrived at Monza by road, loaded with luggage

49

The Rolland-Pilain retained classic lines in the bodywork but it had the advantage of a low centre of gravity

aerodynamic excesses but it had a very low centre of gravity, a point neglected by Ballot and Bugatti.

Sadly to say the Rolland-Pilains, beautiful and sophisticated, driven by those veterans Hémery and Wagner and also by Guyot, proved fragile in the race.

The race itself was run on 15 July on a circuit of 13.4 km, passing by Entzheim, Duttelnheim and Innenheim. All the competitors were started together at 8.18, which allowed the spectators to follow the race more easily. Unhappily for them, Nazzaro's Fiat took the lead from the first lap ahead of Friedrich (Bugatti), Guyot (Rolland-Pilain), and Goux (Ballot). Soon the three Fiats were demonstrating the superiority of their 95 bhp engines. Pietro Bordino, Felice Nazzaro and his nephew Biagio

Nazzaro, dominated the race. Then in an awful moment Biagio went off the road and was killed outright. Felice knew nothing of this, taking the lead and winning his second Grand Prix, fifteen years after his first success of 1907. It was a tragic victory, for he was told of his nephew's death as he got out of his car.

In September the Italian Grand Prix was held on the new autodrome at Monza. The three Fiats came to issue their challenge again, backed by their even greater power output of 112 bhp at 5000 rpm. But there were no takers apart from two compatriot Diattos, two German Heims, and a solitary Bugatti. The French car came by road, fitted with mudguards and covered in luggage, but its tyres proved unsuitable for the circuit and Fiat merely confirmed their technical superiority. So this Italian firm won a second victory, to the applause of its own supporters, a few mutterings from the French, and total disinterest from the other nations.

FRENCH CARS AND THEIR RIVALS						
BALLOT 2 LS	4 cyl	1995 cc	(69.9 × 130 mm)	90 bhp at 5000 rpm	830 kg	170 km/h
BUGATTI T-30	8 cyl	1989 cc	(60 × 88 mm)	86 bhp at 4000 rpm	730 kg	160 km/h
ROLLAND PILAIN	8 cyl	1982 cc	(59.2 × 90 mm)	90 bhp	700 kg	160 km/h
ASTON MARTIN GP	4 cyl	1485 cc	(65 × 112 mm)	55 bhp at 4500 rpm	660 kg	140 km/h
DIATTO	4 cyl	1997 cc	(79.7 × 100 mm)	75 bhp at 4500 rpm	700 kg	150 km/h
FIAT 804	6 cyl	1991 cc	(65 × 100 mm)	112 bhp at 5000 rpm	660 kg	175 km/h
HEIM	6 cyl	1995 cc	(63.5 × 105 mm)	80 bhp at 4300 rpm		155 km/h
SUNBEAM	4 cyl	1975 cc	(68 × 136 mm)	88 bhp at 4500 rpm	700 kg	160 km/h

GENIUS MEETS GENIUS

1923

Very few men in the history of an industry, a technology or a sport have emerged from their own specialized field to take a place among the ranks of the truly great. Of such uncommon men the automobile world has known only a handful. Ettore Bugatti and Gabriel Voisin are among them: two individuals, so different yet resembling each other, contradictory yet driven by the same passion.

The Bugatti tank had a streamlined, all-enveloping body, which contributed to the rigidity of the punt-type chassis

The meeting of these two at the Grand Prix of the ACF in 1923 threw that whole sporting season into a different dimension altogether, both in a technical and a human sense; and practically eclipsed the whole vast range of labour and inspiration provided by all the other manufacturers.

Gabriel Voisin – contentious

Unconventional, tempestuous and a loner, Gabriel Voisin (born 5 February 1880, died 25 December 1973) would accept no compromise, no half-way solutions. After one of his biplanes had become the first to fly a kilometre closed circuit, Gabriel Voisin gave up aeroplanes at a period when that industry was 'slipping through the fingers of clever idiots'. Impetuously, he applied his ideas to cars, his early experience in aeronautics giving its character to his work. In 1922 he took up motor racing and won the Grand Prix du Tourisme at Strasbourg.

When everybody expected him to repeat the performance in 1923, Gabriel Voisin decided to take on the supreme challenge, the Grand Prix itself, driven by a continuous urge to cause a stir.

In six months he created a unique car, with the help of André Lefèvre, who was later one of the brains behind the front-drive Citroën. Gabriel Voisin's car borrowed the front axle of his C5 and had an engine that bore some relationship to that of his four-cylinder C4. It was stretched to six cylinders with an aluminium block and it embodied Knight-type sleeve valves; it had a high compression ratio and extra cooling for racing, the latter assisted by a water pump that actually had a small aircraft-type propeller to drive it, mounted conspicuously ahead of the radiator.

1923		
	ACF Tours, 2/7	**ITALY** Monza, 9/9
1	SUNBEAM Segrave	FIAT Salamano
2	SUNBEAM Divo	FIAT Nazzaro
3	BUGATTI Friedrich	MILLER Murphy
4	SUNBEAM Lee Guinness	BENZ RH Minoia
5	VOISIN Lefèvre	MERCEDES Morner

However, the power output was really insufficient and the 80 bhp of the Voisin could not compete with the 110 bhp of a Sunbeam. It did not matter, for this engineer of genius derived his speed from aerodynamics and light weight.

The structure of the Voisin, called the 'Laboratoire', anticipated monocoque bodies. It was built of sheet aluminium around a wooden framework, reinforced with steel tubes. Very low, it followed an aerodynamic profile directly inspired by the wing of an aircraft. The underside was flat, without any roughness, the wheels were covered with aluminium discs, and the rear ones were recessed into the body. The rear track, reduced to 75 cm (2 ft 5.5 in) avoided the use of a differential and allowed the tail to be kept very narrow. With this body,

the Voisin weighed less than 750 kg and reached nearly 170 km/h (105.6 mph) in spite of its 80 bhp.

Forty years later Gabriel Voisin referred to his own racing in the Grand Prix as a piece of indescribable stupidity!

Ettore Bugatti – aesthete

Ettore Bugatti's whole family was imbued with the arts: sculpture, painting or architecture. Ettore spent his youth between his native Italy and France (he was born in Milan on 15 September 1881 and died at Neuilly on 21 August 1947).

At a young age he opted for France and for things mechanical, but he never denied his Lombard blood and his artistic taste, throughout his life and work. An almost

After the Grand Prix of the ACF, this Bugatti tank was sold to finance the laboratories

maniacal care for beauty governed the creation of all his cars, right up to the extent of paradox itself. Certainly the 'tank', in 1923, was far from beautiful according to the cold tastes of a critic, but there was a kind of mathematical beauty about it, formed by a strange, implacable logic.

The tank appeared to be the end result of a tortuous and complex mental process, with a simple solution. Head-on, it was a perfect rectangle; in profile it was the arc of a circle, drawn with a single flourish of the pencil. The bodywork completely covered the wheels and was built onto a pressed-steel platform with riveted cross-

Opposite page: Very compact, the Bugatti was built on a wheelbase of only two metres

The Voisin 'Laboratoire' had a strange profile, like a section from an aeroplane wing

members. Passing beneath the axles, this platform was only 16 cm (6.3 in) from the ground, which reduced the tendency to stir up the dust.

What was so striking was the compactness of the Bugatti, for with a wheelbase of two metres it was only 3.80 m (12 ft 6 in) long. However, it lost in stability what it had gained in handling, and the drivers complained of the cramped cockpit, in which they suffered from claustrophobia and restricted visibility.

Rivalry

The participation of these two giants must not make us forget the two other French entrants.

During the winter of 1922–23 Delage built an entirely new Grand Prix car, designed by Charles Planchon with the assistance of Albert Lory. Of classic general conception, this Delage 2 LCV created a tremendous sensation because of its superb engine. It was a V12 with cylinders at a 60 degree included angle, having two overhead camshafts per bank, driven from the front of the crankshaft by a cascade of pinions that also served the two magnetos. The duralumin connecting rods had Hoffman roller-bearing big ends. Unsupercharged, the Delage engine really did develop 110 bhp but the car, insufficiently tested, suffered from an overheating problem.

The Delage 2 LCV in its original 1923 version, driven by René Thomas

Rear view of the Voisin, the fuselage entirely covering the very narrow wheel track

54

This failure cost engineer Planchon his job, although he was Louis Delage's cousin.

Rolland-Pilain had made several improvements to their heavy cars from the previous year, but the straight-eight engine was basically the same, while the exhaust had been moved to the other side of the head.

Rolland-Pilain had in their portfolios a six-cylinder cuff-valve engine of 64.8 × 100 mm (1978 cc), but after one had been entered for the Grand Prix of the ACF it was withdrawn and was taken over in 1924 by the Swiss maker Ernest Schmid.

Having won the Spanish Grand Prix at San Sebastian against very little opposition, Rolland-Pilain retired from racing, their appearances in both of these Grands Prix having been marred by retirements.

The Tours Grand Prix

Never had a Grand Prix been so open as the one which took place at Tours in June 1923. To the four French makes listed above must be added the Fiats and the Sunbeams. The latter cars were designed by Vincent Bertarione, one of the authors of the Fiat 804 that won in 1922. But Fiat had a secret weapon: the supercharger, being used for the first time in a Grand Prix. In the end Segrave's Sunbeam was victorious, after the Fiat 805s had demonstrated their speed, far ahead of the French, who had been outclassed. René Thomas in the Delage had been obliged to retire, like the Rolland-Pilains. The single surviving Bugatti, that of Friedrich, finished third in the middle of the Sunbeams and the only Voisin, driven by Lefèvre, was fifth.

At Monza, in the autumn, Fiat again met the Rolland-Pilains and the Voisins and also two newcomers. These were Miller with three type 122 cars, similar to the Indianapolis winner, and Benz with three 'Tropfenwagen' RH, those fantastic cars designed by Hans Nibel,

mid-engined for the first time in history and with the teardrop body shape by Edmund Rumpler. Unhappily, Alfa Romeo withdrew after the fatal accident to Ugo Sivocci and Austro-Daimler stayed away from Monza for similar reasons.

In front of their own public and in possession of the fastest cars, the Fiat team took the first two places, ahead of a redoubtable Miller. It was necessary to come down to seventh place to find the first Frenchman, Guyot, in a Rolland-Pilain.

Thus a magnificent season ended with the first victory for a supercharged engine, one of the richest seasons in technical progress, testing a wide range of different designs against each other.

A Rolland-Pilain won the Spanish Grand Prix but this time, in the Grand Prix of the ACF, it failed to finish

FRENCH CARS AND THEIR RIVALS						
BUGATTI T-30 Tank	8 cyl	1991 cc	(60 × 88 mm)	100 bhp	750 kg	185 km/h
DELAGE 2 LCV	12 cyl	1984 cc	(51.3 × 80 mm)	105 bhp at 6200 rpm	690 kg	180 km/h
ROLLAND PILAIN	8 cyl	1982 cc	(59.2 × 90 mm)	100 bhp	820 kg	175 km/h
VOISIN Laboratoire	6 cyl	1991 cc	(62 × 110 mm)	80 bhp at 4500 rpm	750 kg	170 km/h
ALFA ROMEO P1	6 cyl	1991 cc	(65 × 100 mm)	118 bhp at 5000 rpm	850 kg	185 km/h
AUSTRO DAIMLER ADS IIR	4 cyl	1996 cc	(74 × 116 mm)	90 bhp at 5000 rpm		165 km/h
BENZ RH	6 cyl	1991 cc	(65 × 100 mm)	90 bhp at 5000 rpm	745 kg	175 km/h
FIAT 805	8 cyl	1979 cc	(60 × 87.5 mm)	130 bhp at 5500 rpm	700 kg	190 km/h
MILLER 122	8 cyl	1977 cc	(59.5 × 88.9 mm)	120 bhp at 5000 rpm		185 km/h
SUNBEAM	6 cyl	1988 cc	(67 × 94 mm)	110 bhp at 5000 rpm	670 kg	185 km/h

HONORABLE AMENDS

1924

Still subject to a capacity limit of two litres and a 650 kg minimum weight, the 1924 season marked the birth of one of the most famous Grand Prix cars, the Bugatti type 35.

To get ahead of Fiat and Sunbeam, their new rivals Alfa Romeo, and then those distant adversaries Duesenberg and Miller – not to mention the now reviving Mercedes – the French had created a new wave of cars, all ready to make history.

The Bugatti type 35 was to remain for posterity a symbol of Bugatti's aesthetics, a kind of style that makes itself felt in a very subtle, and altogether timeless way. As much in the harmony of its whole design as in the execution of detail, this car was created as a work of art. Classic lines still permitted a delicacy that was present in every curve: in the pointed tail, in the slim steering linkages, the upright and slightly set-back radiator, the chassis complementing precisely the curves of the body, the forged tubular front axle, the strange cast-aluminium wheels, even in the engine, a perfect parallelepiped, with the marvellous pattern of reflections on the engine-turned surface of the aluminium.

This engine, with its non-detachable cylinder head, was one of the improvements that the type 35 showed over the type 30. It was based on a five-bearing built-up crankshaft, with two ball-races at each end and three sets of rollers.

It retained a single overhead camshaft and three valves per cylinder, a large exhaust and two small inlets, and it

The type 35 Bugatti at the Grand Prix of San Sebastian

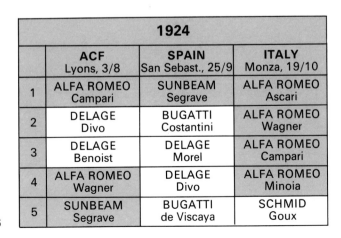

1924		
ACF Lyons, 3/8	**SPAIN** San Sebast., 25/9	**ITALY** Monza, 19/10
1	ALFA ROMEO Campari	SUNBEAM Segrave	ALFA ROMEO Ascari
2	DELAGE Divo	BUGATTI Costantini	ALFA ROMEO Wagner
3	DELAGE Benoist	DELAGE Morel	ALFA ROMEO Campari
4	ALFA ROMEO Wagner	DELAGE Divo	ALFA ROMEO Minoia
5	SUNBEAM Segrave	BUGATTI de Viscaya	SCHMID Goux

The horseshoe radiator, the tubular axle and a thousand other details made the Bugatti a genuine work of art and a legend, despite its rather moderate performance

The aluminium wheels add a special touch of individuality to the type 35 Bugatti. Ettore Bugatti is at the wheel

was without a flywheel. The gearbox was separate from the engine and the multi-disc clutch ran in oil.

The very rigid chassis, braced by the four-point mounting of the engine, possessed the classic Bugatti suspension, with reversed quarter-elliptic rear springs and the front semi-elliptics passing through the tubular axle. For the brake operation, a return had wisely been made to a mechanical system in front, as well as at the rear.

To sum up, the type 35 was a homogeneous, well-balanced machine which, by reason of its road-going qualities – roadholding and handling – could make one forget its lack of horsepower.

However, nothing could cause its defective tyres to be forgotten. Made by Dunlop to a design of Ettore Bugatti, the outer covers came off continually.

At the Delage works, Albert Lory took things in hand after Planchon's departure, while René Thomas organized the racing team. The magnificent design of the V12 engine was touched up here and there, notably as regards

The Bugatti engine: a parallelepiped in engine-turned aluminium

57

Albert Lory modified the design of the Delage for 1924.
The drivers, from left to right, were Benoist, Divo, and
Thomas

the lubrication system, and the speed of revolution went up and up, still without supercharging. The bodywork of the Delage was also modernized and lowered, while a fairing was fitted over the front dumb irons.

The Schmids could be regarded as French in view of their Rolland-Pilain ancestry. However, they were the work of a Swiss, Ernest Schmid, the founder of the SRO ball bearing factory and creator of the 'valveless' engine shown by Peugeot at the 1919 Paris motor show in their 25 hp car. It was precisely by this engine that the cars entered by E. Schmid at San Sebastian, Lyons, and Monza were distinguished. They were 1923 Rolland-Pilains as regards the chassis, but they were fitted with an engine without poppet valves, built in the SRO factory at Annecy. This engine had nothing to do with the Knight type, the ports being controlled by a moving segment and not by sliding sleeves. By an alternating movement, this segment covered and uncovered the inlet and exhaust ports as required, closing both during the compression and firing strokes.

At Lyons and at Monza the Schmids, driven by Goux and Foresti, performed most creditably, especially considering their handicap of excessive weight.

Honourable amends

The French once again used the Lyons circuit on 3 August for the Grand Prix of the ACF, which was also the Grand Prix of Europe that year.

While six type 35 Bugattis arrived by road, one driven by Ettore himself, the rest of the team, the spare parts, and the Bugatti family arrived by train and by lorry in great state.

The superb pale blue cars were impressive, and the Delages also looked formidable, but the foreign entry set themselves a notch higher, Fiat, Sunbeam, and Alfa Romeo all having supercharged engines, which the French had not. In spite of it they defended themselves in fine style, especially Delage, Divo actually finishing second, only one minute 6 seconds behind the uncatchable P2 Alfa Romeo of Campari.

It was their first Grand Prix and the first victory for Alfa Romeo, the start of a brilliant career. Fiat, on the other hand, were leaving the competition world on tiptoe, and gave up altogether in 1927. Struggling with their tyres, the Bugattis finished far behind in 7th and 8th places.

At San Sebastian on 25 September Sunbeam took their revenge and won, ahead of a Bugatti and two Delages, in the absence of Alfa Romeo.

At Monza on 25 October the Alfa Romeos reappeared but Delage and Bugatti remained in their workshops, where they had already started to prepare for 1925. Only Schmid dared to face Alfa and were rewarded with the glory of fifth place. Mercedes awoke from their torpor with a mediocre model, which was christened the Monza type.

In a few months, Alfa Romeo had established their name and the supercharger. Manufacturers wanting to win would in future have to master this technique or give up.

The cuff-valve Schmid was built at Annecy by the Swiss ball bearing manufacturer Ernest Schmid, on a Rolland-Pilain chassis

The front of the Delage chassis was neatly faired in

FRENCH CARS AND THEIR RIVALS						
BUGATTI T-35	8 cyl	1991 cc	(60 × 88 mm)	90 bhp	655 kg	170 km/h
DELAGE 2 LCV	12 cyl	1984 cc	(51.3 × 80 mm)	116 bhp at 8000 rpm	680 kg	185 km/h
SCHMID S.S.	6 cyl	1978 cc	(64.6 × 100 mm)	100 bhp at 5000 rpm	880 kg	180 km/h
ALFA ROMEO P2	8 cyl	1987 cc	(61 × 85 mm)	140 bhp at 5500 rpm	750 kg	200 km/h
FIAT 805	8 cyl	1979 cc	(60 × 87.5 mm)	146 bhp at 5500 rpm	775 kg	200 km/h
MERCEDES MONZA	8 cyl	1980 cc	(61.7 × 82.8 mm)	160 bhp at 7000 rpm	795 kg	215 km/h
MILLER 122	8 cyl	1977 cc	(59.5 × 88.9 mm)	120 bhp at 5000 rpm		185 km/h
SUNBEAM	6 cyl	1988 cc	(67 × 94 mm)	138 bhp at 5500 rpm	790 kg	210 km/h

THE HOPES OF TWO NATIONS

1925

This time, the French understood that to halt the march of the Alfa Romeos it was essential to have recourse to supercharging. Delage at least, because Bugatti still remained handicapped that season by a certain lack of virility.

In 1925 the type 35 Bugatti was still held back by its lack of a supercharger

Since the finish of the Grand Prix of the ACF at Lyons, Delage had been working on the development of their engine and during the winter of 1924–5 it was endowed with two Roots-type superchargers, mounted on the front of the timing case. The power output made a bound up to 205 bhp, giving the Delage a maximum speed around 215 km/h (133.6 mph).

At the same time, a five-speed gearbox was fitted. Externally, the Delage 2 LCV was still further lowered, the bonnet had more vents to assist the cooling and two large exhaust pipes ran the full length of the car. Tyres of greater section gave a squat appearance, promising an aggressiveness of which the Delage was soon to give proof.

On the human side some problems arose and René Thomas was dismissed as team manager, though he continued to drive with Divo, Benoist, Torchy, and Wagner.

Bugatti was content in 1925 to make his type 35 more reliable and to produce copies for customers, but his cars could never equal their rivals without superchargers.

Albert Guyot also defended the colours of France in the Spanish and Italian Grands Prix with his *Guyot-Spéciale*. Like the Franco-Swiss Schmid, it was based on a Rolland-Pilain, which had been fitted with a sleeve-valve engine. In this case, the choice had fallen on a six-cylinder Burt McCollum single-sleeve unit. The Guyot-Spéciale, built at Levallois-Perret, did not leave an imperishable memory after its two discreet appearances.

1925			
BELGIUM Spa, 28/6	**ACF** Montlhéry 28/7	**ITALY** Monza, 6/9	**SPAIN** San Sebast., 19/9
1 ALFA ROMEO Ascari	DELAGE Benoist	ALFA ROMEO Brilli-Péri	DELAGE Divo
2 ALFA ROMEO Campari	DELAGE Wagner	ALFA ROMEO Campari	DELAGE Benoist
3	SUNBEAM Masetti	BUGATTI Costantini	DELAGE Thomas
4	BUGATTI Costantini	DUESENBERG Milton	
5	BUGATTI Goux	ALFA ROMEO de Paolo	

Albert Divo in the Delage 2 LCV, which he drove to victory in the Grand Prix of the ACF in 1925

It was thus upon Delage that all the hopes of French patriotism rested. The first meeting took place at Spa, in Belgium, for the European Grand Prix – but what a disappointment! The Delage team were not really ready and were decimated while Alfa Romeo had a virtual walkover, taking the first two places.

The technicians had to work night and day during the month that separated Spa from the next event, the Grand Prix of the ACF at Montlhéry.

From the start, Antonio Ascari took the lead in an Alfa Romeo P2. Up to the 23rd lap, the Alfas controlled operations and then the accident happened: Ascari left the road and was killed. Campari then led in his Alfa, but when he was told of his team-mate's death at his

For 1925, Albert Lory rebuilt the V12 Delage engine with two Roots superchargers

This Rolland-Pilain chassis was fitted with a Duesenberg engine by Albert Guyot, who also built a sleeve-valve version called Guyot Spéciale

refuelling stop, he retired behind the stands. As a sign of mourning, all the Alfas ceased to race. Behind, there was a struggle between the Sunbeams of Masetti and Segrave and the Delages of Benoist and Wagner. Then Segrave disappeared and Masetti dropped back, leaving the way open for the Delages. Divo, who had replaced Benoist at the wheel of the leading Delage, crossed the finishing line as victor.

Incontestably the withdrawal of the Alfa Romeos took away some of the interest from the first and second places of Delage. However, morally this victory, which rewarded a French car in the national Grand Prix for the first time since 1913, was bound to have repercussions. For the men of the Delage team it was a great encouragement and for their rivals it was a warning.

Although less spectacular, the performance of the Bugattis was not without merit, giving proof of regularity and reliability. Five type 35s started and five finished.

Delage preferred to abstain from the Italian Grand Prix but Bugatti produced some type 35s, reduced to 1500 cc in view of the future formula for 1926. These straight-eights, with dimensions of 52 × 88 mm, differed somewhat from the two-litres, especially in their connecting rods. To these Bugattis and the Guyot-Spéciale, Italy replied with three Alfa Romeos and a Diatto modified by the Maserati brothers. The Englishman, E. A. D. Eldridge, presented one of his streamlined models, with an Anzani engine. Finally, after having won the 500 Miles Race at Indianapolis, Duesenberg made the voyage to Milan.

Brilli-Peri (Alfa Romeo) won the event from his teammate Campari and Costantini's Bugatti.

The last meeting of the season brought Delage and Bugatti to San Sebastian but Alfa Romeo were notable for their absence. The Spanish Grand Prix, the last event run under the two-litre formula, gave a foretaste of what the entries would be like during the next two years. Alfa Romeo subsequently retired from racing, discontented with the change of regulations, and Delage, freed from their most tenacious adversary, had the opportunity to launch into the most sophisticated technical research.

As for Bugatti, these cars began to appear in growing numbers on the starting line at all the races, but they were always seeking their great victory, never finding it.

Sunbeam were in eclipse and were relying on their French sister firm, Talbot.

A great contest was about to begin between the three French firms.

Torchy in the Delage 2 LCV at the Grand Prix of Europe, held at Spa

FRENCH CARS AND THEIR RIVALS						
BUGATTI T-35	8 cyl	1991 cc	(60 × 88 mm)	105 bhp at 5000 rpm	655 kg	175 km/h
DELAGE 2 LCV	12 cyl	1984 cc	(51.3 × 80 mm)	205 bhp at 6500 rpm	720 kg	215 km/h
GUYOT SPÉCIALE	6 cyl	1986 cc	(70 × 86 mm)	125 bhp at 5500 rpm	700 kg	180 km/h
ALFA ROMEO P2	8 cyl	1987 cc	(61 × 85 mm)	155 bhp at 5500 rpm	750 kg	210 km/h
DIATTO	8 cyl	2000 cc		120 bhp		190 km/h
DUESENBERG	8 cyl					
ELDRIDGE	4 cyl	1496 cc	(69 × 100 mm)	80 bhp at 5500 rpm		180 km/h
SUNBEAM	6 cyl	1988 cc	(67 × 94 mm)	150 bhp	750 kg	205 km/h

TECHNICALLY BRILLIANT

1926

The use of the supercharger had catapulted the power of Grand Prix cars towards figures never before attained, beyond 100 bhp per litre. In reducing the maximum capacity to 1500 cc, the organizers intended to put a brake on this debauchery of power. They did not succeed: the three French manufacturers in the arena rivalled each other in technical refinements in a combat which the foreign makes did not wish to join.

As well as the limitation of cylinder capacity (adopted at the same time at Indianapolis), the cars were held to a minimum weight of 700 kg. The era of single-seaters was about to begin, because not only was the presence of a riding mechanic no longer insisted upon, as had been the case in 1925, but the existence of his seat was now optional.

Bugatti had at last adopted the supercharger. It was a Roots compressor, modified by Moglia with three-lobed rotors, which raised the power output to about 110 bhp. Two different engine assemblies were used during the season, one of 60 × 66 mm employing many type 35 parts and the other of 52 × 88 mm with a different design of connecting rod. For the rest, the supercharged 1500 cc Bugatti, called type 39A, followed the characteristics of the type 35 very closely.

Delage, on the contrary, were adopting entirely fresh principles. Albert Lory, then aged 31, had abandoned the design of Planchon to exercise his talents on a completely new straight-eight. Very long, this engine was more 'square' than the V12 with dimensions of 55.8 × 76 mm. The long crankshaft was carried in nine main bearings and the two valves per cylinder were at an included angle of 100°, operated by twin overhead camshafts.

With its two Roots superchargers, the engine of the 15-S-8, fitted with the same five-speed gearbox as the V12, developed 170 bhp at the high crankshaft speed of 8000 rpm. Unhappily, the chassis did not match the high standards of the engine and its lack of rigidity created some roadholding problems. The other object of concern was the location of the exhaust system, which caused overheating of the cockpit and the emission of toxic

The new straight-eight Delage

1926				
ACF Miramas, 27/6	**EUROPE** San Sebast., 18/7	**SPAIN** San Sebastian	**BRITAIN** Brooklands, 7/8	**ITALY** Monza, 5/9
1 BUGATTI Goux	BUGATTI Goux	BUGATTI Costantini	DELAGE Senechal	BUGATTI Sabipa
2 BUGATTI Costantini	DELAGE Morel	BUGATTI Goux	BUGATTI Campbell	BUGATTI Costantini
3	BUGATTI Costantini	DELAGE Wagner	DELAGE Benoist-Dubonnet	
4				
5				

Fitted with a 1500 cc engine, the Bugatti 35 became type 39 A. Here, Costantini is at the wheel in front of the Miramas pits

gases. The drivers suffered burns on their feet and legs from the exhaust manifold, complaining also of sickness, due to the vapour from the benzole, petrol, alcohol, and ether of which the fuel was composed. They had no complaints about the braking system with a Perrot-Piganeau servo.

The return of Talbot

At the beginning of 1926 the Talbot factory at Suresnes was in a state of ferment. It was returning to top-level racing, under the direction of engineer Bertarione, assisted by Becchia. Their engine closely resembled the eight-cylinder Delage, having twin camshafts and two valves per cylinder in hemispherical combustion chambers with single ignition, but it developed 25 bhp less.

If the chassis of the Delage suffered from excessive flexibility, that of the Talbot was a magnificent example of combined lightness and rigidity. Constructed of very deep and liberally pierced side-members, it was also strongly braced transversely. The rear axle, as well as the tubular, two-piece front axle, passed through the side-members. However, both the roadholding and braking proved to be deficient.

Lastly, the engine and transmission were slightly offset to make room for the driver, alongside the propeller shaft.

Thanks to this clever arrangement, which was often copied, the Talbot was very low-built. The chassis was beautifully clothed in body panels of great elegance, from the pointed tail to the radiator cowl which enclosed the dumb irons.

The original Monsieur Violet

Marcel Violet overflowed with new ideas and initiative in that crucible which formed the world of cyclecars. One fine day he wanted to move on so he dreamed up a Grand Prix car. Then he built the engine, a two-stroke because he had mastered that technique; it had four cylinders, horizontally-opposed in pairs, with rotary inlet valves and thermo-syphon cooling. His Grand Prix car was born. Violet, worried about the weight distribution, combined the gearbox with the rear axle. The chassis was a central, tubular backbone, with the engine attached to one end and the gearbox-axle to the other. The front suspension recalled that of the Sizaire Naudin, with the transverse spring mounted very high.

The radiator was placed behind the engine and,

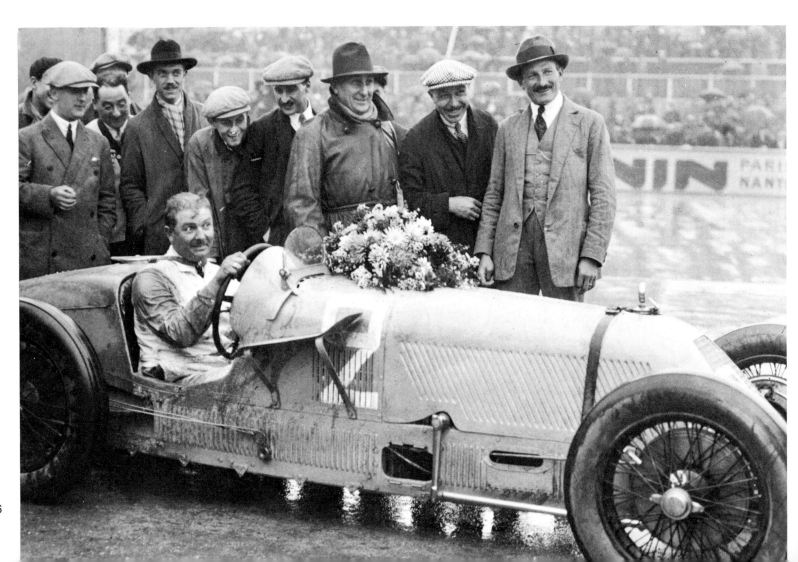

Left: *Albert Divo at Montlhéry, clearly delighted with the performance of his Talbot*

Bertarione designed a new Talbot full of good qualities, but it never attained its real potential

altogether, the Sima-Violet was full of intelligent ideas. Sadly, having run out of money, Violet had to withdraw from the Grand Prix of the ACF, for which he had entered two cars. As the ultra-light Sima-Violet only weighed 500 kg, it would have had to carry a lot of ballast to qualify!

Among the French curiosities of the 1926 season, let us mention the Jean Graf, which was merely a La Perle modified in 1925 to compete in the Grands Prix of Rome (1925) and San Sebastian (1925, 26).

With so much talent and imagination at work in the laboratories, everyone was impatient for the opening of the season, on 27 June, at the new autodrome of Miramas. And nothing happened – one by one the manufacturers withdrew and the Grand Prix of the ACF was a complete fiasco. Three Bugattis, type 39A, were the only starters, and two of them finished – in first and second places.

Serious things began on 18 July on the San Sebastian circuit, where the Grand Prix of Europe took place. Three Delages came face to face with three Bugattis, and here it was seen that their test gallop at Miramas had been useful to the latter team. The Delage drivers found that the heat from the exhaust system was intolerable. Jules Goux won in a Bugatti, in front of a Delage driven successively by Morel, Wagner, Benoist, Thomas, and Sénéchal, taking it in turns to be cooked!

At Brooklands it wasn't so hot and the Delages were a little more at ease. The Bugattis did not cross the Channel

The pierced chassis of the Talbot – a lightweight but very sturdy structure

Talbot engine – an elegant twin-cam straight-eight

Jean Graf modified a La Perle and gave it his name

but Campbell drove a type 39A with the blessing of the importer. The Talbots made their début at the British Grand Prix, of which this was the first. Designed by an Italian, built in France and financed by Englishmen, the Talbots found admirers in all latitudes.

On the British side, Alvis and Thomas were not ready but one Halford and one old Aston Martin started. Initially the Talbots, driven by Divo and Segrave, led the way but the Delages were being saved for the finish. Campbell succeeded in sliding his privately-entered Bugatti between the two Delages driven by Sénéchal-Wagner and Benoist-Dubonnet.

At Monza one hoped to see the completely new Itala 1500 with front-wheel drive, but in vain. Only the type 26 Maseratis, of the model which had won the Targa Florio, gave some opposition to several Bugattis, one of which, driven by Sabipa (alias Charavel), won this pitiful race.

To sum up, whilst the French had had the brief satisfaction of possessing three quite magnificent models, they soon realized that all this clever brainwork had achieved no more than beating the air. It was the fault of the absentees, naturally!

Violet wanted to enter this unusual car in the Grand Prix of the ACF

The Sima-Violet was driven by a two-stroke flat-four engine

FRENCH CARS AND THEIR RIVALS

BUGATTI T-39 A	8 cyl	1495 cc	(52 × 88 mm)	110 bhp	750 kg	185 km/h
		1493 cc	(60 × 66 mm)			
DELAGE 15-S-8	8 cyl	1487 cc	(55.8 × 76 mm)	170 bhp at 8000 rpm	750 kg	200 km/h
SIMA VIOLET	4 cyl	1484 cc	(75 × 84 mm)	60 bhp	700 kg	140 km/h
TALBOT	8 cyl	1488 cc	(56 × 75.5 mm)	145 bhp at 6500 rpm	715 kg	190 km/h
ALVIS	8 cyl	1497 cc	(55 × 78.7 mm)	110 bhp	770 kg	175 km/h
HALFORD	6 cyl	1496 cc	(63 × 80 mm)	96 bhp at 5300 rpm		180 km/h
MASERATI T-26	8 cyl	1493 cc	(60 × 66 mm)	115 bhp at 5300 rpm	720 kg	160 km/h

YEAR OF GLORY

1927

This was a favourable year for France. Led by President Doumergue, the country enjoyed a brief period of euphoria. Prime Minister Poincaré had brought the economy round to a good state of health. Frenchmen could get excited about the exploits of their sports heroes without lack of national confidence.

In motor sport, if the Bugattis were not always very competitive, Delage had come to maturity and was to taste success.

Bugatti in fact marked time and the type 39A could not worry Delage.

It is true that Delage came to the 1927 season very well fitted out. The faults of their 1926 model had been corrected and nothing seemed able to bar the road to the 15-S-8.

The exhaust, which had changed sides, no longer put the drivers in peril. The aerodynamics had been improved by the installation of a sloping radiator cowl that covered the dumb irons. The engine continued to find more horsepower and when a second supercharger was fitted, the power catapulted to 170 bhp, a specific output of 114 bhp per litre. This was in itself a record achievement, and Delage looked invincible.

Talbot seemed unable to match such efforts. Though they had a model that was basically very sound they hardly progressed at all and Talbot abandoned the project after the Grand Prix of the ACF without ever attaining their full potential.

The straight-eight Delage engine had the highest specific power output in 1927

1927			
ACF Montlhéry, 3/7	**SPAIN** San Sebast., 31/7	**ITALY** Monza, 4/9	**BRITAIN** Brooklands, 1/10
1	DELAGE Benoist	DELAGE Benoist	DELAGE Benoist	DELAGE Benoist
2	DELAGE Bourlier	BUGATTI Conelli	OM Morandi	DELAGE Divo
3	DELAGE Morel	DELAGE Bourlier	MILLER Cooper Kreis	DELAGE Bourlier
4	TALBOT Williams		OM Minoïa	BUGATTI Chiron
5				

Just for the record, the Bucciali brothers ran their BUC AB6 at the San Sebastian Grand Prix.

The Grand Prix of the ACF, though not as poor as on the previous year, did not offer a very tempting menu at the Montlhéry autodrome on 3 July. Bugatti having withdrawn, Delage and Talbot grappled with each other in the presence of a solitary Halford; it was total victory for Delage.

The type 39 A Bugattis were beaten by the Delages and Talbots. This is Eyston at the Coupe de la Commission Sportive, Montlhéry

The Talbots never managed to worry the Delages

At the Spanish Grand Prix the official Bugattis gave the Delages a very fair fight, but the fortunes of the race turned towards Robert Benoist (Delage), in front of Conelli (Bugatti).

At Monza there were no Bugattis and a Delage won, ahead of an OM and a Miller. On the same day as the Italian Grand Prix, 4 September, and on the same circuit, an all-comers race was run under the curious title of the Grand Prix of Milan. It was in this not very serious event that Fiat decided to give a discreet demonstration of their new type 806, with two parallel six-cylinder blocks, which actually complied with the 1500 cc formula.

The last Grand Prix of the season, which took place at the Brooklands track, crowned the year for Delage, who took all three places against a pack of Bugattis, the astonishing Thomas 'Flatiron', and the interesting front-drive Alvis.

Delage were decidedly unbeatable in the 1927 season, and the name of Robert Benoist, proclaimed World Champion, was inscribed in the golden book of French sport, beside those of the four tennis stars, Cochet, Brugnon, Borotra, and Lacoste, who had just taken away the Davis Cup from the Americans in August.

But with this success a period of technical prowess came to an end. Talbot sold their cars to an Italian team, and Delage gave up racing. Ettore Bugatti alone remained, competing with his own customers. Grand Prix racing was changing, and it was also entering the trough of a wave.

The BUC AB 6 was nicknamed 'the torpedo', more for its shape than its performance

With his 1500, Delage had a car that could win a driver the World Championship

Refuelling Sénéchal's Delage at the Grand Prix of the ACF

FRENCH CARS AND THEIR RIVALS

BUC AB-6	6 cyl	1490 cc	(61 × 85 mm)	70 bhp at 5000 rpm	800 kg	170 km/h
BUGATTI T-39 A	8 cyl	1492 cc	(60 × 66 mm)	120 bhp at 5500 rpm	750 kg	185 km/h
DELAGE 15-S-8	8 cyl	1487 cc	(55.8 × 76 mm)	177 bhp at 8000 rpm	760 kg	205 km/h
TALBOT	8 cyl	1488 cc	(56 × 75.5 mm)	150 bhp at 7000 rpm	700 kg	200 km/h
ALVIS	8 cyl	1497 cc	(55 × 78.5 mm)	125 bhp	770 kg	190 km/h
FIAT 806	12 cyl	1484 cc	(50 × 63 mm)	175 bhp at 7500 rpm	700 kg	220 km/h
DUESENBERG	8 cyl	1475 cc	(55.5 × 76.2 mm)			
HALFORD	6 cyl	1496 cc	(63 × 80 mm)	100 bhp		180 km/h
MASERATI T-26	8 cyl	1493 cc	(60 × 66 mm)	115 bhp at 5300 rpm	720 kg	160 km/h
MILLER 91	8 cyl	1475 cc	(55.5 × 76.2 mm)	154 bhp at 7000 rpm		200 km/h
OM	8 cyl	1479 cc	(56 × 75 mm)	120 bhp		190 km/h
THOMAS Flatiron	8 cyl	1495 cc	(52 × 88 mm)			195 km/h

REIGN OF MEDIOCRITY

1928

For many years Grands Prix were run under a free formula. However, this was not deliberately arranged as a constructive and creative freedom, it was more the liberty of letting things slide. The Grands Prix lost their cohesion and the cars lost their prime vocation, which was to represent all that was the most advanced in motor engineering; in short, they were becoming debased.

There was now a new interdependence between the formulae for sports and racing cars. It certainly led to the creation of some fabulous multi-purpose cars, but these were not the out-and-out brutes of the race-track that hitherto had been known.

Maserati and then Alfa Romeo in Italy, and Bugatti in France, were well able to to take advantage of the effects of this change by winning more races, but this was at a time when the real Grand Prix car was disappearing. Thus the Bugattis' pre-eminence was no great credit to them in Grand Prix races; and at the same time it was very much to their credit in the difficult Targa Florio, which Bugatti won for six years running from 1925 to 1930. On the Madonie circuit, the type 35s were able to use to the full their qualities of roadholding, braking and steering, which in Grands Prix had not been enough to make up for an engine that was too simple in conception and therefore not sufficiently powerful.

No new cars appeared during 1928, a year in which the only requirement was a weight between 550 and 750 kg.

Having said that, the solitary true Grand Prix, meeting the standard of the AIACR (the international authority) was the Grand Prix of Italy at Monza. It was the only time during the year when the Bugattis and the Talbots raced against each other.

These latter were the 1500 cc cars of the 1926 and 1927 seasons, which had been acquired by an Italian, Emilio Materassi, who killed himself and 23 spectators in this race!

With the circuits practically left to himself, Bugatti carried off all the laurels in 1928

1928	
EUROPE Monza, 9/9	
1	BUGATTI Chiron
2	ALFA ROMEO Varzi
3	BUGATTI Nuvolari
4	BUGATTI Drouet
5	BUGATTI Maggi

The Italian Materassi (sitting in the car), who bought the 1500 cc Talbots. Beside the car are his drivers, Luigi Arcangeli and Antonio Brivio

Some of the Talbots had had their cylinders bored out to give a capacity of 1.7 litres. The Bugattis were divided between type 35B (2.3 litres supercharged) and 35C (2 litres supercharged), which were 1927 models that had recently become production cars. Alfa Romeo brought out the old P2 and Maserati had increased the capacity of the type 26.

At Monza the Bugattis dominated the race against weak opposition, just as they had been scarcely conscious of their adversaries in all the other Grands Prix of the year, all of which had been open to sports cars (ACF, Spain). Only the Mercedes-Benz SSK had fully extended them, in Germany, and we shall be reading some more about that on the next page.

FRENCH CARS AND THEIR RIVALS

BUGATTI T-35 B	8 cyl	2262 cc	(60 × 100 mm)	140 bhp at 5000 rpm	750 kg	210 km/h
BUGATTI T-35 C	8 cyl	1991 cc	(60 × 88 mm)	125 bhp at 5500 rpm	750 kg	200 km/h
TALBOT	8 cyl	1707 cc	(60 × 75.5 mm)	155 bhp	700 kg	210 km/h
ALFA ROMEO P2	8 cyl	1987 cc	(61 × 85 mm)	155 bhp at 5500 rpm	750 kg	225 km/h
MASERATI T-26 B	8 cyl	1980 cc	(62 × 82 mm)	145 bhp at 5300 rpm	715 kg	180 km/h

MONOTONY

1929

After that very dull year of 1928 the regulations were revised. The engine size remained unrestricted but fuel consumption now entered into the equation, with that hidden motive which has come back at regular intervals in the history of motor racing and which consists of making a gesture – hypocritically – towards the car of 'Mr Everyman'.

In brief, 14 kg of fuel and lubricating oil were allowed for every 100 km.

Bugatti, who had a remarkable talent for adaptation, played his cards well with his 35B and C and this year, once again, he ran them in as many races as possible.

Other French names were about to appear on the Grand Prix scene, or at least they had that desire. Alphi, who had already taken part in the 24 Hours Race at Le Mans, decided to adapt their car for Grands Prix by fitting a Cozette supercharger to their CIME engine. And then engineer Causan, who was the designer of the Vernandi, a car with a V8 engine of 1.5 litre capacity, proposed to add a supercharger for the Grand Prix of the ACF. Both these adventures came to naught and Alphi and Vernandi non-started.

Peugeot, on the other hand, honoured their engagement. Since 1922 the 174S (18 CV sleeve-valves) had been representing Peugeot in the touring class. In 1924 the 174S attacked the Targa Florio, then in 1926 it took part in long-distance racing – the 24 hours events at Le Mans and Spa – and the relative success attained here and there encouraged Peugeot to enter the 174S in the Grand Prix of the ACF in 1929.

Conceived originally as a luxurious touring car, the 174S thus found itself climbing, stage by stage, into top-level racing. It put up a good show, too. Bored out from 95 to 97 mm, the engine boasted an output of 100 bhp, and André Boillot succeeded in keeping up to the speed imposed by the Bugatti 35B of Williams.

As for the Talbots, they were now in the hands of Brilli-Peri instead of Materassi.

The first event of the season was not run under the fuel-consumption formula; it was the magnificent Grand Prix of the Principality of Monaco which, for the first time, offered the sinuosities of that city to the roaring of the racing machines. Here was a circuit made to measure for the agile Bugattis and yet, creating something of a surprise, Caracciola entered his white monster of a Mercedes SSK. It seemed a real lorry to drive among the hairpins, but the power of the German car and the skill of its driver made it extremely competitive; and the Englishman Williams (his real name was William Grover) was hard pressed to achieve the victory in a 'works' Bugatti 35B, painted green for the occasion!

The Grand Prix of the ACF used the circuit of the Le Mans 24 Hours Race, from which the Pontlieue corner had been amputated that year. Seven Bugattis opposed by two Peugeots formed the serious part of a rather poor entry list. Williams won this rather insignificant race at the wheel of a 35B, rigged up grotesquely with a cylindrical petrol tank reminiscent of the 1910 era.

At the German Grand Prix, which was open to sports cars, there was again a Bugatti-Mercedes confrontation which turned in favour of the Mercedes. At the Monza track the same freedom of choice for all was granted, but the event at least saw a change from the Bugatti monopoly, thanks to the presence of the works Alfa

1929			
MONACO 14/4	**ACF** Le Mans, 30/6	**SPAIN** San Sebast., 28/7	**MONZA** 15/9
1 BUGATTI Williams	BUGATTI Williams	BUGATTI Chiron	ALFA ROMEO Varzi
2 BUGATTI Bouriano	PEUGEOT Boillot	BUGATTI de Rothschild	TALBOT Nuvolari
3 MERCEDES Caracciola	BUGATTI Conelli	BUGATTI Lehoux	MERCEDES Momberger
4 BUGATTI de Rothschild	BUGATTI Divo	BUGATTI Dreyfus	ALFA ROMEO Brilli Péri
5 BUGATTI Dreyfus	BUGATTI Sénéchal	BUGATTI Bourlier	MERCEDES Caflisch

For the Grand Prix of the ACF, run under a fuel-consumption formula, the type 35 B Bugattis had cylindrical petrol tanks, mounted externally. His smile clearly visible, the British driver Williams won this rather curious Grand Prix

Romeos, the Maseratis (and notably the astonishing type V4 two-engined car), a Mercedes, a Talbot, a Duesenberg, and two front-wheel drive Millers imported from America by Leon Duray. Varzi in a Maserati finished first. At the Tunisian Grand Prix the Bugattis were again beaten; this time the winner was Brilli-Peri's Alfa Romeo P2.

Despite the excessive number of Bugattis on the starting grids and the monotony which that created, the Italians showed their potential here and there. (Molsheim please note . . .)

The only Alphi ever to be entered for a Grand Prix is today preserved in the Musée du Gerier

The Vernandi was withdrawn just before the Grand Prix of the ACF

André Boillot's big Peugeot was able to press the Bugattis hard in the Grand Prix of the ACF

FRENCH CARS AND THEIR RIVALS						
ALPHI	6 cyl	1485 cc	(62 × 82 mm)	70 bhp at 4700 rpm		160 km/h
BUGATTI T-35 B	8 cyl	2262 cc	(60 × 100 mm)	140 bhp at 5000 rpm	750 kg	210 km/h
BUGATTI T-35 C	8 cyl	1991 cc	(60 × 88 mm)	125 bhp at 5500 rpm	750 kg	200 km/h
PEUGEOT 174 S	4 cyl	3990 cc	(97 × 135 mm)	100 bhp	930 kg	175 km/h
VERNANDI	8 cyl	1481 cc	(55.7 × 76 mm)			190 km/h
ALFA ROMEO P2	8 cyl	1987 cc	(61 × 85 mm)	155 bhp at 5500 rpm	750 kg	225 km/h
MASERATI 8 C-2500	8 cyl	2595 cc	(65 × 94 mm)	185 bhp at 5500 rpm	800 kg	235 km/h
MASERATI V4	16 cyl	3961 cc	(62 × 82 mm)	300 bhp at 5200 rpm	955 kg	250 km/h
MERCEDES BENZ SSK	6 cyl	7069 cc	(100 × 150 mm)	225 bhp at 3300 rpm	1200 kg	185 km/h
MILLER 91 FWD	8 cyl	1475 cc	(55.5 × 76.2 mm)	252 bhp at 8000 rpm	635 kg	230 km/h

SOLITUDE

1930

Bugatti continued singlehanded, defending the colours of France in this rather unexciting free formula. But they were not quite alone. Peugeot brought out their ageing 174S with sleeve-valves at San Sebastian and Pau but these cars, series production of which had ceased since 1928, now seemed rather broken-winded.

Sabipa in one of the 15 privately-owned type 35 Bugattis in the Grand Prix of the ACF in 1930

Charles Montier had chosen American machinery to represent France at San Sebastian, Spa and Pau. A Ford specialist since the armistice, he had developed a sports car from the Model A, retaining the brakes, radiator and axle assemblies but modifying the engine with his own special components, which he also supplied to customers (special camshaft, large-diameter valves, 36 mm carburettor, high-geared crown wheel and pinion, etc). Evidently his highest ambition for the Montier-Spéciale was to complete the race reliably.

La Perle made a furtive entry into history on the occasion of the Grand Prix of the ACF. It consisted of a new, lowered chassis, fitted with an engine designed by Causan in 1924 to which a supercharger had been added. In the 1500 cc class the modest La Perle could do nothing against the old Delage of Sénéchal, but it finished second.

Ettore Bugatti (and his customers) remained faithful to types 35B and 35C but, aware of the age of these models, he tried an experiment. He mounted two cylinder blocks side by side, just as he had done with certain aero engines. These were two eight-cylinder blocks, derived from the type 35, united by a single crank-case and connected to the transmission by a train of gears. The superchargers and their carburettors were located behind the two blocks.

The old six-cylinder La Perle, restyled for the 1930 Grand Prix of the ACF at Pau

		1930		
	MONACO 6/4	**BELGIUM** Spa, 20/7	**ITALY** Monza, 7/9	**ACF** Pau, 21/
1	BUGATTI Dreyfus	BUGATTI Chiron	MASERATI Varzi	BUGATT Etanceli
2	BUGATTI Chiron	BUGATTI Bouriat	MASERATI Arcangeli	BENTLE Birkin
3	BUGATTI Bouriat	BUGATTI Divo	MASERATI Maserati	BUGATT Zanelli
4	BUGATTI Zehender		BUGATTI Minozzi	BUGAT Czaykow
5	BUGATTI Dore		MASERATI Fagioli	BUGAT de l'Esp

Louis Chiron trying out the Bugatti T-45 at Geneva

*Charles Montier showing his modified Ford Model A to
the King of Spain*

The Peugeot 174 S reappeared at the 1930 Grand Prix of the ACF

The bodywork of the type 45 followed the style of the 35 but in being enlarged it had lost its graceful proportions. The rear springs were placed outside the chassis side-members and not beneath them. This car, which should have been competitive with the type V4 Maserati that was built to a similar plan, never took part in a Grand Prix, for on its few appearances in hillclimbs it proved to have too many problems in the area of the transmission.

Foreign competition was confined to sports and often even touring cars, converted into Grand Prix cars by simply removing their mudguards and lights and tuning up the machinery.

This applied to some of the French too – Peugeots and Montiers; but very much so to the Mercedes which ran at Monaco and Monza, the Bentley which was not daunted by the difficulties of the Pau circuit, the Austro-Daimler that was more accustomed to the dangers of hillclimbs than to the conditions at the Grand Prix of Monaco, and the model A Duesenberg that appeared at Monza and the Imperia at Spa.

For their part, the Italians were preparing machines which were more in line with the way Grand Prix racing was bound to develop in years to come. Sooner or later these multi-purpose cars, that made such a slight contribution to the advance of engineering research, had to make way for a new generation of Grand Prix cars.

Alfa Romeo and Maserati had understood this and they were hard at work but in the meanwhile they were simply touching up their earlier designs. The revived P2, baptized Alfa Corsa, and the Maserati 8C 2500, filled the gap before the new epoch that was imminent. The balance sheet of the 1930 season was marked down as a total loss.

Bugatti found himself completely isolated, with no competitors except the derivatives of sports cars. The Grand Prix world was passing through a dismal phase of atrophy.

FRENCH CARS AND THEIR RIVALS

BUGATTI T-35 B	8 cyl	2262 cc	(60 × 100 mm)	140 bhp at 5500 rpm	750 kg	210 km/h
BUGATTI T-35 C	8 cyl	1991 cc	(60 × 88 mm)	125 bhp at 5500 rpm	750 kg	200 km/h
BUGATTI T-45	16 cyl	3800 cc	(60 × 84 mm)	250 bhp at 5000 rpm	1000 kg	250 km/h
LA PERLE	6 cyl	1493 cc	(60 × 88 mm)	85 bhp at 4500 rpm		170 km/h
MONTIER	4 cyl					
PEUGEOT 174 S	4 cyl	3990 cc	(97 × 135 mm)	100 bhp	930 kg	190 km/h
ALFA ROMEO P2	8 cyl	1987 cc	(61 × 85 mm)	175 bhp at 5500 rpm	750 kg	230 km/h
AUSTRO DAIMLER	6 cyl	3644 cc	(82 × 115 mm)	200 bhp		
BENTLEY 4.5 l	4 cyl	4398 cc	(100 × 140 mm)	240 bhp		185 km/h
DUESENBERG	8 cyl					
MASERATI 8 C-2500	8 cyl	2495 cc	(65 × 94 mm)	185 bhp at 5500 rpm	800 kg	235 km/h
MASERATI V4	16 cyl	3961 cc	(62 × 82 mm)	300 bhp at 5200 rpm	900 kg	250 km/h
MERCEDES BENZ SSK	6 cyl	7069 cc	(100 × 150 mm)	250 bhp	1200kg	190 km/h

AN END TO STAGNATION

1931

Motor sport was making a slow recovery from its depressed state. Ettore Bugatti himself consented to present a new model: type 51.

Certainly, from the outside it differed very little from the 35B, with which it shared the wider radiator. However, some of the details served for identification: the hole for the supercharger blow-off valve was placed lower down in the side of the bonnet, the wheels were cast in one piece without a bolted-on rim, and the magneto had gone from the dashboard. It was under the bonnet that the 51 was really new. The 2.3-litre engine now had a twin overhead camshaft cylinder head, with two valves per cylinder at an included angle of 90°. The design bore some resemblance to that of the Millers, which Leon Duray had sold to Ettore Bugatti after the Grand Prix of Italy in 1929.

The 51 was catalogued from 1931 at a price of Frs 135 000; it was the last Grand Prix Bugatti to be offered to the public. In September, another Bugatti appeared at Monza; this one was reserved for the factory and carried the type number 54. The lines followed the general style first seen in the type 35, but the dimensions were altogether more generous. The type 54 was a large and powerful car with an engine derived from the type 50. It had an imposing cast-iron cylinder block with a non-detachable head and twin overhead camshafts. With 300 bhp, the type 54 attained 250 km/h (155.3 mph) but at that speed some alarming deficiencies in roadholding, stability, and braking became apparent, limiting the full use of its potential. Some tyres of larger section were therefore mounted on new wheels, which were cast separately from the brake drums. The Bugatti type 54 was conceived for fast circuits and short races, and at

Louis Chiron — victorious at Monaco with his agile Bugatti

1931		
MONACO 19/4	**ITALY** Monza, 24/5	**ACF** Montlhéry, 21/6
1	BUGATTI Chiron	ALFA ROMEO Campari	BUGATTI Chiron
2	MASERATI Fagioli	ALFA ROMEO Borzacchini	ALFA ROMEO Campari
3	BUGATTI Varzi	BUGATTI Divo	MASERATI Biondetti
4	BUGATTI Bouriat	BUGATTI Wimille	MASERATI Birkin
5	ALFA ROMEO Zehender	MERCEDES Ivanowski	DELAGE Sénéchal

The new type 51 Bugatti twin-cam could be recognized by its wheels, cast in one piece, and the lower position of the orifice in the bonnet side

Monza it achieved an honourable third place against cars as monstrous as itself, such as the type A two-engined Alfa Romeo and the Mercedes SSKL.

The Bugatti type 51, infinitely better balanced, more manageable, and less brutal, followed the tradition of the 35 and it shone at all the circuits which made great demands on roadholding qualities. Chiron won at Monaco and Brno, Varzi at Tunis, Williams and Conelli at Spa, and Chiron and Varzi at Montlhéry.

Nevertheless, the Alfa Romeo 8C 2300 and the Maserati 8C 2500 and 2800 were a permanent and growing menace: the former won the Grand Prix of Italy in May, the latter, in its 2.8 litre version, the Monza race in September.

As for the Mercedes-Benz SSKL, it was just as phenomenal as its driver, Rudy Caracciola, who threw it around with astonishing skill at Monaco and at Nurburgring, where he carried off the German Grand Prix.

Let us note that among all the events of the year, only three were contested for a duration of ten hours, which was obligatory by international regulations. These were the Grands Prix of Italy, the ACF and Belgium.

The year 1931 represented a turning point. It marked a renewal of interest in the Grand Prix formula and it gave notice of the first warning issued to Bugatti by the Italians. It was absolutely the last year of French domination – for a very, very long time.

FRENCH CARS AND THEIR RIVALS						
BUGATTI T-51	8 cyl	2262 cc	(60 × 100 mm)	180 bhp at 5500 rpm	750 kg	230 km/h
BUGATTI T-54	8 cyl	4972 cc	(86 × 107 mm)	300 bhp at 4400 rpm	940 kg	250 km/h
ALFA ROMEO 8 C-2300	8 cyl	2336 cc	(65 × 88 mm)	165 bhp at 5400 rpm	820 kg	210 km/h
ALFA ROMEO TIPO A	8 cyl	3504 cc	(65 × 88 mm)	230 bhp at 5200 rpm	930 kg	240 km/h
MASERATI 8 C-2800	8 cyl	2731 cc	(68 × 94 mm)	198 bhp at 6000 rpm	810 kg	240 km/h
MERCEDES BENZ SSKL	6 cyl	7069 cc	(100 × 150 mm)	300 bhp at 3300 rpm	1150 kg	210 km/h

BUGATTI DISMISSED

1932

The economic crisis, born at Wall Street on that sad Thursday evening of October 1929, was still shaking France. Tardieu was practising spend-thrift policies (for instance, the construction of the Maginot line!) which led to a growing national debt. The motor industry was hard hit, factories closing their doors one by one.

In the space of a few months, the pioneers of the French motor industry disappeared: de Dion Bouton, Léon Bollée, Rochet-Schneider, Rolland-Pilain, and Lorraine-Dietrich each in turn stopped producing motor cars. Some among those who survived had to be content to live in a precarious and temporary state of equilibrium; they continued to respect quality and to conduct research but obtained very little in the way of productivity. Hispano-Suiza, Voisin, and Bugatti were in this position.

Bugatti prepared for the season with the same devoted enthusiasm as in times of prosperity. The type 51 was still put in the races, although the independent drivers were turning more and more towards the Italian vehicles – the Alfa Romeo 8C 2300 Monza, a dual-purpose sports-racing car, or the Maserati 8C 2500. For the ultra-rapid circuits Bugatti still had the enormous type 54, which was always ready to face the twin-engined Maserati V5 or the Mercedes SSKL, specially streamlined by Koenig-Fachsenfeld, but it remained just as perilous to drive as its rivals.

The tyres and chassis had difficulty in coping with the colossal power of these great machines.

Thus it was that the question of roadholding caused a lot of concern to Ettore Bugatti, who was split between two concepts; that of the 51, balanced and responsive but limited in power, and that of the 54, over-powered and undriveable. Antonio Pichetto, one of the engineers who worked at Molsheim, thought he had the solution: four-wheel drive. Bugatti let himself be convinced and had two examples built of a new type, the 53, based on a totally new system. Like the 54 it had the type 50 engine, but this drove a combined gearbox and differential, with two propeller shafts to the front and rear axles.

	MONACO 17/4	AVUS 22/5	EIFEL Nurburgring, 29/5	ITALY Monza, 5/6	ACF Reims, 3/7	GERMANY Nurburgring, 17/7	CZECHOSLOVAKIA Brno, 4/9	MONZA 11/9
1	ALFA ROMEO Nuvolari	MERCEDES Brauchitsch	ALFA ROMEO Caracciola	ALFA ROMEO Nuvolari	ALFA ROMEO Nuvolari	ALFA ROMEO Caracciola	BUGATTI Chiron	ALFA ROMEO Caracciola
2	ALFA ROMEO Caracciola	ALFA ROMEO Caracciola	BUGATTI Dreyfus	MASERATI Fagioli	ALFA ROMEO Caracciola	ALFA ROMEO Nuvolari	MASERATI Fagioli	MASERATI Fagioli
3	MASERATI Fagioli	BUGATTI Stuber	MERCEDES Brauchitsch	ALFA ROMEO Borzacchini	BUGATTI Chiron	ALFA ROMEO Borzacchini	ALFA ROMEO Nuvolari	ALFA ROMEO Nuvolari
4	BUGATTI Howe	MERCEDES Stück		ALFA ROMEO Campari	ALFA ROMEO Borzacchini			ALFA ROMEO Borzacchini
5	ALFA ROMEO Zehender			BUGATTI Dreyfus	BUGATTI Dreyfus			BUGATTI Varzi

Table title: **1932**

Chiron's type 51 Bugatti looks small beside Divo's type 54

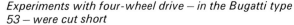

Experiments with four-wheel drive – in the Bugatti type 53 – were cut short

The rear suspension retained the usual reversed quarter-elliptic springs but in front one must record the appearance, almost miraculous with Bugatti, of independent suspension by two transverse leaf springs. The body owed nothing to traditional Bugatti styling. This was a pity, one must say, for the effect produced by the large inclined radiator cowl and the exposed petrol tank of the 53 was not exactly one of elegance!

However, in justice we must concede that it was compact, by virtue of the removal of all overhanging weight outside the wheelbase. This car only made sense on very winding circuits and Bugatti took a 53 to Monaco. Divo used it during practice for the race but he was not impressed by his few laps of the circuit, and so it was that the career of the 'four-wheel drive' was confined to hillclimbs.

Bugatti continued to race his type 51, but this year his great adversary, Alfa Romeo, had produced a formidable new weapon in collaboration with Vittorio Jano: the type B, which was later known as the P3. It was the first true single-seater and its transmission included two shafts from the rear of the gearbox, which solved some of the roadholding problems of such powerful cars. The 51 was made to feel its age cruelly, in comparison with this new single-seater.

Alfa Romeo carried off almost all the Grands Prix of the season, thanks to Nuvolari (victories at the Grands Prix of Italy and the ACF) and Caracciola (1st in the Grands Prix of Germany and Monza), and still with the 8C 2300 (victories at Monaco and Eifel). Alfa Romeo were only beaten at Avus, by the great streamlined Mercedes of Von Brauchitsch, and at Brno in Czechoslovakia, by Louis Chiron's type 51 Bugatti.

Let us leave aside the secondary French races, for while it is true that they added to the list of Bugatti victories, they brought no great merit (Grands Prix of Tunis, Oran, Dieppe, la Boule, Nice, Lorraine, etc.).

The reign of Bugatti was truly over, and perhaps we should say the heyday of the small independent manufacturers too; for behind Alfa Romeo a whole nation had thrown itself headlong into the battle.

With his enormous type 54 Bugatti, Lord Howe was unable to beat the fast Alfa Romeos at the Grand Prix of the ACF

FRENCH CARS AND THEIR RIVALS						
BUGATTI T-51	8 cyl	2262 cc	(60 × 100 mm)	180 bhp at 5500 rpm	750 kg	230 km/h
BUGATTI T-54	8 cyl	4972 cc	(86 × 107 mm)	300 bhp at 4400 rpm	940 kg	250 km/h
BUGATTI T-53	8 cyl	4972 cc	(86 × 107 mm)	300 bhp at 4400 rpm	940 kg	240 km/h
ALFA ROMEO 8 C-2300	8 cyl	2336 cc	(65 × 88 mm)	178 bhp at 5400 rpm	920 kg	225 km/h
ALFA ROMEO P3	8 cyl	2654 cc	(65 × 100 mm)	215 bhp at 5600 rpm	700 kg	235 km/h
MASERATI 8 C-2800	8 cyl	2731 cc	(68 × 94 mm)	198 bhp at 6000 rpm	810 kg	240 km/h
MASERATI V5	16 cyl	4906 cc	(69 × 82 mm)	360 bhp at 5500 rpm	980 kg	260 km/h
MERCEDES BENZ SSKL	6 cyl	7069 cc	(100 × 150 mm)	270 bhp	1200 kg	230 km/h

FRATRICIDAL COMBAT

1933

His tall figure was already well known in sporting circles, but he had never before occupied a post of such great responsibility. He had been a racing driver, but now he became the Sports Director of the most distinguished team in Grand Prix racing.

This legendary personage was Enzo Ferrari, and his Prancing Horse emblem was to grace the flanks of Grand Prix Alfa Romeos for many years.

With the 'Tipo B' (P3), which demolished its adversaries in 1932, and the 8C Monza enlarged from 2.3 to 2.6 litres, Enzo Ferrari confronted his compatriots the Maseratis, and Ettore Bugatti.

Maserati, with more modest means than the Scuderia Ferrari, defended themselves with heads held high, using the 8C 3000, which was replaced in March 1933 by the 8CM with hydraulic brakes, the first single-seater of this make. A front-wheel drive model also appeared, in September 1932, but it never took part in a race. Ettore Bugatti was preparing an absolutely new Grand Prix car but until it was ready the type 51 assured some good pace-making on the circuits. For tracks demanding pure speed, the big type 54 was always available.

The new car, type 59, did not appear before September, just in time to run in the final Grand Prix of the season at San Sebastian. The last of the Grand Prix Bugattis, it really did constitute the fullest development of a tradition. We shall speak of it again further on.

Charles Montier, whom we have already met, continued to juggle with Ford bits and to divert them from their original purpose, which had never been top-class motor racing. With two Ford A engines, mounted end-to-end to make a straight-eight, and installed in his 1930 chassis, he had created a single-seater which he ran in the smaller French events, such as the Grands Prix of Dieppe or La Baule.

At Monaco, practice times decided the positions on the starting grid. This logical arrangement was adopted here for the first time, overtaking being a very delicate matter

Presentation of the T-59 Bugatti, San Sebastian

	MONACO 3/4	AVUS 20/5	EIFE Nurburgrin
1	BUGATTI Varzi	BUGATTI Varzi	ALFA RC Nuvol
2	ALFA ROMEO Borzacchini	BUGATTI Czaykowski	MERCE Brauch
3	BUGATTI Dreyfus	ALFA ROMEO Nuvolari	ALFA RC Taru
4	ALFA ROMEO Chiron		
5	ALFA ROMEO Trossi		

on this particular circuit. Varzi, in a Bugatti 51, drove a superb race against a pack of Alfa Romeos and won the Grand Prix, but in spite of that Bugatti withdrew from the Grand Prix of the ACF. The fact was that his type 59 was not ready, and at Montlhéry the roadholding of the type 51 would not have sufficed to counteract the sheer horsepower of the Alfas and Maseratis, which therefore found themselves fighting for the lead. On the last lap, Campari (Maserati 8C 3000) overtook Etancelin (Alfa Romeo), but the latter took his revenge at Rheims in the Grand Prix of the Marne.

The angry Nuvolari, disgusted with the mechanical preparation of his car, left the Scuderia Ferrari and acquired a new Maserati 8 CM, which he drove to victory in the Belgian Grand Prix, but the following Grands Prix, of Italy, Czechoslovakia, and Spain, went to Alfa Romeo.

There had been a tragedy at the Grand Prix of Monza. Count Czaikowski owned a Bugatti type 54, with which he had finished second at the Avusrennen to Varzi in a similar car. At Monza he was to confront Count Trossi in the big Duesenberg, entered by Enzo Ferrari. After some laps, the engine of the American car broke down and the oil spilt over the track. Coming behind them, Campari and Borzacchini both skidded on the slippery surface and crashed fatally. Soon afterwards, Count Czaikowski himself lost control of his type 54 and was the third victim of this sinister race.

Let us come back to the Spanish Grand Prix, won by the Alfa Romeo of Chiron ahead of his team-mate Fagioli, and let us salute the performance of the type 59 Bugattis at their first appearance. They finished fourth (Varzi) and sixth (Dreyfus).

Under the long bonnet of the Montier Spéciale, two Ford engines were mounted end-to-end

1933				
CF éry, 11/6	**BELGIUM** Spa, 9/7	**ITALY** 10/9	**CZECHOSLOVAKIA** 17/9	**SPAIN** San Sebast., 24/9
ERATI npari	MASERATI Nuvolari	ALFA ROMEO Fagioli	ALFA ROMEO Chiron	ALFA ROMEO Chiron
ROMEO ncelin	BUGATTI Varzi	ALFA ROMEO Nuvolari	ALFA ROMEO Fagioli	ALFA ROMEO Fagioli
ROMEO ston	BUGATTI Dreyfus	MASERATI Zehender	ALFA ROMEO Wimille	BUGATTI Lehoux
ROMEO nmer	BUGATTI Lehoux	ALFA ROMEO Lehoux	BUGATTI Dreyfus	BUGATTI Varzi
	ALFA ROMEO Siena	ALFA ROMEO Brivio	BUGATTI Zdeneck	ALFA ROMEO Wimille

The type 59 was designed for the new formula which was to be set up in 1934. But what would this magnificent car be able to achieve in the face of the German machines which were shortly to make a devastating appearance, prior to dominating the next six years of motor sport?

In 1933 the type 51 Bugatti once again dominated the Monaco Grand Prix

Count Czaykowski was one of the rare drivers to domesticate the type 54 Bugatti. Here he is at Avus

FRENCH CARS AND THEIR RIVALS						
BUGATTI T-51	8 cyl	2262 cc	(60 × 100 mm)	180 bhp at 5500 rpm	750 kg	230 km/h
BUGATTI T-54	8 cyl	4972 cc	(86 × 107 mm)	300 bhp at 4400 rpm	940 kg	250 km/h
BUGATTI T-59	8 cyl	2820 cc	(67 × 100 mm)	240 bhp at 5400 rpm	750 kg	250 km/h
ALFA ROMEO T TIPO B	8 cyl	2654 cc	(65 × 100 mm)	215 bhp at 5600 rpm	700 kg	235 km/h
ALFA ROMEO 8 C-2600	8 cyl	2557 cc	(68 × 88 mm)	180 bhp at 5600 rpm	920 kg	225 km/h
DUESENBERG	8 cyl	4370 cc	(88.4 × 89 mm)		990 kg	230 km/h
MASERATI 8 C-3000	8 cyl	2991 cc	(69 × 100 mm)	230 bhp at 3500 rpm	700 kg	240 km/h
MASERATI 8 CM	8 cyl	2991 cc	(69 × 100 mm)	240 bhp at 3500 rpm	745 kg	240 km/h
MERCEDES BENZ SSK	6 cyl	7069 cc	(100 × 150 mm)	270 bhp	1200 kg	230 km/h

THE MOST BEAUTIFUL CAR IN THE WORLD

1934

This is simply an open boast and a subjective statement, and at all events it is a matter of relative values. The Bugatti type 59 was the last car of a very distinguished lineage, a lineage that had, in the course of its history, established a style and a school of thought all of its own.

Superb wheels, refinement in every detail, majestic proportions: the type 59 Bugatti was an aesthetic masterpiece

Ten years after the type 35, the type 59 took up once more the same favourite themes, this time developed to their peak. It was done with that rare combination, a sense of harmony in the overall design, and a refinement of detail. Apart from these praises for truly classic beauty, we must not overlook the other face of the type 59; it had not broken with the techniques used on earlier models that had by now become out of date.

The Bugatti 59 was not a single-seater. The chassis, modelled on that of the type 54, was constructed with two pierced side-members, very deep at the scuttle area, tapering elegantly towards the front on both sides of the pretty radiator and meeting at the rear within the slim tail. And still there was the same suspension: rigid tubular front axle in two parts, reversed quarter-elliptic springs behind, in this case mounted outside the body.

The engine looked very much like that of the type 57, which Bugatti had introduced at the Paris Motor Show of 1933. It was a straight-eight, with twin overhead camshafts operating two valves per cylinder and single ignition. Henceforth, the crankshaft was on six plain bearings, whereas the previous Grand Prix engines had rollers.

The original capacity of the type 59 engine was 2.8 litres but, as from the 1934 Grand Prix of the ACF, it was increased to 3.3 litres. Even this figure remained timid compared with the competition as did that of the power output: 250 against 350 bhp!

					1934		
	MONACO 2/4	**AVUS** 27/5	**EIFEL** 3/6	**ACF** 1/7	**GERMANY** 15/7	**BELGIUM** 29/7	**PESCAR** 15/8
1	ALFA ROMEO Moll	ALFA ROMEO Moll	MERCEDES Brauchitsch	ALFA ROMEO Chiron	AUTO UNION Stück	BUGATTI Dreyfus	MERCED Fagioli
2	ALFA ROMEO Chiron	ALFA ROMEO Varzi	AUTO UNION Stück	ALFA ROMEO Varzi	MERCEDES Fagioli	BUGATTI Brivio	MASERA Nuvolar
3	BUGATTI Dreyfus	AUTO UNION Momberger	ALFA ROMEO Chiron	ALFA ROMEO Moll-Trossi	ALFA ROMEO Chiron	MASERATI Sommer	BUGATT Brivio
4	ALFA ROMEO Lehoux			BUGATTI Benoist	MASERATI Nuvolari	BUGATTI Benoist	ALFA ROM Varzi-Ghe
5	BUGATTI Nuvolari				MERCEDES Geier		AUTO UNI Sébastia

TZERLAND 26/8	ITALY 9/9	SPAIN 23/9	CZECHOSLOVAKIA 30/9
TO UNION Stück	MERCEDES Caracciola	MERCEDES Fagioli	AUTO UNION Stück
TO UNION omberger	AUTO UNION Stück	MERCEDES Caracciola	MERCEDES Fagioli
UGATTI Dreyfus	ALFA ROMEO Trossi	BUGATTI Nuvolari	MASERATI Nuvolari
A ROMEO Varzi	ALFA ROMEO Chiron	AUTO UNION Stück	AUTO UNION Leiningen
A ROMEO Chiron	MASERATI Nuvolari	ALFA ROMEO Varzi	ALFA ROMEO Varzi

The engine of the type 59 looked very much like that of the type 57

'Le Patron', Ettore Bugatti, with one of his most beautiful creations, the type 59. At the wheel, probably his son, Jean

Whilst the type 59 was mechanically of a rather orthodox design, there was one feature that did deserve great gasps of admiration: the wheels! A multitude of fine wire spokes glittered in front of a disc that was splined to the countersunk brake drum and embraced the hub, also splined; the whole assembly was machined and polished in aluminium. This was both an aesthetic and a technological success; or you could say it was a fine example of art that is born of the very constraints and the sheer logic of engineering.

The type 59 Bugatti was designed under the new formula, which was in force for three years from 1934. It specified three dimensions: the car must weigh less than 750 kg (1650 lbs), without tyres and dry, and the minimum cockpit width was 85 cm: furthermore, the race distance was at least 500 km.

Alfa Romeo widened the body of the P3 slightly to comply with the regulations and Maserati similarly adapted their 8 CM; they also created the six-cylinder type 34, although unlike Alfa, they received no government subsidy. They won races of secondary importance only (Dieppe, Donington, etc).

But the event of the year 1934 erupted from the other side of the Rhine: Daimler-Benz and Auto-Union entered the Grand Prix circus, and with what splendour! The Mercedes, designed by Hans Nibel, was of conventional architecture except that all four wheels were independently sprung; and the Auto-Union, dreamed up by Professor Ferdinand Porsche, had a centrally-mounted V16 engine.

The grasping of power by Adolf Hitler on 30 January 1933 was already having repercussions in the German automobile industry. Very quickly, the new Chancellor had shown his understanding of the problems of this sector by giving Professor Porsche the job of designing his people's car (the Volkswagen).

As for Bugatti, he was struggling with financial realities. On the production front, for 1934 he had come down to a single model, the type 57, which was to remain in the catalogue until the war in numerous versions. For racing he had three 59s, still limited to 2.8 litres, which were available from the very start of the season, at Monaco. Third on the starting grid, Dreyfus finished the race in the same position, the victory going to the Alfa Romeo of Moll.

The Italian make won all the races in the early part of the season, at Alexandria and Tripoli, and on the Avus track where the P3 carried aerodynamic bodywork and was equipped with a bigger engine. However, on that day, 27 May, all eyes were on the Auto-Unions which achieved a third place on their first outing.

A week later, at the Eifelrennen, the Mercedes team, directed by Alfred Neubauer, entered the scene and won, but the first genuine international confrontation was at Montlhéry, at the Grand Prix of the ACF. Both the

German makes failed to finish, Alfa took the first three places and Robert Benoist, his type 59 enlarged to 3.3 litres, was fourth and last. At Nurburgring, the Germans put things in perspective with Auto-Union (Stuck) first and Mercedes-Benz second. At Spa another false step: the Germans were absent and left the victory to Bugatti. With Dreyfus first, Brivio second and Benoist fourth after breaking the lap record, the future began to look very promising; but this was to be the only important victory of the type 59.

Mercedes-Benz and Auto-Union took it in turns to win after this and the rest of the season was a veritable pas-de-deux between Fagioli and Stuck, the respective chief drivers. The first took three Grands Prix (Pescara, Italy where Caracciola won, and Spain), the second two (Switzerland and Czechoslovakia).

On just one occasion, the type 59 Bugatti was honourably placed, when Nuvolari took third place at the Spanish Grand Prix. But very often Bugatti was only represented by one car, the finances of Molsheim now beginning to find the travelling expenses for an ever-growing number of races to be something of a strain.

The type 59 Bugatti had above all shown that it was a sensible, well-balanced car, endowed with excellent roadholding qualities like its predecessors. Unfortunately the cable-operated brakes were as much of a handicap as its lack of power.

Jean-Pierre Wimille and Piero Taruffi about to take the wheels of their type 59 Bugattis

BUGATTI AND ITS RIVALS						
BUGATTI T-59	8 cyl	3257 cc	(72 × 100 mm)	250 bhp at 5750 rpm	750 kg	250 km/h
ALFA ROMEO P3	8 cyl	2905 cc	(68 × 100 mm)	255 bhp at 5400 rpm	720 kg	260 km/h
AUTO UNION A-Type	16 cyl	4358 cc	(68 × 75 mm)	295 bhp at 4500 rpm	840 kg	280 km/h
MASERATI T-34	6 cyl	3325 cc	(84 × 100 mm)	260 bhp at 5000 rpm	680 kg	260 km/h
MASERATI 8 CM	8 cyl	2991 cc	(69 × 100 mm)	260 bhp at 5800 rpm	745 kg	260 km/h
MERCEDES BENZ W-25	8 cyl	3363 cc	(78 × 88 mm)	314 bhp at 5800 rpm	855 kg	280 km/h
	8 cyl	3719 cc	(82 × 88 mm)	348 bhp at 5800 rpm	855 kg	290 km/h
	8 cyl	3992 cc	(82 × 94.5 mm)	370 bhp at 5800 rpm	855 kg	300 km/h

FRANCE VERSUS THE AXIS POWERS

1935

Following the example of his German friend, Benito Mussolini now adopted motor sport as an organ of propaganda. He went on neglecting Maserati, who were bringing out a new V8 model, while giving encouragement to Alfa Romeo.

The P3 was now showing its age and, pending the arrival of the entirely new type 8C, which did not appear until September, it was fitted with independent front suspension (as developed in France by André Dubonnet); it was given reversed quarter-elliptic springs at the rear and a bigger engine of 3.2 litres, enlarged to 3.8 litres for the Grand Prix of the ACF.

Then Enzo Ferrari produced, in his own workshops, a special model for ultra-rapid circuits, such as Tripoli and Avus, a single-seater equipped with two engines: one in front and one behind!

Mercedes were still developing their W25. Starting with 3.3 litres, the capacity was successively increased to 3.7 litres, 4 litres and finally 4.3 litres. Max Sailer had become technical director in succession to Hans Nibel in November 1934.

Auto-Union had also increased their engine size and they had adopted torsion-bar rear suspension.

These were the serious and habitual Grand Prix competitors. However, in July 1935 the veil was lifted from an astonishing project. Count Trossi had produced a single-seater driven by a 16-cylinder radial engine. Its designer was Augusto Monaco, and its home the splendid castle of Gaglianico, where the car was built in secret.

However, the Trossi-Monaco did not race. A similar enigma in France was called the SEFAC. Hiding behind these initials was la Societé d'Études et de Fabrication d'Automobiles de Course. A special subscription had been set up to promote a French racing car, and with its resources SEFAC had built a Grand Prix car, under the

The SEFAC, driven by Lehoux and designed by Emile Petit, was one of the most memorable fiascos of French motor sport

	1935							
	MONACO 22/4	**TRIPOLI** 12/5	**AVUS** 26/5	**EIFEL** 16/6	**ACF** 23/6	**BELGIUM** 14/7	**GERMANY** 28/7	**SWITZERL** 25/8
1	MERCEDES Fagioli	MERCEDES Caracciola	MERCEDES Fagioli	MERCEDES Caracciola	MERCEDES Caracciola	MERCEDES Caracciola	ALFA ROMEO Nuvolari	MERCED Caraccio
2	ALFA ROMEO Dreyfus	AUTO UNION Varzi	ALFA ROMEO Chiron	AUTO UNION Rosemeyer	MERCEDES Brauchitsch	MERCEDES Fagioli	AUTO UNION Stück	MERCED Fagiol
3	ALFA ROMEO Brivio	MERCEDES Fagioli	AUTO UNION Varzi	ALFA ROMEO Chiron	MASERATI Zehender	ALFA ROMEO Chiron	MERCEDES Caracciola	AUTO UN Rosemey
4	MASERATI Etancelin	ALFA ROMEO Nuvolari			MERCEDES Fagioli	ALFA ROMEO Dreyfus	AUTO UNION Rosemeyer	AUTO UN Varzi
5	ALFA ROMEO Chiron	ALFA ROMEO Chiron			AUTO UNION Varzi	BUGATTI Benoist	MERCEDES Brauchitsch	ALFA RO Nuvola

FRENCH CARS AND THEIR RIVALS						
BUGATTI T-59	8 cyl	4744 cc	(84 × 107 mm)	320 bhp	750 kg	260 km/h
SEFAC	8 cyl	2771 cc	(70 × 90 mm)	250 bhp at 6500 rpm	910 kg	240 km/h
ALFA ROMEO P3	8 cyl	3167 cc	(71 × 100 mm)	265 bhp at 5400 rpm	725 kg	270 km/h
	8 cyl	3827 cc	(78 × 100 mm)	330 bhp at 5400 rpm	725 kg	275 km/h
ALFA ROMEO 8C	8 cyl	3827 cc	(78 × 100 mm)	330 bhp at 5400 rpm	820 kg	275 km/h
ALFA ROMEO Bimotore	16 cyl	6335 cc	(71 × 100 mm)	540 bhp at 5400 rpm	1030 kg	325 km/h
AUTO UNION B-Type	16 cyl	4954 cc	(72.5 × 75 mm)	375 bhp at 4800 rpm	820 kg	300 km/h
MASERATI V8 R1	8 cyl	4788 cc	(84 × 108 mm)	320 bhp at 5300 rpm	770 kg	270 km/h
MASERATI T-34	6 cyl	3724 cc	(84 × 112 mm)	280 bhp at 5300 rpm	680 kg	260 km/h
MERCEDES BENZ W25	8 cyl	4309 cc	(82 × 102 mm)	402 bhp at 5500 rpm	750 kg	300 km/h
TROSSI MONACO	16 cyl	3982 cc	(65 × 75 mm)	250 bhp at 6000 rpm	710 kg	240 km/h

ITALY 8/9	SPAIN 22/9	CZECHOSLOVAKIA 29/9
TO UNION Stück	MERCEDES Caracciola	AUTO UNION Rosemeyer
A ROMEO Nuvolari	MERCEDES Fagioli	ALFA ROMEO Nuvolari
TO UNION semeyer	MERCEDES Brauchitsch	ALFA ROMEO Chiron
A ROMEO Marinoni	BUGATTI Wimille	
JGATTI Taruffi	AUTO UNION Rosemeyer	

But now no-one was watching these pretty light-blue cars anyway. Mercedes took first place all the time, their silver single-seaters throbbing with all their 400 bhp, eating up the race-track, quite indifferent to whether it might be one of the difficult, winding circuits, or else a high-speed track. At Monaco, Tripoli, Avus, Montlhéry, Spa, Berne and San Sebastian, the chequered flag had fallen to the W25; the driver in the lead was Caracciola, except at Monaco and Avus where the winner was Fagioli. Alfa Romeo, with a single victory in the German Grand Prix, and Auto-Union with two (Italy and Czechoslovakia) picked up the crumbs while Mercedes simply dominated the season.

technical direction of Émile Petit, an elderly man who had worked for Salmson. It was perhaps surprising to find in the SEFAC some rather modern ideas, such as helical springs and a 'V8' engine. This was actually composed of two parallel cylinder blocks, each with its own crankshaft enclosed in a communal crank-case. The four camshafts operated the valves on a semi-desmodromic system (each cam was between two others which returned the tappet assemblies, the springs having only to close the valves). A Cotal electromagnetic gearbox served this unusual engine.

The SEFAC completed several practice laps in the hands of Marcel Lehoux before the Grand Prix of the ACF, but it retired bashfully behind the stands for the race.

There remained Bugatti, but optimism was no longer in season at Molsheim. Dreyfus, Brivio and Nuvolari had left the French team to put their talent – not to let it stagnate – at the service of Alfa Romeo. The official drivers for 1935 were Wimille, Benoist, Veyron and Taruffi. Four cars from the past year crossed to the other side of the Channel into the good care of Brian Lewis, C. E. C. Martin, Lord Howe and Lindsay Eccles.

The Bugatti 59 no longer appeared regularly in the big races, and the best result was a fourth place by Wimille at the Spanish Grand Prix. Otherwise the type 59 had to content itself with mediocre successes, like the Grand Prix of Picardy. At the Grand Prix of the ACF, before their own public, Bugatti only entered a single car, fitted with a 4.7-litre engine, type 50B, a cowled radiator, and a riveted central fin on the tail. Benoist finished the race without a bonnet and with no success.

During this time the English owners of type 59s scarcely left their island, racing each other at Brooklands, at Donington, and the Mannin Moar.

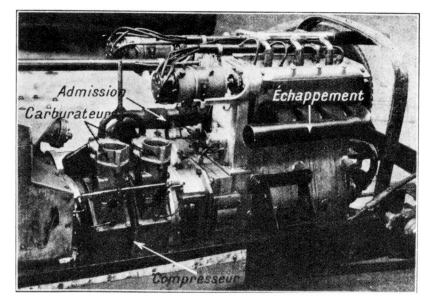

The weird engine of the SEFAC had two parallel four-cylinder blocks

Opposite page: *In the Grand Prix of the ACF the type 59 Bugatti of Robert Benoist had a modified radiator cowl*

FRANCE LOSES FAITH

1936

France was sinking; she had lost all faith in her future. With the arrival of the Popular Front Government there was a change of complexion, but the agony continued. French motor sport withdrew within itself.

The single-seater Bugatti had the same chassis as the normal type 59

The Automobile Club of France decided to open its Grand Prix to sports cars and no longer to racing cars, in order to turn away the German terror. The stratagem worked and Delage, Delahaye, Talbot, Amilcar and certainly Bugatti responded favourably; they produced sports cars bearing some relationship to their production models. Bugatti thus prepared a car which they called the 57G tank for Le Mans (which did not take place) and the Grand Prix of the ACF. But, it was difficult to reconcile this sort of racing with an event called a Grand Prix.

Nevertheless, the type 59 stayed faithfully at its post, now fitted with a 3.8-litre engine. Wimille drove for all he was worth at Monaco, Nurburgring and Berne, but without success. At Comminges and Deauville, with no real opposition, he won.

At practice for the Grand Prix of Monaco the first single-seater Bugatti was seen. Still treated in the style of the 59, the single-seater had the rounded radiator cowl that was later fitted to the 'Million' car and the three-litre model, and central steering. Driven by the 50B engine with nine main bearings, this single-seater retained the complete chassis of the 59.

Alfa Romeo played on two tables. In the same chassis they could mount either an eight or a twelve-cylinder engine, but they obtained no great victories. Maserati were letting go their hold before giving up racing at the end of 1936, but they maintained the V8 R1 in good order and it won the Pau Grand Prix. On the other side of the Rhine, the Third Reich continued to defile the sporting world with its combination of ostentation and trickery. Hitler's furious outburst when Long, a German, congratulated the black American, Jesse Owens, was an indication of the spirit in which the Olympics took place at Berlin in August 1936. The nobility and the neutrality of sport were no more than

	MONACO 12/4	TRIPOLI 10/5	PENYA 7/6
1	MERCEDES Caracciola	AUTO UNION Varzi	ALFA RO Nuvo
2	AUTO UNION Varzi	AUTO UNION Stück	MERCE Carac
3	AUTO UNION Stück	MERCEDES Fagioli	ALFA RO Fari
4	ALFA ROMEO Nuvolari	MERCEDES Caracciola	AUTO U Deli
5	ALFA ROMEO Brivio	ALFA ROMEO Pintacuda	AUTO U Rosem

BUGATTI AND ITS RIVALS						
BUGATTI T-59	8 cyl	3800 cc				
BUGATTI 4.71	8 cyl	4744 cc	(84 × 107 mm)	370 bhp at 5700 rpm	750 kg	270 km/h
ALFA ROMEO 8 C	8 cyl	3827 cc	(78 × 100 mm)	330 bhp at 5400 rpm	820 kg	275 km/h
ALFA ROMEO 12 C	12 cyl	4064 cc	(70 × 88 mm)	370 bhp at 5800 rpm	820 kg	290 km/h
AUTO UNION C-Type	16 cyl	6008 cc	(75 × 85 mm)	520 bhp at 5000 rpm	820 kg	310 km/h
MASERATI V8 R1	8 cyl	4788 cc	(84 × 108 mm)	320 bhp at 5300 rpm	770 kg	270 km/h
MERCEDES BENZ W25	8 cyl	4740 cc	(86 × 102 mm)	453 bhp at 5800 rpm	750 kg	310 km/h

empty phrases. The propaganda that was extracted from the performance of Mercedes and Auto-Union was typical.

For 1936 Daimler-Benz once more used the W25, which was three years old. The Auto-Union had evolved more systematically and was on top at the Grands Prix of Tripoli, Eifel, Germany, Switzerland and Italy. Most of the time, Rosemeyer obtained the Auto-Union victories, save at Tripoli where Varzi was best. Nuvolari managed to slide in front with the Alfa 8C at the Grands Prix of Penya Rhin at Barcelona and of Hungary at Budapest.

At the end of the year an unusual race was organized on the other side of the Atlantic. The Americans revived the Vanderbilt Cup, abandoned since 1916. The German teams were not interested but Alfa Romeo, Maserati and Bugatti took the boat. Wimille and the British driver Lewis drove a type 59 and the Frenchman finished second behind Nuvolari's Alfa Romeo 12C.

In June the Bugatti tank had won the Grand Prix of the ACF and this success had helped Bugatti's performance on the French market, doing more good at any rate than those pitiful but nevertheless costly appearances in the real Grands Prix, run under the racing car formula. Thus

the choice really made itself, and Bugatti concentrated on the Le Mans 24 Hours Race for 1937, giving up Grands Prix. For the first time in fifteen years, Bugatti was not involved in the struggle at the summit.

For the practice period at Monaco, Bugatti took along this single-seater with central steering

1936					
FEL 4/6	HUNGARY 21/6	MILAN 28/6	GERMANY 26/7	SWITZERLAND 23/8	ITALY 13/9
UNION meyer	ALFA ROMEO Nuvolari	ALFA ROMEO Nuvolari	AUTO UNION Rosemeyer	AUTO UNION Rosemeyer	AUTO UNION Rosemeyer
ROMEO volari	AUTO UNION Rosemeyer	AUTO UNION Varzi	AUTO UNION Stück	AUTO UNION Varzi	ALFA ROMEO Nuvolari
ROMEO ivio	AUTO UNION Varzi	ALFA ROMEO Farina	ALFA ROMEO Brivio	AUTO UNION Stück	AUTO UNION Delius
ROMEO rina			AUTO UNION Hasse	MERCEDES Lang	ALFA ROMEO Dreyfus
CEDES ng		MERCEDES Fagioli	AUTO UNION Delius-Hasse	ALFA ROMEO Pintacuda	

ONE LAST FLING

1938

Nazi Germany was all-powerful. Its economy, which had collapsed after the depression of 1929, had taken off spectacularly, thanks to Doktor Schacht who put it back on its feet. Exports were doing well, and unemployment had become insignificant.

Germany now possessed the necessary means for satisfying its desire to dominate Eastern Europe. Austria and the Sudetenland were annexed, while France and England were being distracted by skilful diplomatic manoeuvres. For Hitler, the motor industry was more than ever the iron of the lance in his flourishing economy. Germany's technological and racial superiority ought to find its expression, according to him, in motor sport as well. Organized in a semi-military fashion, it had become an affair of the state.

The formula in force from 1938 for Grands Prix very soon proved itself a fiasco from a technical point of view. After ten years of free formula, capacity was limited to three litres supercharged or 4.5 litres unsupercharged.

With so little difference, engines with atmospheric induction (without a supercharger) suffered an insurmountable handicap. Mercedes extracted 140 bhp per litre from a supercharged engine while Delahaye must be content with a little over 50 bhp per litre.

Whatever technological advance resulted from the work of Mercedes or Auto-Union, this was a flagrant inequality and served to widen the gulf that separated Delahaye from their rivals.

Otherwise the 1938 season showed some noticeable if not spectacular progress in aerodynamics. The streamlining of the bodywork, as well as the lowering of the centre of gravity, were given a good deal of attention. Unfortunately this was another of the areas where the difference was very apparent between the French cars, which were more or less adaptations of earlier models, and the German and Italian single-seaters, which were designed on a clean sheet of paper.

Bugatti's last stand

Ettore Bugatti decided to develop a car in conformity with the current formula from the single-seater seen at

1938						
PAU 10/4	**TRIPOLI** 15/5	**ACF** 3/7	**GERMANY** 24/7	**SWITZERLAND** 21/8	**ITALY** 11/9	**DONINGTON** 22/10
1 DELAHAYE Dreyfus	MERCEDES Lang	MERCEDES Brauchitsch	MERCEDES Seaman	MERCEDES Caracciola	AUTO UNION Nuvolari	AUTO UNION Nuvolari
2 MERCEDES Caracciola-Lang	MERCEDES Brauchitsch	MERCEDES Caracciola	MERCEDES Caracciola	MERCEDES Seaman	ALFA ROMEO Farina	MERCEDES Lang
3 DELAHAYE Comotti	MERCEDES Caracciola	MERCEDES Lang	AUTO UNION Stück	MERCEDES Brauchitsch	MERCEDES Caracciola	MERCEDES Seaman
4 MASERATI Raph	ALFA ROMEO Sommer	TALBOT Carrière	AUTO UNION Nuvolari-Kautz	AUTO UNION Stück	ALFA ROMEO Biondetti	AUTO UNION Muller
5 BUGATTI Trintignant	MASERATI Taruffi			ALFA ROMEO Farina	ALFA ROMEO Ghersi	MERCEDES Brauchitsch

Monaco in 1936. Well versed in the technicalities of supercharging, he chose the capacity of three litres, which he obtained from a reduced version of the nine-bearing type 50B engine. This single-seater used the type 59 chassis with the old suspension by rigid axles, with semi-elliptic front springs and reversed quarter-elliptics behind. Robust trailing arms to locate the rear axle were anchored well forward, but this was the only novelty. Though still based on the type 59 chassis, the body of the three litre differed from that of the 1936 single-seater in having a faired headrest, while the grille was extended forwards to cover the oil radiator.

The rest of the car followed previous models, including the superb wire-spoked wheels, but also unhappily the obsolescent, cable-operated brakes. The Bugatti 3 litre only appeared twice in 1938, at Cork and Rheims. It proved to be as fast as it was fragile, a consequence of hasty preparation and an inadequate budget.

Bugatti also possessed another model complying with the current formula, but this time equipped with an unsupercharged engine of 4.5 litres capacity. This resembled the 3 litre except for an exposed oil radiator in front. The 4.5 litre was used for the 'Million Francs Grand Prix' in 1937, but in 1938 Bugatti preferred to throw the supercharged car into the battle.

Delahaye

The firm of Delahaye was as much a special case as were the men who ran it: Charles Weiffenbach, the managing director, and Jean François, his engineer. While Bugatti was well aware that 1938 was the year of his last stand, Delahaye on the other hand were just making their entry on the sporting scene. Delahaye had high ambitions and long teeth: victorious in the 1937 Monte Carlo Rally and the Le Mans 24 Hours Race in 1938, they were winning every sort of event. But Delahaye had a secret desire: to make a dent in Germany's supremacy in the Grand Prix world.

Since 1936 Jean François had been developing a dual-purpose racing car, which could equally well be used in Grands Prix or endurance races. To propel it, he designed a 60° V12 engine with unusual valve gear, a central camshaft operating the inlets in both banks, with two outside camshafts for the exhausts.

Jean François did not adopt overhead camshafts but his V12 incorporated some modern ideas nevertheless, such as hemispherical combustion chambers, double ignition, and dry-sump lubrication. He used many magnesium-alloy castings, which presented serious machining problems, but this did not prevent the engine from weighing 268 kg (590 lbs) on the scales.

Preoccupied with the design of this V12, Jean François used his earlier designs for the chassis. The frame of the 135 was the basis of the 145 which, though considerably

Delahaye carried off the Grand Prix du Million in 1937 with the type 145 two-seater, which was used again in 1938

THE MILLION FRANCS GRAND PRIX, 1937

The Automobile Club of France did not organize a Grand Prix for racing cars in 1937; instead they invited contributions towards a Racing Fund, which was then used for prize money in a special event for sports cars. Their unspoken hope was that this would help revive the industry's flagging skills.

The prize, to the value of a million francs, was for beating, before 31 August 1937, an average speed of 146.508 km/h (91.03 mph) established by Mercedes-Benz at Montlhéry in 1935. SEFAC and Bugatti tried their luck but on 27 August René Dreyfus grabbed the stake from his adversaries at the wheel of a Delahaye 145. He had averaged 146.654 km/h, as a reward for which Charles Weiffenbach was handed the million-franc cheque, by Count de Rohan, the President of the ACF.

Bugatti's entry for the Grand Prix du Million in 1937 — an unsupercharged 4.5-litre single-seater

Against the German opposition the Delahaye had only its reliability and moderate fuel consumption in its favour. The keenness and perserverance of the team were therefore all the more to be admired.

Talbot for the formula

After having won the sports-car Grand Prix of the ACF in 1937, Talbot were tempted by the racing-car formula under which the event was repeated in 1938. At their works in Suresnes they began construction of a supercharged three-litre engine, which they exhibited during development before the Racing Fund Committee, receiving an immediate and generous reaction in hard cash. Unfortunately Antonio Lago did not have time to finish his three-litre for the Grand Prix of the ACF, but to fulfil his entry he raced two sports models in that event, modifying them to the extent of removing their lamps.

At the same race, there was an opportunity to watch the 1935 SEFAC with a new radiator grille, but only for three laps.

A demoralizing season

The Grand Prix of Pau, which opened the 1938 season, constituted a sort of miracle for Delahaye. Mercedes had not hesitated to bring into action an absolutely new car which was, however, not well adapted to the circuit, and above all heavy on fuel.

Two Delahayes, infinitely less thirsty, were the main challengers in a rather motley selection in which only the newcomer Maurice Trintignant, in an old Bugatti, stood

Attractive on paper, the single-seater Delahaye 155 never lived up to its promise in a race

lowered, was of impressive proportions. The suspension followed the Delahaye tradition, with a transverse leaf spring in front and a rigid rear axle.

As for the body, a temporary construction was used to get the car onto the circuits. It was a simple and somewhat ungraceful shell in two-seater form, but Delahaye had no intention of leaving it at that and a genuine single-seater was already in the portfolios.

Later they built this single-seater. It was appreciably lighter than the two-seater but its 'tip-toe' outline made it hard to disguise its origins: the chassis was derived directly from the two-seater, apart from the De Dion rear axle. It made an appearance at the German Grand Prix and was seen no more. Delahaye preferred to continue racing with the 145 two-seater that was more thoroughly developed and which had carried off the 'Million Francs Grand Prix' in 1937.

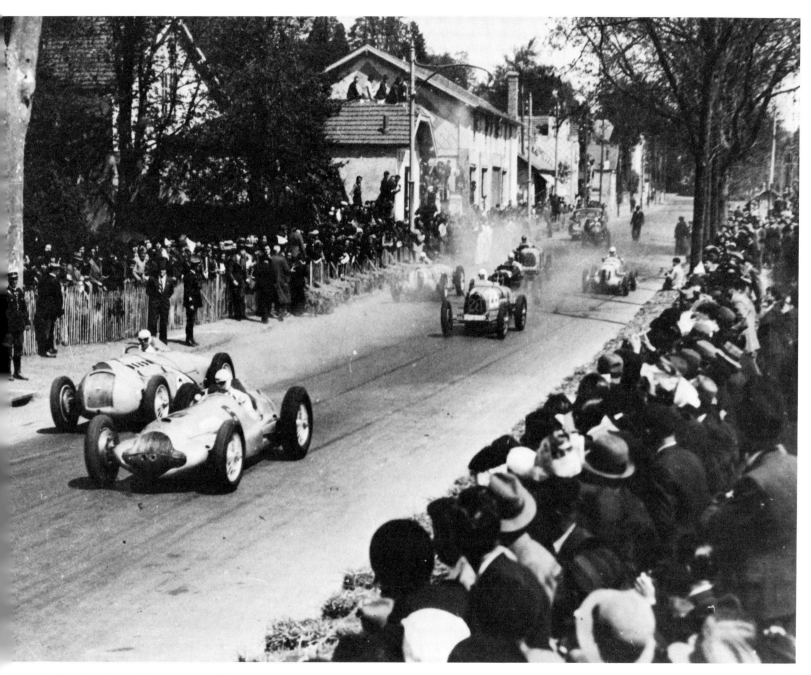

Left: *The Delahaye 145 two-seater. This was not a real Grand Prix car but it was the best that France had in 1938*

Above: *Thanks to lower fuel consumption, Dreyfus in his Delahaye beat the Mercedes W-154 at the 1938 Pau Grand Prix. Behind them is Maurice Trintignant, starting his career in an old Bugatti type 35.*

The Bugatti 3 litre of 1938 was derived from the 4.5 litre of the 'Million'

out. While the Mercedes stood at its pit refuelling Dreyfus gnawed away the seconds of its lead. He won, for although the Mercedes was much faster, it consumed 100 litres of fuel for 100 km. To complete the triumph of Delahaye, Comotti finished third.

At Cork in Ireland the French driver repeated his performance. His principal opponent on this occasion was Jean-Pierre Wimille in the Bugatti 3 litre.

The serious business of the season began with the Grand Prix of Tripoli in May 1938. Mercedes lined up an impressive armada of W154s while the Italians, who particularly wanted to shine at this venue, were present in force. Alfa Romeo had stretched their entry to three 312s, a 316 and a 308. Maserati introduced their new 8 CTF. Beside all these Delahaye cut a poor figure with their 145 two-seater, fitted for this ultra-fast race with a faired

For the high-speed circuit of Tripoli, the Delahaye was fitted with a special streamlined body. René Dreyfus accompanying it to the quayside at Marseilles

radiator and side pods. What was bound to happen took place, and Mercedes finished in the first three places, with Dreyfus an honourable seventh.

The French did not have their revenge at the Grand Prix of the ACF, run at Rheims at the beginning of July. After the Racing Fund Committee had decided to make a grant to Talbot, Delahaye sulked and non-started. To confront Mercedes and Auto-Union there only remained the fragile Bugatti, the phantom-like SEFAC and two sports Talbots. Four cars finished the race, three Mercedes leading and a Talbot, ten laps behind.

The same story was repeated at every event. Mercedes arrogantly made a clean sweep of the German Grand Prix, the Coppa Ciano (at Leghorn), the Coppa Acerbo (at Pescara) and the Swiss Grand Prix; they conceded two victories to their compatriots, Auto-Union, at the Grands Prix of Italy and Donington.

For the whole length of that season, the only chance for the French was to lie in wait for any weakness on the part of their adversary, merely playing a passive role where events were entirely in the hands of the Germans.

The fact was that the French had relatively slight financial means. Of course, the same resources at any earlier time would have been enough for them either to win or at least to do justice to their talents.

For Mercedes and Auto-Union motor racing had taken on another dimension. It was no longer a simple meeting of sportsmen but the impact of nations. The whole of German life was founded on the same nationalistic ideal, upon which all economic, military, and sporting ambitions were built, as well as every other human activity. In this context the importance attached to the engineers of Mercedes and Auto-Union was immense. In addition, Mercedes were able to profit from regulations which had condemned unsupercharged engines in advance.

The Talbot for the 1938 Grand Prix of the ACF was nothing but a sports car with its lamps removed

Here is the SEFAC again, this time with a streamlined nose

FRENCH CARS AND THEIR RIVALS

BUGATTI 3 l*	8 cyl	2982 cc	(78 × 78 mm)	270 bhp at 6000 rpm		280 km/h
BUGATTI 4.5 l	8 cyl	4500 cc				
DELAHAYE 145	12 cyl	4490 cc	(75 × 84.7 mm)	225 bhp at 5500 rpm	1060 kg	225 km/h
DELAHAYE 155	12 cyl	4490 cc	(75 × 84.7 mm)	235 bhp at 5000 rpm	860 kg	250 km/h
SEFAC*	8 cyl	2771 cc	(70 × 90 mm)	250 bhp at 6500 rpm	910 kg	240 km/h
TALBOT	6 cyl	4467 cc	(92 × 112 mm)			210 km/h
ALFA ROMEO 308*	8 cyl	2991 cc	(69 × 100 mm)	295 bhp at 6000 rpm	870 kg	260 km/h
ALFA ROMEO 312*	12 cyl	2996 cc	(66 × 73 mm)	350 bhp at 6500 rpm	880 kg	285 km/h
ALFA ROMEO 316*	16 cyl	2959 cc	(58 × 70 mm)	440 bhp at 7500 rpm	920 kg	300 km/h
AUTO UNION D-Type*	12 cyl	2986 cc	(65 × 75 mm)	420 bhp at 7000 rpm	850 kg	300 km/h
MASERATI 8 CTF*	8 cyl	2991 cc	(69 × 100 mm)	360 bhp at 6500 rpm	780 kg	270 km/h
MERCEDES BENZ W154*	12 cyl	2961 cc	(67 × 70 mm)	468 bhp at 7800 rpm	980 kg	310 km/h

* supercharged

HOPE FOR BETTER DAYS TO COME

1939

Jean Renoir's film, 'The Rules of the Game', was showing in the cinemas in Paris. But every day in Europe, real life was becoming a more sinister game. Hitler had Europe at his mercy. On the circuits, Mercedes and Auto-Union towered above their rivals with engines touching 500 bhp. For the poor French, entering the race at all was only a symbolic gesture.

Delahaye, preoccupied with more urgent military activities, could no longer concentrate on motor sport; nevertheless, René Dreyfus appeared in a 145 two-seater at the German Grand Prix.

SEFAC remained obscure in 1939 and Tremoulet's few laps at the Pau Grand Prix, no more than a gesture of respect for French public opinion, did not convince the spectators.

Bugatti was concentrating all his efforts (and his money) on the Le Mans 24 Hours race. The 4.5 litre single-seater that he had built for Wimille was not seen at any of the Grands Prix. This car, which was really a disguised type 59 that hid the lines of its old chassis with a body that was all curves, appeared in 1939 only at the Prescott and La Turbie hillclimbs, and at Montlhéry; it slept all through the war until its time came to win the Liberation Grand Prix in the Bois de Boulogne in 1945. It did not have the quality for great races.

Curiously enough, at Suresnes the racing workshop continued to be active. Antonio Lago, with Becchia at his shoulder, prepared for the 1939 season as if there was nothing amiss. This Venetian, born in 1893, had already saved the name of Talbot in 1935, and now he wanted it to take the plunge into the racing pool once again.

Three cars were being assembled in the Talbot factory. The first two, with steering offset to the right, were directly developed from the sports model and did not boast ultra-modern machinery. It was enough to cast a pitying glance at the leaf springs, transverse in front and longitudinal behind. The engine repeated well-tried features such as a lateral camshaft and single ignition. However, the cylinder block was cast in aluminium and the head had hemispherical combustion chambers.

	1939							
	PAU 2/4	**TRIPOLI** 7/5	**EIFEL** 21/5	**BELGIUM** 25/6	**ACF** 9/7	**GERMANY** 23/7	**SWITZERLAND** 20/8	**YUGOSLAVIA** 3/9
1	MERCEDES Lang	MERCEDES Lang	MERCEDES Lang	MERCEDES Lang	AUTO UNION Muller	MERCEDES Caracciola	MERCEDES Lang	AUTO UNION Nuvolari
2	MERCEDES Brauchitsch	MERCEDES Caracciola	AUTO UNION Nuvolari	AUTO UNION Hasse	AUTO UNION Meier	AUTO UNION Muller	MERCEDES Caracciola	MERCEDES Brauchitsch
3	TALBOT Etancelin	ALFA ROMEO Villoresi	MERCEDES Caracciola	MERCEDES Brauchitsch	TALBOT Le Bègue	MASERATI Pietsch	MERCEDES Brauchitsch	AUTO UNION Muller
4	ALFA ROMEO Sommer	MASERATI Taruffi	MERCEDES Brauchitsch	ALFA ROMEO Sommer	TALBOT Etancelin	DELAHAYE Dreyfus	AUTO UNION Muller	
5	DELAHAYE Paul	MASERATI Hug	AUTO UNION Hasse	DELAHAYE Mazeaud	ALFA ROMEO Sommer	DELAHAYE Raph	AUTO UNION Nuvolari	

The third car was a single-seater with a central driving position: the offset cars were only transitory in Lago's plan, and it was the single-seater which was later to carry the supercharged three-litre V16 engine.

But that project had only reached the design stage and the single-seater made its first appearance, with the classic six-cylinder engine, at the Grand Prix of the ACF at Rheims. Raymond Mays was the test driver of the single-seater and at Rheims, as had also happened earlier during private testing at Montlhéry, the fuel tank sprang a leak, wasting 10 litres per kilometre. In compensation, Le Bêgue and Etancelin finished – miraculously – third and fourth behind two Auto-Unions, driving their offset cars.

However, the Talbots were never again able to interfere in the battle of the titans between Mercedes and Auto-Union, which finally saw the triumph of Mercedes. Lang won the Grands Prix of Paris, Eifel, Belgium, and Switzerland, leaving to his team-mate, Caracciola, the honour of winning in Germany.

Talbot returned to competition, thanks to Antonio Lago. The first single-seater had a slightly offset driving position

Delahaye 145 two-seater, driven here by René Dreyfus at the Grand Prix of the ACF

Talbot single-seater at the 1939 Grand Prix of the ACF

Auto-Union were victorious on two occasions only: at the Grand Prix of the ACF with Muller and in Yugoslavia with Nuvolari. As for Alfa Romeo and Maserati, they were completely out-distanced, the Germans taking their revenge in the process for a certain display of low cunning on the part of the Italians. The latter had very craftily limited engine sizes in the Tripoli Grand Prix to 1500 cc.

The Italians were tired of seeing the Germans winning and they already had some little 1500 cc cars that were well prepared, the Alfetta and the Maserati 4 CL. But Daimler-Benz demonstrated their incredible potential and their inexhaustible flair for adaptation. In eight months the engineers designed, built and developed the W165 and the two examples dominated the Tripoli Grand Prix! Whatever ruse was employed, the Germans were unbeatable.

But, while the Auto-Union of Nuvolari and the Mercedes of Manfred von Brauchitsch were crossing the finishing line at the Grand Prix of Yugoslavia, France and Britain declared war on Germany. A brutal end came to that particular chapter in the history of motor sport. Its chief legacy was that gigantic advances in motor technology had taken place, the product of a rivalry fuelled by propaganda.

Germany's scientific knowledge had certainly been augmented by these years of domination in sport, and she had also gained self-confidence. Her racing activities had brought out the excellence in many people who were involved; and they had led to progress in technology too. From now on all these accomplishments were to be directed in the pure pursuit of nationalism, by means of war.

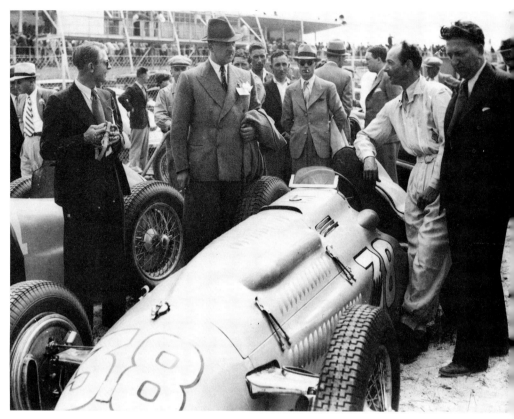

The 'real' Grand Prix Talbot was this single-seater, tried out by the British driver, Raymond Mays, at Rheims

FRENCH CARS AND THEIR RIVALS						
DELAHAYE 145	12 cyl	4490 cc	(75 × 84.7 mm)	235 bhp at 5000 rpm	1060 kg	230 km/h
TALBOT	6 cyl	4434 cc	(94 × 106.5 mm)			240 km/h
TALBOT Single-seater	6 cyl	4483 cc	(93 × 110 mm)	210 bhp at 4500 rpm	850 kg	250 km/h
ALFA ROMEO 316*	16 cyl	2959 cc	(58 × 70 mm)	440 bhp at 7500 rpm	920 kg	300 km/h
AUTO UNION D-Type*	12 cyl	2986 cc	(65 × 75 mm)	485 bhp at 7000 rpm	850 kg	340 km/h
MASERATI 8 CTF*	8 cyl	2991 cc	(65 × 75 mm)	360 bhp at 6500 rpm	850 kg	270 km/h
MERCEDES BENZ W163*	12 cyl	2961 cc	(67 × 70 mm)	483 bhp at 7800 rpm	895 kg	330 km/h

* supercharged

LIVING
ON A SHOESTRING

1946

Europe arose slowly from the apocalypse. Devastated by six years of uninterrupted warfare, it was reborn from its cinders and once more dared to hope. This was a time of slow awakening and, through sheer human effort, of revival. An immense task of reconstruction, political, moral and material, was imposed upon the Allies by their total victory.

In September 1945 the curtain rose on motor sport in the Bois de Boulogne. The circuit was an improvised one, merely marked out with straw bales, but the public were there in force, and they were enjoying themselves. Jean-Pierre Wimille won the Liberation Grand Prix in the single-seater Bugatti, built in 1939. On the other hand, the new type 60, dreamed up by 'le Patron' during the war, remained on the drawing board at Molsheim.

Six years of war had not improved the financial position for any maker of racing cars. Not only Bugatti; neither Talbot nor Delahaye were in a position to produce new models. Nevertheless, the organizers agreed on a new formula, which imposed a limit of 4.5 litres for engines with atmospheric induction or 1.5 litres supercharged. At last the supercharger was reasonably handicapped compared with the naturally aspirated engine.

Alfa Romeo and Maserati had quickly settled for supercharging, as they already possessed well-tried machines using that principle. They were happy to fall back on their pre-war types 158 and 4CL because on the French side, the shortage of cars had caused drivers and teams to carry out veritable prehistoric excavation.

The 'Ecurie France' had collected several *Delahaye* 135 Spéciales, which were re-bodied in more or less good taste for Georges Grignard, Charles Pozzi, or Eugène Chaboud. The dust was blown off the *Talbots* for the attention of Pierre Levegh and Louis Chiron.

At the same time a brand new French single-seater had been promised. Enguerrand de Coucy had been working on it during the last months of the war and at the beginning of the winter of 1945–46 the Societé Guérin, a subsidiary of the Air-Industrie firm, undertook to build this car. Initially the Guerin-de Coucy seemed an interesting enough car, with a twin-cam straight-eight

The Guérin, designed by de Coucy, but never seen in a race

1946		
NICE 22/4	**NATIONS** 21/7	**TURIN** 1/9
1	MASERATI Villoresi	ALFA ROMEO Farina	ALFA ROMEO Varzi
2	ALFA ROMEO Sommer	ALFA ROMEO Trossi	ALFA ROMEO Wimille
3	DELAHAYE Chaboud	ALFA ROMEO Wimille	MASERATI Sommer
4	DELAHAYE Grignard	MASERATI Nuvolari	DELAHAYE Chaboud
5	MASERATI Ruggieri	MASERATI De Graffenried	MASERATI Platé

engine and two-stage supercharging, a gearbox combined with the final drive, and all four wheels independently sprung. Gearchanges could be made without declutching, thanks to an ingenious semi-automatic system: finally, the low-built body had a slightly awkward-looking tail combined with the headrest. An agreeable car, it never started in a Grand Prix, although it appeared once at Rheims with a less ambitious engine of 1100 cc.

In that year of recovery the races could be counted on the fingers of one hand, and the two Italian makes shared the laurels. Maserati won the Grands Prix of Nice and Marseilles (Villoresi and Sommer) while Alfa Romeo took the Grands Prix of Geneva and Turin. The Delahaye of Chaboud only won the Belgian Grand Prix, but in every race a French car managed to get among the places of honour, encouraged by a fanatical public: Chaboud was

third at Nice and fourth at Turin, Grignard third at Marseilles, all in their renovated Delahayes.

The participation of these patched-up cars and the shoe-string organization of races showed that motor sport possessed a real will to live, both on the part of its active exponents and of the public, that was full of enthusiasm. They all wanted to join together in sporting life, and were prepared to make the sacrifices that were necessary.

This Bugatti, built in 1939, won the Grand Prix de la Libération in the Bois de Boulogne in 1945

This 4.5 litre Talbot was a sports coupé before the war. Re-bodied, it ran in Grands Prix from 1946 to 1950

FRENCH CARS AND THEIR RIVALS						
DELAHAYE 135 Sp.	6 cyl	3557 cc	(84 × 107 mm)	152 bhp at 4300 rpm	900 kg	185 km/h
GUERIN-DE COUCY	8 cyl	1487 cc	(59 × 68 mm)	255 bhp at 8200 rpm		
TALBOT Single-seater	6 cyl	4483 cc	(93 × 110 mm)	210 bhp at 4500 rpm	850 kg	250 km/h
ALFA ROMEO 158/46 B	8 cyl	1479 cc	(58 × 70 mm)	254 bhp at 7500 rpm	620 kg	250 km/h
MASERATI 4 CL	4 cyl	1491 cc	(78 × 78 mm)	220 bhp at 6600 rpm	630 kg	240 km/h

RECONSTRUCTION

1947

It seemed that motor sport itself was subject to rationing!

Walter Watney's type D6 *Delages* joined the Delahaye 135 Spéciales in becoming the mainstay of the postwar reconstruction period. These three-litre cars, built by Arthur Michelat before the war, were fitted with new bodies and survived for several seasons, turning up again at the Le Mans 24 Hours Race in 1949 and 1950.

At the *Talbot* factory all efforts were concentrated on the new car, which was completed in 1948; but in the meantime some improvements were made to the 1939 single-seater. The suspension received detail modifications, the brakes were given hydraulic operation, and another 10 bhp was coaxed from the engine. These improvements helped Louis Chiron to win the Grand Prix of the ACF at Lyons.

But the main hopes of the French lay in another car: the CTA-Arsenal. This esoteric title referred to *Le Centre d'Études Techniques de l'Automobile et du Cycle* and a former arsenal in which the car was constructed, near to Paris. The man in charge was Albert Lory. The creator of the Delages in 1926–7, he was 52 and he had not forgotten his bold ideas concerning engines.

He designed a twin-cam V8, with two Roots superchargers at the front and the timing pinions situated at the rear. The double ignition was entrusted to two magnetos. On the test bench the engine promised more than 260 bhp, but how much of that arrived at the wheels? The CTA-Arsenal was inadequate in its transmission, and its chassis.

Albert Lory designed an impressive V8 engine for the CTA-Arsenal

1947			
SWITZERLAND 8/6	**BELGIUM** 29/6	**ITALY** 7/9	**ACF** 21/9
1 ALFA ROMEO Wimille	ALFA ROMEO Wimille	ALFA ROMEO Trossi	TALBOT Chiron
2 ALFA ROMEO Varzi	ALFA ROMEO Varzi	ALFA ROMEO Varzi	MASERATI Louveau
3 ALFA ROMEO Trossi	ALFA ROMEO Trossi	ALFA ROMEO Sanesi	TALBOT Chaboud
4 MASERATI Sommer	ERA Gerard	ALFA ROMEO Gaboardi	TALBOT Rosier
5 ALFA ROMEO Sanesi	DELAGE Trintignant	MASERATI Ascari	DELAHAYE Pozzi

The CTA-Arsenal on its first drive ever. In the cockpit, Raymond Sommer

In the CTA-Arsenal workshop: one complete car and another under construction

Louis Chiron beside the Talbot single-seater at Marseilles

The Talbot single-seater winning the 1947 Grand Prix of the ACF at Lyons

112

The gearbox and final drive formed a compact assembly at the rear and all four wheels were independently sprung on torsion bars. But all that was installed in an archaic chassis with side members braced by curved tubular cross-members. The axis of the engine inclining 8° towards the rear, the driver sat relatively low.

The CTA-Arsenal turned its wheels at Montlhéry for the first time one morning in September. Raymond Sommer was the test-driver, but this unhappy pilot never managed to sort out the caprices of the Arsenal, nor its disastrous roadholding. On the starting line of the Grand Prix of the ACF the clutch seized, and when he released the pedal it brutally wrecked the transmission.

In 1948 the CTA-Arsenal was finally withdrawn from racing, after being left far behind during practice by the Italian cars; the two examples that had been built finished up with Antonio Lago.

In May 1947 Benoît Falchetto was to be seen at the wheel of a Bugatti single-seater, a 4.5 litre improvised by a mechanic in Nice who used a type 35 chassis and a type 50 B engine, covered by a home-made body. In fact (and thank God!) this hybrid model never took part in a Grand Prix.

On the other side of the Alps, Alfa Romeo continued to develop their 158 while Maserati gave the 4 CL a tubular chassis, thus making it the 4 CLT – and there was nothing home-made about that.

In the circumstances it was obvious that the 1947 season was going to be an Alfa Romeo festival, Jean-Pierre Wimille winning the Swiss and Belgian Grands Prix, and Trossi winning in Italy. By not taking part in the Grand Prix of the ACF, Alfa Romeo left the remaining place on the podium to Talbot, which was indeed fair play.

Louis Chiron, aged 48, took the single-seater to victory under a leaden sky and to the applause of a French crowd, who would never again see 'their' Grand Prix won by a team that was a hundred per cent French. This was at Lyons on 21 September and it gave encouragement for the following season, when Talbot planned to race a new single-seater.

The year 1947 had really and truly seen the restoration of Grands Prix.

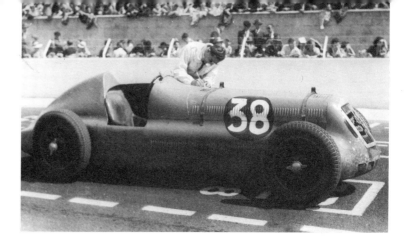

Walter Watney built up a stable of D6 Delages, left over from the Le Mans 24 Hours Race before the war

Two generations together in the Grand Prix of Pau: at the centre the single-seater Talbot, on the left the D6 Delage, and on the right two Delahaye 135s

FRENCH CARS AND THEIR RIVALS						
CTA ARSENAL	8 cyl	1482 cc	(60 × 65.5 mm)	266 bhp at 7500 rpm		240 km/h
DELAGE D 6	6 cyl	2988 cc	(83.7 × 90.5 mm)	142 bhp at 5300 rpm		180 km/h
DELAHAYE 135 SP.	6 cyl	3557 cc	(84 × 107 mm)	152 bhp at 4300 rpm	900 kg	185 km/h
TALBOT Single-seater	6 cyl	4483 cc	(93 × 110 mm)	220 bhp	850 kg	250 km/h
ALFA ROMEO 158/46 B	8 cyl	1479 cc	(58 × 70 mm)	275 bhp at 7500 rpm	620 kg	260 km/h
MASERATI 4 CLT	4 cyl	1491 cc	(78 × 78 mm)	250 bhp at 6000 rpm	630 kg	250 km/h

THE RETURN

1948

Ettore Bugatti died on 21 August 1947. The last 'real' Bugatti, built under his direction, was enthroned on the stand at the Paris Motor Show, under the glass roof of the Grand Palais.

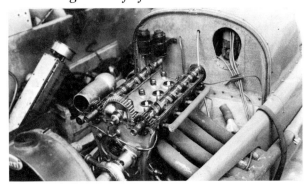

The Bugatti engine, type 73 C: a little four-cylinder with twin overhead camshafts

It was the little 1500 cc type 73A saloon. A racing version had also been proposed, with a twin-cam engine, fitted for the first time with a detachable cylinder head. Two chassis were built but they were discreetly put away and forgotten. The curtain had fallen at Molsheim; later on, Roland Bugatti and Pierre Marco attempted to breathe fresh life into that legendary name – but only for a final spasm.

Emile Petit emerged from obscurity in 1948, but his SEFAC was unrecognizable with its new bodywork in Duralinox. It now carried the trade mark of the *Dommartin* engine company. Nevertheless, all the ingredients of the original SEFAC were still present. Let us begin with the engine, that double four-cylinder with semi-desmodromic valve operation and with two crankshafts, the left one driving the water pump and the other the dynamo. The capacity had simply been stretched, by over-boring, from 2.7 litres to 3.6 litres to compensate for the disappearance of the supercharger. The Dommartin retained the drum brakes with six shoes.

Yves Giraud-Cabantous was chosen to drive this machine but, luckily for him, capital ran short and the Dommartin, now an obsolete type of car altogether, spent many years neglected in an abandoned workshop.

Antonio Lago's Masterpiece

At Suresnes the Talbot factory was far from being abandoned, and feverish activity prevailed as Lago and his chief engineer, Carlo Marchetti, supervised the construction of the first type 26 C. For financial reasons the Talbot Lago was not a revolution compared with the 1939 single-seater. The suspension followed that of the previous model scrupulously, with a rigid rear axle and a transverse front spring. The engine also preserved a classic architecture.

1948						
	NATIONS 9/5	**MONACO** 16/5	**SWITZERLAND** 4/7	**ACF** 18/7	**ITALY** 5/9	**BRITAIN** 2/10
1	MASERATI Farina	MASERATI Farina	ALFA ROMEO Trossi	ALFA ROMEO Wimille	ALFA ROMEO Wimille	MASERATI Viloresi
2	MASERATI de Graffenried	TALBOT Chiron	ALFA ROMEO Wimille	ALFA ROMEO Sanesi	MASERATI Villoresi	MASERATI Ascari
3	FERRARI Sommer	MASERATI de Graffenried	MASERATI Villoresi	ALFA ROMEO Ascari	FERRARI Sommer	ERA Gerard
4	DELAHAYE Chaboud	SIMCA GORDINI Trintignant	ALFA ROMEO Sanesi	TALBOT Comotti	MASERATI Ascari	TALBOT Rosier
5	DELAGE Louveau	MASERATI Villoresi	MASERATI Ascari	TALBOT Raph	MASERATI Parnell	MASERATI Bira

The new Talbot-Lago type 26 C was outclassed by the Alfettas. Philippe Etancelin racing at Rheims

To the rather costly valve operation by overhead camshafts, Lago preferred the solution of two side-camshafts placed high in the block, operating valves inclined at 95°. The cylinder head, with hemispherical combustion chambers, and the block were cast in light alloy.

With 240 bhp, the Talbot approached the Maseratis which boasted 260 bhp, but it was still far behind the Alfa Romeos. It had the advantage of greater reliability because it developed its maximum power at a far less frenzied rate of revolutions than its Italian rivals (4700 rpm as opposed to more than 7000!).

Numbers on the starting grids were increased by a valuable new recruit when the first Formula 1 Ferrari made its debut at the Italian Grand Prix.

In fact, 1948 was the first year when people used the expression, 'Formula 1'. Thanks to the appearance of a competitive new Talbot, and also to the growing number of races, the 1948 season took on a less makeshift appearance than those that had gone before.

The city of Pau welcomed the first Formula 1 Grand Prix in March 1948. It saw a Maserati victory. During the first part of the season, with no entries from Alfa Romeo, the Maseratis continued to occupy the leading places, Farina winning at Geneva and Monaco.

It was in Monaco that the type 26 C Talbot first officially turned a wheel. Louis Rosier, who drove

Eugène Chaboud built himself a single-seater Delahaye
175

115

This Bugatti was re-bodied with a lot of bad taste and no attempt at authenticity

The fantastic-looking Dommartin was only a re-bodied SEFAC with the supercharger removed

The engine of the Talbot-Lago type 26 C was a classic six-cylinder with two side camshafts

it, had to retire, but Louis Chiron was second in the 1939 single-seater. In fourth place there was a little car of 1200 cc, lively and easily handled, a Simca from the Gordini stable driven by Trintignant. The year 1948 in fact marked the entry into Grand Prix racing of Amédée Gordini, but his promising single-seater was not yet a full Formula 1 car – we shall speak of this later on.

All through the spring, Talbot were developing their new car. A second example was ready for the European Grand Prix at Berne on 4 July. At the Grand Prix of the ACF, run at Rheims on 18 July, Talbot were in a position to line up four new type 26 Cs for Comotti, Raph, Rosier and Etancelin. The last named retired, but the other drivers finished in that order in 4th, 5th and 6th places behind the Alfas.

Alfa Romeo were hard to beat and they were well backed up by their compatriots, Maserati and Ferrari. The Italian Grand Prix of Italy saw nothing but victory for the Italians all down the line: first Alfa Romeo, second Maserati, third Ferrari! The best Talbot finished in sixth place. At the British Grand Prix at Silverstone, neither Alfa Romeo nor Ferrari took part. Louis Rosier managed fourth place, beaten all the same by the ancient C-type ERA of Gerard.

At the Coupe du Salon, a minor event organized at Montlhéry, the Talbot-Lagos had their first victory, Rosier, Levegh, and Giraud-Cabantous taking the three leading places. During this time, the Ecurie France had acquired two Lagos, for Louis Chiron and Eugène Chaboud, thus bringing up to six the number of users of the new car. Until then, Chaboud had been using an astonishing Delahaye, a single-seater whose mechanism was derived from the type 175.

The year ended with the Monza Grand Prix, where all the candidates for victory faced each other for the last time. Once again that great driver, Jean-Pierre Wimille,

Yves Giraud-Cabantous at the 1948 Grand Prix of the
ACF — still in his old Talbot with offset driving position

gave Alfa Romeo a splendid success, ahead of his three team-mates, Trossi, Sanesi and Taruffi. Jean-Pierre Wimille had already won the Grands Prix of the ACF and Italy, with a second place at Geneva. At the same time he was putting the finishing touches to his own highly original saloon, with a central engine and a body by Philippe Charbonneaux. It is painful to record that Jean-

Pierre Wimille was killed in the first weeks of 1949 while testing a Simca Gordini in Argentina.

The death of Wimille, which followed that of Varzi, deprived Alfa Romeo of their best drivers, especially as Trossi was soon to fall ill. In fact Alfa Romeo, having dominated the 1948 season, withdrew from racing for a year.

FRENCH CARS AND THEIR RIVALS						
BUGATTI T-73 C	4 cyl	1488 cc	(76 × 82 mm)	250 bhp	800 kg	230 km/h
DOMMARTIN	8 cyl	3619 cc	(80 × 90 mm)	200 bhp	920 kg	220 km/h
TALBOT LAGO T-26 C	6 cyl	4483 cc	(93 × 110 mm)	240 bhp at 4700 rpm	915 kg	260 km/h
ALFA ROMEO 158/47	8 cyl	1479 cc	(58 × 70 mm)	310 bhp at 7500 rpm	700 kg	280 km/h
ERA Type B/C	6 cyl	1483 cc	(57.5 × 95.2 mm)	240 bhp at 7500 rpm	710 kg	240 km/h
ERA Type E	6 cyl	1496 cc	(63 × 80 mm)	270 bhp at 7500 rpm	655 kg	270 km/h
FERRARI 125	12 cyl	1497 cc	(55 × 52.5 mm)	230 bhp at 7000 rpm	700 kg	240 km/h
MASERATI 4 CLT/48	4 cyl	1491 cc	(78 × 78 mm)	260 bhp at 7000 rpm	630 kg	260 km/h

THANKS TO ABSENT FRIENDS

1949

Thanks to the Americans, who came to the rescue with the Marshall Plan, Europe dressed its wounds, but the East-West tension now weighed more and more heavily on international relations. The cold war was breaking out.

In contrast to this, 1949 was a more relaxing year for motor sport. Alfa Romeo had parked their Alfettas in the workshops and their racing organization took a rest. Three of the team drivers had died, and the Alfa management preferred to forget competition work to concentrate on the introduction of the 1900 saloon.

The withdrawal of Alfa Romeo was a relief to Antonio Lago and all the Talbot team. They had successfully completed the preparation of eight cars which faced, without false modesty, the Ferraris that were still young and vulnerable and the Maseratis, especially those supplied to an Argentine team led by Juan Manuel Fangio.

Alta continued their efforts despite a crippling lack of capital. The ancient ERAs, more than ten years old, still attracted attention, especially Gerard's R14B of 1936, which gave much greater satisfaction than the more recent and sophisticated E type.

The highly original Cisitalia, built by Piero Dusio and Rodolpho Hruska to Ferdinand Porsche's design, failed to make an appearance; it is true that the development of a four-wheel drive, mid-engined 12-cylinder car was a heavy assignment for so small a team. Outdone in acceleration by the supercharged cars, the Talbots had their revenge in the long run. Sturdy and reliable, in long-distance races they left behind the Italian cars, which were more often delayed by refuelling, tyre changing or simply by deterioration of their engines.

At Spa-Francorchamps, on 19 June, Louis Rosier achieved the first great victory for the Talbot-Lago in this way. The early part of the race was dominated by the fast Italian cars; Fangio (Maserati) and then Villoresi (Ferrari) took the lead; but far behind them Louis Rosier was steadily gaining places. The supercharged cars were breaking up fast and the Talbot got on the heels of the Ferrari, then overtook it.

1949					
BRITAIN 14/5	**BELGIUM** 19/6	**SWITZERLAND** 3/7	**FRANCE** 17/7	**ITALY** 11/9	**CZECHOSLOVAKIA** 25/9
1	MASERATI de Graffenried	TALBOT Rosier	FERRARI Ascari	TALBOT Chiron	FERRARI Ascari	FERRARI Whitehead
2	ERA Gerard	FERRARI Villoresi	FERRARI Villoresi	MASERATI Bira	TALBOT Etancelin	TALBOT Etancelin
3	TALBOT Rosier	FERRARI Ascari	TALBOT Sommer	FERRARI Whitehead	MASERATI Bira	FERRARI Cortese
4	ERA Hampshire	FERRARI Whitehead	TALBOT Etancelin	TALBOT Rosier	MASERATI de Graffenried	TALBOT Levegh
5	TALBOT Etancelin	TALBOT Claes	MASERATI Bira	TALBOT Sommer	FERRARI Sommer	MASERATI Louveau

*Big road wheels, big steering wheel, it took a lot of
sheer muscle to steer a Talbot if there were many corners*

119

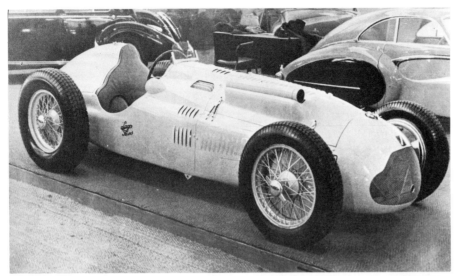

Victorious from the French and Belgian Grands Prix, the Talbot-Lago on its stand at the Paris Motor Show in October 1949

That victory, won fairly and brilliantly, remains one of the most gallant achievements of the Talbot-Lago. Ferrari made no mistake, and that day the supercharged engines signed their own death warrant, at least as far as 'the Commendatore' was concerned. For the next year, Ferrari also started the development of a 4.5-litre unsupercharged engine.

Meanwhile, the Ferrari 125 was not inactive; Ascari drove it to victory in the Grands Prix of Switzerland and Italy, and Peter Whitehead was triumphant in Czechoslovakia. In between, the Talbot-Lago again distinguished itself. That year, the ACF reserved its Grand Prix for sports cars, but a Grand Prix of France was nevertheless organized at Rheims on 17 July. Following their usual tactics, the Talbot drivers let the Ferraris and Maseratis fly ahead but, thanks to their refuelling stops, Louis Chiron was second at half distance, 25 seconds behind Bira. On lap 47 Bira had to stop for fuel and Chiron took the lead, to the frenzied applause of the spectators. During the final laps, the Talbot driver managed to ward off the attacks of Bira (Maserati) and Whitehead (Ferrari) with coolness and skill.

In this memorable French Grand Prix, Talbot introduced a new engine with double ignition. Philippe Etancelin was the only driver to enjoy this advantage, but he unfortunately was forced to retire. In the Grands Prix of Italy and Czechoslovakia he again used this new engine with an extra 14 bhp, finishing second in both races. The test bench was conclusive and the 12-plug engine was generally adopted for 1950.

But already the fortunes of Alfa Romeo were waning. The firm was later to make its comeback with an improved 158, more unbeatable than ever. Meanwhile, Antonio Lago and his drivers took good advantage of this temporary absence of the best single-seater in Grand Prix racing.

At the French Grand Prix Talbot introduced a new engine with double ignition

TALBOT-LAGO AND ITS RIVALS						
TALBOT LAGO T-26 C	6 cyl	4483 cc	(93 × 110 mm)	240 bhp at 4700 rpm	915 kg	260 km/h
ALTA	4 cyl	1491 cc	(78 × 78 mm)	230 bhp at 7000 rpm	610 kg	250 km/h
CISITALIA 360	12 cyl	1492 cc	(50 × 50.5 mm)	296 bhp at 8500 rpm		
ERA Type B/C	6 cyl	1483 cc	(57.5 × 95.2 mm)	240 bhp at 7500 rpm	710 kg	240 km/h
FERRARI 125 F1	12 cyl	1497 cc	(55 × 52.5 mm)	300 bhp at 7500 rpm	700 kg	270 km/h
MASERATI 4 CLT/48	4 cyl	1491 cc	(78 × 78 mm)	260 bhp at 7000 rpm	630 kg	260 km/h

FAREWELL TO TALBOT

1950

Like Ettore Bugatti and also Antonio Lago, Amédée Gordini was born in Italy (in 1899 at Bazzano, near Bologna) and, like his fellow expatriates, for several years he was to be the representative of the French motor industry on the circuits.

Very early on he found out how to cast a spell on Fiat engines. Step by step, by tuning and rebuilding, he completely transformed the engines that passed through his hands.

In the nineteen-thirties he had converted the Simca Five and Eight into really competitive machines for the Le Mans 24 Hours Race. After the war he began to develop, in his workshop at Boulevard Victor, Paris, some single-seaters based on Simca-Fiat components.

His first car, in 1946, was derived from the 6CV Simca of 1100 cc; the next year it grew to 1220 cc and 70 bhp; then in 1948 Gordini went up a peg and created the 1430.

Complying with Formula 1

Henceforth, Gordini had at hand a block that could comply with Formula 1 regulations. For the 1950 season he fitted a type RL 15 Wade comressor, driven at one and a half times engine speed, or approximately 10 000 rpm, for single-stage supercharging.

The basic Simca cylinder block had only three main bearings, which proved fragile when stressed by supercharging. The valves too were simply over-whelmed. Similarly, the chassis had a somewhat frail appearance with its slim side-members and standard Simca front suspension, but all that made sense when one talked about weight. The Simca Gordini was lighter than all its Grand Prix rivals, for the very good reason that it was one of those rare cars that could be adapted to Formula 1 or 2 (only the HWM of Stirling Moss was similarly placed). Gordini of course removed the supercharger for Formula 2.

As for Antonio Lago, he was always dreaming of his supercharged V16 engine, until the realities of his bank balance counselled moderation and he stayed with his faithful type 26 C. For 1950 this engine had made a certain amount of progress, using the double ignition seen on Etancelin's car the previous season and a compression

1950						
	BRITAIN 13/5	MONACO 21/5	SWITZERLAND 4/6	BELGIUM 18/6	FRANCE 2/7	ITALY 3/9
1	ALFA ROMEO Farina	ALFA ROMEO Fangio	ALFA ROMEO Farina	ALFA ROMEO Fangio	ALFA ROMEO Fangio	ALFA ROMEO Farina
2	ALFA ROMEO Fagioli	FERRARI Ascari	ALFA ROMEO Fagioli	ALFA ROMEO Fagioli	ALFA ROMEO Fagioli	FERRARI Serafini
3	ALFA ROMEO Parnell	MASERATI Chiron	TALBOT Rosier	TALBOT Rosier	FERRARI Whitehead	ALFA ROMEO Fagioli
4	TALBOT Giraud-Cabantous	FERRARI Sommer	MASERATI Bira	ALFA ROMEO Farina	SIMCA GORDINI Manzon	TALBOT Rosier
5	TALBOT Rosier	MASERATI Bira	MASERATI Bonetto	FERRARI Ascari	TALBOT Etancelin	TALBOT Etancelin

Amédée Gordini entered Formula 1 with this
supercharged Simca single-seater: Manzon racing at
Pau

ratio raised from 8 to 11:1, with three Zenith 50 HN
horizontal carburettors. The power attained was a
somewhat strained 280 bhp. Externally, this new type
could be recognized instantly by its side-mounted air
intake for the horizontal carburettors, instead of the
former location on top of the bonnet. There remained that
devilish weight, the eternal enemy of the Talbot. In spite
of fitting lighter brakes, the type 26 C still weighed

around 910 kg, or just under 18 cwt.

In 1950, Lago deployed his cars on two fronts: in
Grands Prix certainly, but also at the Le Mans 24 Hours
Race, for which the body was converted into a two-seater
and fitted with mudguards and lamps to conform with
the regulations. With Louis Rosier driving for 23 hours,
the Talbot won the great endurance race. Shall we ever
again see a Grand Prix car victorious at Le Mans?

On the Grand Prix front, the opposition was fierce indeed. The Alfa Romeos had returned, more effective than ever with 350 bhp under their bonnets and Fangio, Farina, and Fagioli as drivers.

At the Ferrari works, Aurelio Lampredi had almost forsaken the supercharged 125, turning his research towards large engines (successively of 3.3, 4.1, and 4.5 litres). The reliability of the Talbots had made an impression on the management of Ferrari. Peter Berthon's BRM looked terrifying on paper, with its complex 16-cylinder engine of more than 400 bhp, but after long and patient hours of development it still achieved nothing.

The Alfa Romeos literally overwhelmed the season and won all the World Championship events. Fangio and Farina shared the honours, but on points it was finally the Italian who was declared World Champion, a title which was bestowed that year for the first time. He was victorious in the Grands Prix of Europe, Switzerland and Italy, while Fangio won at Monaco, Belgium and the ACF.

Behind the Alfas, Talbots often took places of honour. In Switzerland and in Belgium Rosier came third. He even had one first place, but in a non-Championship event, the Dutch Grand Prix at Zandvoort, on 23 July. The Alfa Romeos were absent and Juan-Manuel Fangio exceptionally took the wheel of a Maserati; it was only after a beautifully judged pursuit that he had to concede victory to Louis Rosier.

As for the tiny, fragile Simcas, they had often shocked the drivers of more powerful cars, as in the Grand Prix of the ACF when Manzon took an excellent fourth place; but for them the leading places were inaccessible. In this they found no great consolation.

It had come to the point where two entirely different languages were being spoken in the Grand Prix world: Italian cars were perpetually in a state of evolution, whilst French cars simply could not break free from old-fashioned ideas. Talbot had played their last cards, while Gordini was waiting for his turn.

Pau was not ideal for the cumbersome Talbot-Lago

Georges Grignard winning the Paris Grand Prix in his Talbot-Lago

FRENCH CARS AND THEIR RIVALS						
SIMCA-GORDINI	4 cyl	1430 cc				235 km/h
TALBOT-LAGO T-26 C	6 cyl	4483 cc	(93 × 110 mm)	280 bhp at 5000 rpm	910 kg	270 km/h
ALFA-ROMEO 158/50	8 cyl	1479 cc	(58 × 70 mm)	350 bhp at 8500 rpm	700 kg	290 km/h
ALTA	4 cyl	1491 cc	(78 × 78 mm)	255 bhp at 6500 rpm		265 km/h
BRM Type 5	16 cyl	1472 cc	(49.5 × 47.8 mm)	405 bhp at 8000 rpm	900 kg	290 km/h
FERRARI 125 F1 DD	12 cyl	1497 cc	(55 × 52.5 mm)	315 bhp at 7800 rpm	600 kg	275 km/h
FERRARI 275 F1	12 cyl	3322 cc	(72 × 68 mm)	300 bhp at 7300 rpm	820 kg	270 km/h
FERRARI 340 F1	12 cyl	4102 cc	(80 × 68 mm)	335 bhp at 7000 rpm	850 kg	275 km/h
FERRARI 375 F1	12 cyl	4494 cc	(80 × 74.5 mm)	350 bhp at 7000 rpm	850 kg	275 km/h
HWM FII	4 cyl	1971 cc	(83.5 × 90 mm)	120 bhp at 5000 rpm		210 km/h
MASERATI 4 CLT/48	4 cyl	1491 cc	(78 × 78 mm)	320 bhp		630 kg	280 km/h

A DESPERATE STRUGGLE

1951

This was the last year in which the World Championship was based on the formula of 4.5 litres unsupercharged or 1.5 litres supercharged. For this encounter the single-seaters, which we have seen in course of development during the previous years, had now reached their maturity.

Alfa Romeo had given the final touches to the 158, which thus became the 159 at the 1950 Italian Grand Prix. Ferrari had made a useful intermediate version of his type 375. The name of Maserati remained on the circuits only through the intermediary of private teams, such as one called the Milan team who uprated the 4 CLT/48.

The Maserati brothers themselves set off on a new adventure with the complex Osca V12. BRM continued their laborious development, and Tony Vandervell started his Ferrari transformations under the name of Thinwall.

Amédée Gordini in confusion

In the French camp, faces were long. Amédée Gordini had built an entirely new engine which owed nothing to his previous Simca units. The cylinder block carried a five-bearing crankshaft and it had the very square dimensions of 78 × 78 mm, while the head contained two valves per cylinder, inclined at 90° and operated by twin gear-driven camshafts. The ultra-light chassis remained virtually unchanged.

Gordini's problems stemmed from the diversification of his efforts. All through the year he was switching back and forth between Formula 1 and Formula 2. The mechanics spent days and nights either fitting or removing superchargers. Men and cars arrived at the circuits tired and ill-prepared. On top of all that, Gordini stubbornly insisted on taking part in the Le Mans 24 Hours Race. The final result was that he obtained no success in either category, and the President of Simca, Theodore Pigozzi, was so dissatisfied that he withdrew his support at the end of 1951. The only Formula 1 victory was obtained by Maurice Trintignant in the Grand Prix of Albi, an event outside the Championship.

	SWITZERLAND 27/5	BELGIUM 17/6	FRANCE 1/7	BRITAIN 14/7	GERMANY 29/7	ITALY 16/9	SPAIN 28/10
1951							
1	ALFA ROMEO Fangio	ALFA ROMEO Farina	ALFA ROMEO Fangio	FERRARI Gonzalez	FERRARI Ascari	FERRARI Ascari	ALFA ROMEO Fangio
2	FERRARI Taruffi	FERRARI Ascari	FERRARI Ascari	ALFA ROMEO Fangio	ALFA ROMEO Fangio	FERRARI Gonzalez	FERRARI Gonzalez
3	ALFA ROMEO Farina	FERRARI Villoresi	FERRARI Villoresi	FERRARI Villoresi	FERRARI Gonzalez	ALFA ROMEO Farina	ALFA ROMEO Farina
4	ALFA ROMEO Sanesi	TALBOT Rosier	THINWALL Parnell	ALFA ROMEO Bonetto	FERRARI Villoresi	FERRARI Villoresi	FERRARI Ascari
5	ALFA ROMEO de Graffenried	TALBOT Giraud-Cabantous	ALFA ROMEO Farina	BRM Parnell	FERRARI Taruffi	FERRARI Taruffi	ALFA ROMEO Bonetto

Louis Rosier wrestling with his Talbot-Lago in the streets of Pau

Philippe Etancelin, cap turned back to front, driving the Talbot-Lago type 26 C in the 1951 Grand Prix of the ACF

The Simca-Gordini was particularly at ease on the winding roads of the Nurburgring

The end of Talbot

For Antonio Lago things were not to improve. The type 26C was the descendant of a 1939 design. The weight handicap of 150 kg, added to the power handicap of 150 bhp, deprived it of all hope. Even the drivers of the Talbot team were getting old : Louis Rosier was 46, Yves Giraud-Cabantous was 47 and Philippe Etancelin was 55 ; surely they could no longer have the fire of a Gonzalez or a Fangio.

It was no good counting on sales of Grand Touring Talbots to replenish the coffers. The Lago Grand Sport shared a rather pitiful market with the Bugatti 101 and the Delahaye 235.

Ferrari and Alfa : closely matched

In the top class of motor racing Ferrari and Alfa Romeo were waging a relentless battle, from which Juan Manuel Fangio emerged as World Champion with the Alfa, in front of Alberto Ascari with the Ferrari. Of the seven events counting for the Championship, three went to Ferrari (Britain, Germany and Italy) and four to Alfa Romeo (Switzerland, Belgium, ACF and Spain).

The best Talbot performance was at the Belgian Grand Prix, where the cars of Rosier and Giraud-Cabantous were placed fourth and fifth. Outside the Championship, Talbot again carried off the Dutch Grand Prix. Rosier repeated his 1950 success with Etancelin second, but neither the Ferraris nor the Alfa Romeos had travelled to the sand dunes of Zandvoort.

Talbots would never again be seen in a Grand Prix. The make survived until the 1960 Paris Motor Show and Antonio Lago died in December 1960. There was nothing for him to do, for his factory had been taken over by Simca.

As for Amédée Gordini, he had learnt a lot during his two seasons of Formula 1, where his fragile cars had often seemed out of place. The opening of the 1952 World Championship to Formula 2 single-seaters was to offer him a splendid chance, for here his little cars would feel at home, no longer engaged in his desperate struggle against giant adversaries.

FRENCH CARS AND THEIR RIVALS						
SIMCA GORDINI	4 cyl	1491 cc	(78 × 78 mm)			240 km/h
TALBOT LAGO T-26 C	6 cyl	4483 cc	(93 × 110 mm)	280 bhp at 5000 rpm	910 kg	270 km/h
ALFA ROMEO 159	8 cyl	1479 cc	(58 × 70 mm)	425 bhp at 9300 rpm	710 kg	305 km/h
BRM Type 5	16 cyl	1472 cc	(49.5 × 47.8 mm)	465 bhp at 11 000 rpm	900 kg	305 km/h
FERRARI 212	12 cyl	2562 cc	(68 × 58.8 mm)	200 bhp at 7500 rpm	600 kg	260 km/h
FERRARI 375 F1	12 cyl	4494 cc	(80 × 74.5 mm)	384 bhp at 7500 rpm	720 kg	280 km/h
MASERATI MILAN	4 cyl	1491 cc	(78 × 78 mm)	325 bhp at 7000 rpm	630 kg	280 km/h
OSCA Type G	12 cyl	4472 cc	(78 × 78 mm)	395 bhp at 5500 rpm		280 km/h
THINWALL	12 cyl	4494 cc	(80 × 74.5 mm)	350 bhp at 7000 rpm	850 kg	275 km/h

THE HAND OF PROVIDENCE

1952

In those days providence lavished its attention on Amédée Gordini. In October 1951 the FIA announced that the rules of Formula 1 and Formula 2 were to remain in force for another two years, but that the World Championship would be judged on Formula 2 results only. At that time, with Talbot senile and Alfa Romeo again in retirement, Formula 1 was asleep.

Less sophisticated and less of a closed shop, Formula 2 opened its ranks to a greater number of candidates. Unsupercharged engines had their capacity limited to two litres, which would evidently call for less creative work and less burning of the midnight oil by the technicians. If the field of action was reduced, so was the cost of construction, and that inspired numerous modest constructors with the hope of winning the World Championship.

In the smallest, dingiest, and most sordid of workshops in England a swarm of 'F2' cars were being created. Many of them only made irregular appearances but Cooper, HWM and Connaught became involved in the contest for the summit. The Germans, Veritas and AFM, joined in more discreetly.

The car to beat was the Ferrari 500, Lampredi's four-cylinder, which was driven by Ascari, Farina, Taruffi, and Villoresi. Maserati were more cautious and took time to produce their new type A6 GCM. Meanwhile, Enrico Platé represented the trident with a 4 CLT, deprived of its supercharger and stretched to two litres.

And now Gordini

During the winter of 1951–2, Amédée Gordini was virtually bankrupt. Simca had just abandoned him. But these were just the conditions which stimulated this sorcerer of a man. Freed from all constraints – other than financial ones – he excelled. He designed a new engine, a six-cylinder with the square dimensions of 75 × 75 mm and a dry sump, the oil tank being located under the seat.

The tubular chassis and the compact body followed the lines of previous Gordinis and therein lay the trump card of this French car: its lightness. With 450 kg (990 lbs) and 155 bhp, the Gordini obtained a favourable

1952						
SWITZERLAND 18/5	**BELGIUM** 22/6	**FRANCE** 6/7	**BRITAIN** 19/7	**GERMANY** 3/8	**NETHERLANDS** 17/8	**ITALY** 7/9
1 FERRARI Taruffi	FERRARI Ascari	FERRARI Ascari	FERRARI Ascari	FERRARI Ascari	FERRARI Ascari	FERRARI Ascari
2 FERRARI Fischer	FERRARI Farina	FERRARI Farina	FERRARI Taruffi	FERRARI Farina	FERRARI Farina	MASERATI Gonzalez
3 GORDINI Behra	GORDINI Manzon	FERRARI Taruffi	COOPER BRISTOL Hawthorn	FERRARI Fischer	FERRARI Villoresi	FERRARI Villoresi
4 FRAZER-NASH Wharton	COOPER BRISTOL Hawthorn	GORDINI Manzon	CONNAUGHT Poore	FERRARI Taruffi	COOPER BRISTOL Hawthorn	FERRARI Farina
5 COOPER BRISTOL Brown	HWM Frère	GORDINI Trintignant	CONNAUGHT Thompson	GORDINI Behra	GORDINI Manzon	MASERATI Bonetto

power to weight ratio of 2.9 kg/bhp. The torsion bar front suspension was more elaborate than the preceding example, but the rear axle was stubbornly rigid.

The Gordini lapped briefly at Pau, during practice for the Grand Prix, but it did not take part in the race. Its real introduction took place at the Marseilles Grand Prix, with Robert Manzon as its first driver. The first leg of the World Championship took place in Switzerland and it was there that serious racing began.

The blue Gordini lorry arrived at the circuit in time. Robert Manzon started preparing his car. Back in Paris at the Boulevard Victor at that very moment, the second Gordini was still being built. The mechanics completed its assembly, Jean Behra the driver standing by. When it was ready at last, 'trade' number plates were fitted, for the only way to reach the circuit in time to qualify was by road. Jean Behra headed for Berne, weaving his agile racing car along the roads of Burgundy and the Jura. After a few formalities at the frontier post, the Swiss customs officers push-started the Gordini. It made it in time to qualify for the Grand Prix.

On the first lap, Robert Manzon took the lead in front of Taruffi! The miracle lasted until fifteen laps from the end, and then Manzon's engine failed. Taruffi won ahead of Fischer, both in Ferraris; Jean Behra took third place, and a good deal of credit for it.

That 4 May 1952, at Berne, Amédée Gordini had won the confidence of the public and the respect of his adversaries.

Grand Prix of the Marne. Formula 2 Gordinis 2, 4 and 6, on even terms with Ferrari 500s 10, 12 and 14, and Cooper Bristol 32. Jean Behra in no. 4 won the race

With restricted means and simple techniques, he had proved that he could worry a professional team like that of Ferrari. However, he was never able to surmount that unbeatable duo, Ferrari-Ascari, who, apart from the Swiss Grand Prix won ALL the great races (Belgium, ACF, Britain, Holland, Germany, Italy). But one day – outside the championship – his efforts were rewarded.

In June the Grand Prix of the Marne was organized, on the Rheims-Gueux circuit. As well as the two models for Manzon and Behra, Gordini produced another car for Prince Birabongse of Thailand. On his car, Manzon employed some new ventilated brake drums. Right from the start Jean Behra dictated the race, ahead of Farina and Ascari in their Ferraris, and never gave way to their pressure. If only the Grand Prix of the Marne counted for the World Championship!

By the end of the season Gordini's resources had melted away. Development was halted, and production became more and more cursory.

128 *The Gordini in the Paris Grand Prix, at Montlhéry*

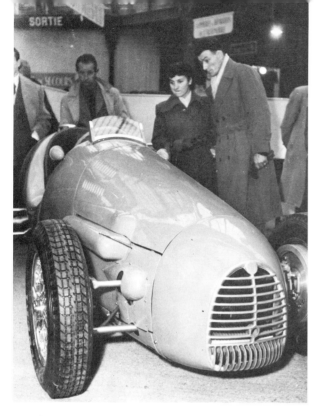

The Gordini at the 1952 Paris Motor Show, resting up after an encouraging first season

In 1952 Gordini still used drum brakes

At the Pau Grand Prix, the Gordini Formula 2 still had the same body as the 1951 Simca Gordini

GORDINI AND ITS RIVALS

GORDINI	6 cyl	1988 cm	(75 × 75 mm)	155 bhp at 6000 rpm	450 kg	250 km/h
AFM	8 cyl	1992 cm	(67.3 × 70 mm)	160 bhp at 8200 rpm		250 km/h
ALTA	4 cyl	1971 cm	(83.5 × 90 mm)	150 bhp at 6000 rpm	585 kg	245 km/h
ASTON BUTTLEWORTH	4 cyl	1984 cm	(87.5 × 82,5 mm)		420 kg	210 km/h
CONNAUGHT A-Type	4 cyl	1960 cm	(79 × 100 mm)	140 bhp at 6000 rpm	560 kg	240 km/h
COOPER BRISTOL T-20	6 cyl	1970 cm	(66 × 96 mm)	130 bhp at 5800 rpm	510 kg	245 km/h
ERA G-Type	6 cyl	1970 cm	(66 × 96 mm)	130 bhp at 5800 rpm		230 km/h
FERRARI 500 F2	4 cyl	1985 cm	(90 × 78 mm)	170 bhp at 7500 rpm	560 kg	260 km/h
FRAZER-NASH	6 cyl	1970 cm	(66 × 96 mm)	130 bhp at 5800 rpm		230 km/h
H.A.R.	6 cyl	1985 cm	(63.5 × 104,5 mm)			220 km/h
H.W.M.	4 cyl	1971 cm	(83.5 × 90 mm)	150 bhp at 6000 rpm	560 kg	245 km/h
MASERATI A6 GCM	6 cyl	1988 cm	(75 × 75 mm)	177 bhp at 8000 rpm	620 kg	255 km/h
MASERATI PLATE 4 CLT	4 cyl	1995 cm	(84 × 90 mm)	140 bhp at 6500 rpm	620 kg	240 km/h
OSCA	6 cyl	1987 cm	(76 × 73 mm)	166 bhp at 6700 rpm		250 km/h
VERITAS	6 cyl	1988 cm	(75 × 75 mm)	140 bhp at 6500 rpm	560 kg	240 km/h

BATTLE SCARS

1953

The streets of Levallois are sad in winter. But in January 1953 in a dull, anonymous warehouse, an atmosphere of excitement centred round one small group of people. Huddled in their mackintoshes, Sacha Gordine and two engineers, Vigna and Perkins, posed with pride before their creation: a Formula 2 single-seater.

Sacha Gordine was a rich film producer (among other films he financed Max Ophuls' *La Ronde*). Passionately interested in motor racing, he had taken part as an amateur in a few rallys, but his dream was to build his own car. He called in M Vigna, an engineer of Italian origin who had worked with Professor Porsche on the Cisitalia 360 project. Vigna's assistant was called Perkins, and came from Thailand.

Vigna was greatly influenced by his apprenticeship with Porsche: the Sacha Gordine bore no resemblance to any existing F2 car. Crouching low between the large wheels, the wide, flat body had an unusual shape. The radiator cowl with two symmetrical air intakes, such as Ferrari were to use in 1961, was one of the brilliant touches. The influence of Porsche technique was obvious in every part: central engine, torsion bars, De Dion rear axle.

Sacha Gordine took care of the details. The magnesium V8 cylinder block was machined all over and contained detachable finned wet liners, the combustion chambers were hemispherical and the exhaust valves were sodium-cooled. Cooling of the engine was achieved with the aid of glycol, which was contained in a little radiator placed at the front, alongside a fuel tank and the oil radiator. For admirers of refined engineering, merely to read the specification is mouth-watering – and it continues. The rear axle was entirely made of magnesium (Perkins, who came from the aircraft industry, was doubtless no stranger to such rare materials). The weight distribution was ingenious. The enormous fuel tanks were carried low down against the two tubes that formed the chassis. The very compact gearbox was in unit with the ZF limited-slip differential.

	ARGENTINA 18/1	NETHERLANDS 7/6	BELGIUM 21/6	FRANCE 5/7	BRITAIN 18/7	GERMANY 2/8	SWITZERLAND 23/8	ITALY 13/9
1	FERRARI Ascari	FERRARI Ascari	FERRARI Ascari	FERRARI Hawthorn	FERRARI Farina	FERRARI Ascari	FERRARI Ascari	MASERATI Fangio
2	FERRARI Villoresi	FERRARI Farina	FERRARI Villoresi	MASERATI Fangio	MASERATI Fangio	MASERATI Fangio	FERRARI Farina	FERRARI Farina
3	MASERATI Gonzalez	MASERATI Bonetto	MASERATI Marimon	MASERATI Gonzalez	FERRARI Farina	FERRARI Hawthorn	FERRARI Hawthorn	FERRARI Villoresi
4	FERRARI Hawthorn	FERRARI Hawthorn	MASERATI de Graffenried	FERRARI Ascari	MASERATI Gonzalez	MASERATI Bonetto	MASERATI Bonetto	FERRARI Hawthorn
5	MASERATI Galvez	MASERATI de Graffenried	GORDINI Trintignant	FERRARI Farina	FERRARI Hawthorn	MASERATI de Graffenried	MASERATI Lang	GORDINI Trintignant

The Gordini in the 1953 Grand Prix of Pau

The very modern Sacha-Gordine bore an undeniable resemblance to Dr Porsche's Cisitalia

A model of the Sacha-Gordine, clearly showing the similarity of the two forward air intakes to those of the 1961 Ferrari

No doubt to finance such a machine single-handed weighed heavily on Gordine's resources. And one day he realized that to pursue the project any further would be his ruin. He drew back and awoke from his dream. The other projects he had planned were suspended and all work stopped: a 1.5-litre supercharged engine remained on the drawing board, and the Le Mans model, whose chassis already existed, went no further.

And nothing more was ever heard of the Sacha Gordine.

As for Amédée Gordini, he was not happy either. He could not produce a new model for 1953; this being so, the old model would have to do, despite its dumpy, awkward, high-built look. It is true that the other competitors in Formula 2/1953 were also pausing for breath, excepting Maserati, for whom Gioacchimo Colombo had taken in hand the work of Massimino.

The Gordini retained its qualities of lightness and high maximum speed but it began to prove less and less reliable, especially in the area of the transmission. Preparation of the single-seaters was carried out in a rather piecemeal fashion, always overshadowed by that wretched Le Mans 24 Hours Race, which drained Gordini of energy and funds.

That year again, Ferrari flattened all their competitors: in Argentina, Holland, Belgium, France, Britain, Germany and Switzerland, the Ferrari 500, backed up by the 'Squalo 552', was victorious! One had to wait for the last Grand Prix, in Italy, to see Juan Manuel Fangio put his Maserati on top. It was there that the Gordini team accomplished their best performance of the year, all the three cars entered reaching the finish, but no Gordini gained a higher place than fifth in any Championship race of 1953. Amédée got nothing out of it but the scars of battle.

For the Grand Prix of Italy, the Gordini had two exhaust pipes, and the nosecone was surrounded by a deflector

Vigna designed a complex magnesium V8 engine for the Sacha-Gordine

Above left: *The chassis of the Sacha-Gordine, partly assembled in February 1952*

FRENCH CARS AND THEIR RIVALS						
GORDINI	6 cyl	1988 cc	(75 × 75 mm)	160 bhp	450 kg	250 km/h
SACHA GORDINE	8 cyl	1970 cc	(70 × 64 mm)	191 bhp at 8000 rpm	470 kg	280 km/h
CONNAUGHT A-Type	4 cyl	1960 cc	(79 × 100 mm)	165 bhp	560 kg	250 km/h
COOPER BRISTOL T-23	6 cyl	1970 cc	(66 × 96 mm)	150 bhp at 5800 rpm	510 kg	255 km/h
COOPER ALTA T-24	4 cyl	1971 cc	(83.5 × 90 mm)	186 bhp	510 kg	260 km/h
COOPER SPECIAL	4 cyl	1971 cc	(83.5 × 90 mm)	200 bhp at 6000 rpm	520 kg	270 km/h
FERRARI 500 F2	4 cyl	1985 cc	(90 × 78 mm)	180 bhp at 7500 rpm	560 kg	275 km/h
FERRARI 553 F2	4 cyl	1997 cc	(93 × 73.5 mm)	190 bhp at 7500 rpm		280 km/h
H.W.M.	4 cyl	1971 cc	(83.5 × 90 mm)	175 bhp at 7000 rpm	560 kg	255 km/h
MASERATI A6 GCM	6 cyl	1970 cc	(76.2 × 72 mm)	200 bhp at 8000 rpm	580 kg	280 km/h
NARDI	6 cyl	1991 cc	(72 × 81.5 mm)	135 bhp		
OSCA	6 cyl	1987 cc	(76 × 83 mm)	170 bhp		250 km/h
TURNER	4 cyl	1960 cc	(79 × 100 mm)	160 bhp		
VERITAS	6 cyl	1988 cc	(75 × 75 mm)	140 bhp at 6500 rpm	560 kg	240 km/h

ON THE BRINK

1954

In 1952–3 Formula 1 had so seriously declined that the World Championship had been fought out solely under Formula 2. The effect was like a return to those chaotic times of 1909–12 or 1928–33. But each time the decadent period was followed by a spectacular revival. It was the Renaissance after the middle ages, as if according to some universal law of alternation.

After two seasons of atrophy, the World Championship started off on the right foot in 1954. New rules opened the door to further experiments, cylinder capacity being limited to 2.5 litres with atmospheric induction, or 750 cc if supercharging was applied.

Except for Taraschi and Giannini, who prepared a supercharged 750 cc Giaur for the Grand Prix of Rome, all the makers chose the 2.5-litre engine. This cylinder capacity was sufficiently close to that of F2/53 to permit some adaptation: the Maserati A6 GCM became the 250F, the Ferrari 500 grew into the 625, while the Squalo 553 was transformed into the 555. At a lower level, HWM and Cooper-Bristol managed to stretch their engines a little. In all that, there was nothing unexpected.

But the appearance in the entry lists of three famous names caused some excitement: Lancia with a V8-engined car having laterally-mounted fuel tanks, Alfa Romeo with a mysterious 12-cylinder engine, and Mercedes-Benz with a car as advanced aerodynamically as mechanically.

It turned out that Alfa Romeo abandoned their project, after their engine's promise on the test bench of 300 bhp. As for the Lancia, it was not ready until the end of the season; but the Mercedes entered the arena at the French Grand Prix, with its awe-inspiring silver silhouette.

Amédée Gordini, of course, was among those who had to live from their winnings from Formula 2 racing. His financial situation was even worse than before and the Gordini that was so familiar on all the circuits would have to be used again for one more season. To bring his engine up to 2500 cc he had simply replaced the crankshaft and the cylinder liners, without even changing the head. 'Why innovate?' said Amédée.

1954							
ARGENTINA 17/1	**BELGIUM** Spa 20/6	**ACF** Rheims 4/7	**BRITAIN** Silverstone 17/7	**GERMANY** Nurburgring 1/8	**SWITZERLAND** 22/8	**ITALY** Monza 5/9	**SPAIN** 24/10
1 MASERATI Fangio	MASERATI Fangio	MERCEDES Fangio	FERRARI Gonzalez	MERCEDES Fangio	MERCEDES Fangio	MERCEDES Fangio	FERRARI Hawthorn
2 FERRARI Farina	FERRARI Trintignant	MERCEDES Kling	FERRARI Hawthorn	FERRARI Gonzalez	FERRARI Gonzalez	FERRARI Hawthorn	MASERATI Musso
3 FERRARI Gonzalez	MASERATI Moss	FERRARI Manzon	MASERATI Marimon	FERRARI Trintignant	MERCEDES Hermann	FERRARI Maglioli	MERCEDES Fangio
4 FERRARI Trintignant	FERRARI Hawthorn	MASERATI Bira	MERCEDES Fangio	MERCEDES Kling	MASERATI Mieres	MERCEDES Hermann	MASERATI Mieres
5 GORDINI Bayol	GORDINI Pilette	MASERATI Villoresi	FERRARI Trintignant	MASERATI Mantovani	MASERATI Mantovani	FERRARI Trintignant	MERCEDES Kling

NEW AMBITIONS

1955

At this time French motor sport was entering its darkest days. Still without any financial help, Amédée Gordini continued to make sacrifices. Practically unchanged, his single-seater was outclassed by all its rivals.

This situation bore some resemblance to the state of the French economy, which was thus reflected on the circuits. Engaged in an inconclusive war in Indochina, facing greater and greater difficulties in North Africa, France of the Fourth Republic was losing its grip in economic terms.

A new model in preparation

The new model which Amédée Gordini had designed was under construction, but in the meanwhile the good old six-cylinder had to act as substitute. But without Jean Behra: the talent of this French driver had aroused a certain amount of envy – and in 1955 he was driving a Maserati 250F.

For their part, the foreign makes had made no real changes and the hierarchy had become accepted: still there was the same superiority of Mercedes and Fangio, with Ferrari and Maserati always lying in wait.

With barely time to attend the races, the Gordini team were toiling away in the workshop on their new car. Then one morning in July some journalists arrived early at the Montlhéry autodrome. They were waiting for the Gordini lorry. Amédée was nervous; he had his normal worried expression, which gave him an appearance of shyness, but one caught a glimpse of an immense inner joy. Juan Manuel Fangio himself was there, out of sympathy.

The doors of the lorry opened: Gordini unveiled his new eight-cylinder. At last he had a modern car, competitive, a real Formula 1 and not just a Formula 2 substitute. Broad but carefully profiled, especially at the level of the wheels, the Gordini was very impressive, and in no way resembled the six-cylinder model, which looked quite delicate in comparison.

Among the technical innovations which abounded,

1955					
ARGENTINA 16/1	**MONACO** 22/5	**BELGIUM** 5/6	**NETHERLANDS** 19/6	**BRITAIN** 16/7	**ITALY** 11/9
1 MERCEDES Fangio	FERRARI Trintignant	MERCEDES Fangio	MERCEDES Fangio	MERCEDES Moss	MERCEDES Fangio
2 FERRARI Trintignant	LANCIA Castellotti	MERCEDES Moss	MERCEDES Moss	MERCEDES Fangio	MERCEDES Taruffi
3 FERRARI Farina	MASERATI Behra	FERRARI Farina	MASERATI Musso	MERCEDES Kling	FERRARI Castellotti
4 MERCEDES Hermann	FERRARI Farina	FERRARI Frère	MASERATI Mieres	MERCEDES Taruffi	MASERATI Behra
5 MASERATI Mieres	LANCIA Villoresi	MASERATI Mieres	FERRARI Castellotti	MASERATI Musso	MASERATI Menditigny

Bordeaux Grand Prix: no. 2 is the 1954 6-cylinder Gordini driven by Manzon; next to it is Bayol's 1955 model, no. 6

the eight-cylinder stood out particularly by its independent suspension of all four wheels. Each wheel was supported by a cranked arm, oscillating around a horizontal pivot attached to the chassis. On one side, these bars were connected to a hydraulic shock absorber and on the other to a torsion bar. Gordini had adopted Messier disc brakes, with which he had already experimented on the six-cylinder, placed within the wheels in front and mounted inboard at the rear.

For the chassis itself Gordini had not, unfortunately, discarded his habitual design. Instead of adopting the multi-tubular space frame chosen by Mercedes, Ferrari, Maserati and Lancia, he had retained his 'ladder' made of two large tubes with cross-bracing.

The five-speed gearbox, formerly tried on Behra's car in 1955, was also employed. Finally, the engine lay at full length in the form of an elegant and classic straight-eight, over-square, with twin overhead camshafts, and a battery of four twin-choke carburettors. On the bench, it developed 256 bhp at 7300 rpm, but as installed it was probably giving 230 bhp.

The eight-cylinder Gordini should have made its first appearance at the Grand Prix of the ACF on 3 July, but the Le Mans catastrophe upset the calendar. The Grand Prix was cancelled and the début of the Gordini was delayed until the Italian Grand Prix in September. Manzon was to have driven the new car but he had to

Amédée Gordini's totally new single-seater, the type 32

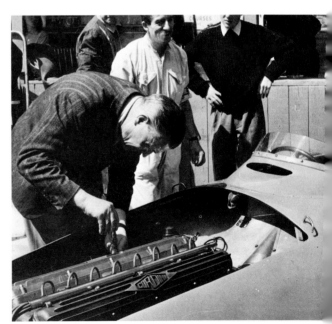

Amédée Gordini making the final adjustments to his new 8-cylinder engine

Juan Manuel Fangio, driver of the Mercedes W196, was at Montlhéry for the presentation of the Gordini type 32 in August 1955

return to France in an unexpected emergency, leaving his car to Jean Lucas, who only completed a discreet eight laps.

Previously Gordini had been dealing with cars that were too old, but suddenly he was exposed to the terrors of youth. The new eight-cylinder had not lost the weaknesses of the six-cylinder (fragility, uncertainties in the preparation before a race, limited power), but it

René Bonnet transformed his DB-Panhard Monomill by the simple addition of a supercharger. It was an interesting idea, but it was to have no future

Gordini and Messier introduced disc brakes in France

Above right: The supercharger of the DB was directly coupled to the front of the crankshaft

lacked its qualities of lightness and compactness. The eight-cylinder was large and heavy with its weight of 875 kg ready for the circuit. All the winter remained for Amédée Gordini to prove that he had not made a mistake.

A supercharged car

Decidedly, if France did not produce cars that won, she did not shy away from any difficulty or any original idea. At the Grand Prix of Pau, a liliputian car hid behind the monsters of Formula 1: weighing 350 kg, less than three metres long, shaped like a wasp, with an engine the size of a coffee grinder, it was a DB Monomill, among the Fis!

Charles Deutsch and René Bonnet had – like Giaur in 1954 – applied the letter of the law and created a supercharged Formula 1 car. They had taken their Monomill as a base, which itself stemmed from the 500 cc racers of 1948 – 51. It retained the slim and spidery appearance and the large and prominent nose which hid the overhanging engine.

This was a twin-cylinder, air-cooled Panhard, with front wheel drive and forced induction, a technique of which Deutsch and Bonnet already had experience on their record-breaking cars. The Mag compressor, modified by René Bonnet, was directly driven from the end of the crankshaft and consequently turned at engine speed. The chassis was hardly strengthened at all but braking was improved, with disc brakes, and roadholding was as marvellous as before. With its supercharger the flat-twin delivered 85 bhp instead of 50, but even with as little as 350 kg, or about 4 kg/bhp, that was not enough to trouble the Ferraris with their 250 bhp and 2.4 kg/bhp.

Nevertheless, the idea was fascinating and the courageous experiment needed to be made, if only to prove the viability of the Formula to those who doubted it. The Monomill had not lost everything: it had before it a useful career in Formula Junior.

FRENCH CARS AND THEIR RIVALS						
DB Monomill	2 cyl	746 cc	(79.6 × 75 mm)	85 bhp	350 kg	180 km/h
GORDINI	6 cyl	2473 cc	(80 × 82 mm)	230 bhp at 6500 rpm	560 kg	260 km/h
GORDINI Type 32	8 cyl	2474 cc	(75 × 70 mm)	256 bhp at 7300 rpm	650 kg	270 km/h
ARZANI VOLPINI	4 cyl	2498 cc	(94 × 90 mm)	220 bhp	630 kg	235 km/h
BRM P-25	4 cyl	2490 cc	(102.8 × 75 mm)	235 bhp	540 kg	260 km/h
CONNAUGHT B-Type	4 cyl	2472 cc	(93.5 × 90 mm)	240 bhp at 7000 rpm		260 km/h
COOPER T-40	6 cyl	1970 cc	(66 × 96 mm)	190 bhp		250 km/h
FERRARI 625 A	4 cyl	2497 cc	(100 × 79.5 mm)	250 bhp at 7500 rpm	600 kg	285 km/h
FERRARI 555	4 cyl	2497 cc	(100 × 79.5 mm)	270 bhp at 7500 rpm		290 km/h
LANCIA D-50	8 cyl	2488 cc	(73.6 × 73.1 mm)	260 bhp at 8000 rpm	620 kg	285 km/h
MASERATI 250 F	6 cyl	2494 cc	(84 × 75 mm)	240 bhp at 7000 rpm	630 kg	280 km/h
MERCEDES BENZ W196	8 cyl	2497 cc	(76 × 68.8 mm)	290 bhp at 8500 rpm	680 kg	290 km/h
VANWALL	4 cyl	2490 cc	(96 × 86 mm)			

FAREWELL

1956

A day in late November 1955, on the Entzheim track in Alsace; with a look of excitement about them, an engineer, a mechanic and a financier stood wrapped up in their overcoats. Just think, they were bringing out a new Bugatti! Roland Bugatti, heir to 'le Patron' himself, had revived his father's firm with the help of Pierre Marco, Ettore's faithful colleague since 1919.

The Molsheim factory had dressed its wounds and the two men had chosen a radical way to start its new life. They had called in the Italian designer, Gioacchimo Colombo. This hardy engineer was born in 1903 and had behind him a prolific career, with Alfa Romeo from 1924 to 1937 and 1951–2, with Ferrari from 1945 to 1950, and finally with Maserati in 1953. With such a personality among the new Bugatti men, public opinion was scenting out a spectacular return to competition.

The type 251 Bugatti, the posthumous work of Ettore Bugatti completed by Colombo, could justly be called original in every way. Compact and low-built in the extreme, the body looked corpulent but it was very well streamlined (CX factor 0.54). The radiator intake filled the whole width of the chassis and there were fairings on either side of it, in front of the wheels, which gave the Bugatti an entirely different shape from its longer and slimmer rivals.

The secret of the reduced length was in the architecture of the car; the engine was mounted transversely in the centre, an arrangement that was revived ten years later in the Lamborghini Miura. Designer of the V12 Ferrari, Colombo here chose a straight-eight configuration, born from the marriage of two four-cylinder units with the timing gears between them. With double ignition and twin overhead camshafts, the Bugatti engine conformed with modern racing practice.

The gearbox was arranged parallel with the engine and concealed synchromesh kindly lent by Porsche. The suspension also contained several surprises. The De Dion rear axle was suspended on helical springs, inclined at 45° transversely and deflected by long rockers. In front, a rigid axle perpetuated the pre-war tradition (a pity). The accessories very neatly filled the spaces that remained free in the multi-tubular chassis: water radiator and oil tank at the front, fuel tanks at the sides between

1956						
ARGENTINA 22/1	**MONACO** 13/5	**BELGIUM** Spa 3/6	**ACF** Rheims 1/7	**BRITAIN** Silverstone 14/7	**GERMANY** Nurburgring 5/8	**ITALY** Monza 2/9
FERRARI Fangio	MASERATI Moss	FERRARI Collins	FERRARI Collins	FERRARI Fangio	FERRARI Fangio	FERRARI Moss
MASERATI Behra	FERRARI Collins	FERRARI Frère	FERRARI Castellotti	FERRARI de Portago	MASERATI Moss	FERRARI Collins
MASERATI Hawthorn	MASERATI Behra	MASERATI Moss/Perdisa	MASERATI Behra	MASERATI Behra	MASERATI Behra	CONNAUGHT Flockhart
MASERATI Landi	FERRARI Fangio	VANWALL Schell	FERRARI Fangio	CONNAUGHT Fairman	MASERATI Godia	MASERATI Godia
FERRARI Gendebien	GORDINI da Silva Ramos	MASERATI Villoresi	MASERATI Perdisa	MASERATI Gould	MASERATI Rosier	CONNAUGHT Fairman

*Monaco Grand Prix, 1956: the six-cylinder Gordini
behind the eight-cylinder*

*The Gordini type 32 number 2 was more round-bellied
than the first and had eight separate exhaust pipes.
Manzon at the Italian Grand Prix*

142

the front and rear wheels. The weight distribution seemed ideal and this could have been a car of the 1970s.

But from there on – an abrupt change of tone. Maurice Trintignant, an official Vanwall driver for 1956, agreed with enthusiasm to drive the type 251 for a single race. Between races driving for Vanwall, he returned to test-drive the blue car. 'When I brake, the front wheels go mad and the steering becomes uncontrollable.'

Roadholding was relatively good but the Bugatti described graceful arabesques down the road: the front axle had insufficient weight. However, Raymond Roche insisted that the car should be at the Grand Prix of the ACF at Rheims on 1 July. After much persuasion he succeeded, and it was not one but two Bugatti type 251s which arrived at Rheims. The second chassis was visibly different from the first: the body was longer and less corpulent, while the rear suspension was more conventional, with vertical springs. The disc brakes, tried in practice, were replaced by the drums of the type 57.

Trintignant did not have time to sort out the new car and elected to start in the prototype which they therefore simply fitted with the newer engine from the other car. He was in 17th position on the grid, having lapped 18 seconds slower than Juan Manuel Fangio in a Ferrari.

The Bugatti lacked power and only developed 230 bhp though 275 bhp was claimed. Its roadholding quickly deteriorated and the courageous 'Petoulet' was soon driving practically without shock absorbers. But he

Type 251 Bugatti in its first version: November 1955

The second Bugatti type 251 as it appeared at practice for the Grand Prix of the ACF, 1956

143

The chassis of the second Bugatti type 251 exhibited today at the Fondation Schlumpf

retaining his everlasting six-cylinders. Eight-cylinder number two had a more curvaceous body and could be distinguished by its eight separate exhaust pipes, which ran along its left side. But at Monaco, Manzon and Hermanos da Silva Ramos both preferred the six-cylinders, while Bayol and Pilette shared the earlier of the eight-cylinder models. The Portuguese driver had good intuition, for he finished fifth, ahead of Bayol.

After the Monaco Grand Prix, Gordini stayed away from the circuits more and more; he did not go to Belgium, but he made a supreme effort and fielded three cars for the Grand Prix of the ACF: both eights and a six. It was a wasted effort, da Silva Ramos, Manzon, and Pilette finishing very far back in eighth, ninth, and eleventh places. It was discouraging but he persevered to the end of the season – without result.

The opposing teams had made some notable progress. The Ferrari ex-Lancias were approaching the performance of the 1955 Mercedes; and the Vanwalls, revised by Frank Costin and Colin Chapman, had made enormous strides. And it was against this background that the position of Gordini was growing weaker. As far as power is concerned, he was at the bottom of the ladder, the eight-cylinder never fulfilling the hopes that were held out for it. It was at the beginning of the 1957 season, after one last attempt in the Grand Prix of Naples that Amédée Gordini decided to give up racing. He accepted an invitation to enter the Régie Renault, where he found a new lease of life in the job of transforming the Dauphine, the R8 and the R12.

Gordini's withdrawal signalled a long period in the wilderness for French motor sport, especially at the higher levels of competition. France had other pre-occupations, centring on the Mediterranean basin. In 1956 Morocco and Tunisia gained their independence and the Suez crisis came hard and fast upon the loss of the North African colonies. And the rebellion in Algeria which had broken out in 1954 was still continuing, more bitterly and violently than ever.

One need hardly say that the troubles of motor sport were of little interest at this time.

pressed on regardless for 18 laps, when the accelerator seized. This brought the history of Bugatti to its true end. Exposed to financial and family problems, the Molsheim firm ceased production of cars with this type 251 and a type 252 cabriolet, its contemporary.

The Sorcerer lays down his arms

Gordini was also about to make his farewells as an independent constructor. In the course of the winter of 1955–6 he had built a second eight-cylinder, though still

FRENCH CARS AND THEIR RIVALS						
BUGATTI T-251	8 cyl	2431 cc	(75 × 68.8 mm)	230 bhp at 7500 rpm	750 kg	260 km/h
GORDINI T-32	8 cyl	2474 cc	(75 × 70 mm)	235 bhp	650 kg	270 km/h
BRM P-25	4 cyl	2490 cc	(102.8 × 75 mm)	250 bhp at 9000 rpm	540 kg	270 km/h
CONNAUGHT B-Type	4 cyl	2472 cc	(93.5 × 90 mm)	245 bhp at 7500 rpm		275 km/h
FERRARI 8 CL	8 cyl	2488 cc	(73.6 × 73.1 mm)	270 bhp at 8000 rpm	630 kg	290 km/h
FERRARI 8 CL	8 cyl	2486 cc	(76 × 68.5 mm)	270 bhp at 8000 rpm	630 kg	290 km/h
MASERATI 250 F	6 cyl	2494 cc	(84 × 75 mm)	250 bhp at 7200 rpm	630 kg	290 km/h
VANWALL	4 cyl	2490 cc	(96 × 86 mm)	260 bhp at 7400 rpm	605 kg	285 km/h

*Renault Type AK 1906
dessin d'Édouard Montaut.*

Delage 15-S-8 1927
collection Briggs S. Cunningham Museum, Costa-Mesa,
◀ *U.S.A.*

Bugatti T-35 B 1928
collection André Binda. **147**

Talbot-Lago T-26 C 1950
collection Henri Malartre-Ville de Lyon, La Rochetaillée-
148 *sur-Saône.*

Gordini 1954
collection Henri Malartre-Ville de Lyon, La Rochetaillée-
sur-Saône.

Renault RS 01 1978
dessin (Grâce-E.T.A.I.)

ENGLISH, SCOTS AND FRENCH TOGETHER

1968

In April 1967 the French Government, led by Georges Pompidou, made a grant of six million francs to Matra-Sports for the development of a Formula 1 car.

French motor sport, in a state of hibernation for eleven years, at all events at Grand Prix level, was able to come out of the tunnel with assured financial backing. Why Matra-Sports? This company, founded in October 1964, took over the small sports-car business of René Bonnet, but Matra is not to be counted among the small businesses. It is a marginal subsidiary of the giant Engins Matra group, which is an aerospace concern and therefore closely allied with armaments and defence. The competition Matras had the double task of boosting the sales of Matra-Sports production cars and also, to a secondary extent, of speeding up the advance of technology for French industry.

The national oil company, Elf, took part in this venture alongside Matra. An agreement was concluded on 19 January 1967 at Monaco, providing for technical and financial co-operation. Immediately, engineers in the lubricants department set to work to prepare a castor-base oil.

Where was Formula 1 in 1968?

After a period of 1500 cc between 1961 and 1965, Formula 1 events were run under a three-litre capacity

The Matra MS 9, used in the South African Grand Prix of 1968, was an experimental Formula 1 car built on a Formula 2 chassis

Johnny Servoz-Gavin testing the Matra MS 11 with the V12 engine, March 1968

The Matra V12 engine was a very fine piece of foundry-work but unfortunately it was not quite powerful enough

	SOUTH AFRICA 1/1	SPAIN 12/5	MONACO 26/5	BELG 9/6
1	LOTUS Clark	LOTUS G. Hill	LOTUS G. Hill	McLA McLa
2	LOTUS G. Hill	McLAREN Hulme	BRM Attwood	BR Rodri
3	BRABHAM Rindt	COOPER Redman	COOPER Bianchi	FERR Ick
4	FERRARI Amon	COOPER Scarfiotti	COOPER Scarfiotti	MAT Stev
5	McLAREN Hulme	MATRA Beltoise	McLAREN Hulme	LOT Oli

In a deluge of rain, Jackie Stewart taking the Matra-Ford MS 10 to its first victory — the Dutch Grand Prix

	1968						
ERLANDS 23/6	**FRANCE** 7/7	**BRITAIN** 20/7	**GERMANY** 4/8	**ITALY** 8/9	**CANADA** 22/9	**USA** 6/10	**MEXICO** 3/11
MATRA ewart	FERRARI Ickx	LOTUS Siffert	MATRA Stewart	McLAREN Hulme	McLAREN Hulme	MATRA Stewart	LOTUS G. Hill
MATRA ltoise	HONDA Surtees	FERRARI Amon	LOTUS G. Hill	MATRA Servoz-Gavin	McLAREN McLaren	LOTUS G. Hill	McLAREN McLaren
RM riguez	MATRA Stewart	FERRARI Ickx	BRABHAM Rindt	FERRARI Ickx	BRM Rodriguez	HONDA Surtees	LOTUS Oliver
RRARI ckx	COOPER Elford	McLAREN Hulme	FERRARI Ickx	BRM Courage	LOTUS G. Hill	McLAREN Gurney	BRM Rodriguez
BHAM oser	McLAREN Hulme	HONDA Surtees	BRABHAM Brabham	MATRA Beltoise	COOPER Elford	LOTUS Siffert	HONDA Bonnier

First appearance of the MS 11 at Monte Carlo, with its cut-off nose

Matra MS 11 with hydraulic transmission to all four wheels. The hydraulic receivers and curved suspension arms can be seen next to the front wheels

limit. The regulations created fantastic rivalry between the engine builders and the chassis constructors. After two seasons of trials and experiments, the numerous teams seemed ready to face 1968. Ferrari, BRM, Honda, Brabham and Eagle had produced their own engines, while Lotus and McLaren chose the Ford Cosworth, and Cooper used the V12 BRM.

The Matra team were playing it both ways. While they were developing their own hundred-per-cent French V12, they raced their single-seater with a V8 Cosworth engine.

Their first experimental Formula 1 single-seater saw the light of day in December 1967. This was the MS 9, and it incorporated numerous existing components: the monocoque of the MS 7 (Formula 2) and various parts from the front and rear suspensions of the 630 sports prototype. The MS 9 ran in the South African Grand Prix only. Jackie Stewart recorded the third fastest practice lap, but in the race he was let down by his engine. However, the Matra, with its truncated nose, did not pass unnoticed, for Beltoise finished sixth in the Formula 2 MS 7.

The first true Formula 1 Matra appeared at the Spanish Grand Prix on 15 May 1968, with Jean-Pierre Beltoise at the wheel. The MS 10, as it was called, had a structure that was entirely its own: the monocoque ended behind the driver's seat, for the Cosworth was designed to withstand rear suspension stresses without any chassis to reinforce it. A tubular frame was used while changing engines, to hold the rear-end assembly, so as to avoid having to dismantle the suspension and brakes every time. Jean-Pierre Beltoise was sixth in the Spanish Grand Prix and made the fastest lap. Two weeks later, Johnny Servoz-Gavin starred at the Monaco circuit. For the first three laps he led the race with astonishing ease, until his rear suspension collapsed.

At the Belgian Grand Prix Jackie Stewart reappeared, together with the Matra-International team, directed by the master-hand of Ken Tyrrell. The Scots driver finished fourth. This result was soon forgotten, however, as the real date to remember was 23 June. This was the day of the Dutch Grand Prix, held at Zandvoort and, as usual, in the rain.

For this occasion Jackie Stewart introduced the MS 10/02, which was lighter than the 01 he had driven hitherto. The lightening of this car had been given a high priority by the technicians at Vélizy. According to Beltoise, the excessive weight showed itself in the handling of the car by 'a certain propensity to exaggerate the oversteering or understeering characteristic that one has chosen, in setting up the car for a particular circuit'. It also produced 'heaviness and excessive reversibility of the steering'.

Whatever it was, Jackie Stewart won a masterly victory at Zandvoort, helped by Dunlop tyres with a central channel in the tread, which defeated the problem of aquaplaning. Jackie Stewart also won the Grands Prix of Germany and the United States. He thus became runner-up to Graham Hill for the World Championship.

The 1968 season had been notable for the sudden proliferation of ailerons. This aerodynamic feature often tended to be applied in an irrational and exaggerated style. On the Matra, the first aileron was fitted for practice at the British Grand Prix; low and flat, it was secured to the chassis at four points. At the Italian Grand Prix a broader aerofoil was fitted, placed higher and attached directly to the rear hub carriers. Also for Monza, the shape of the fairing surrounding the cockpit was redesigned.

Matra's first season was a resounding success. Thanks to the talent of Stewart, to the impeccable organization of Ken Tyrrell, and to the qualities of the Ford Cosworth engine, Matra went to the top of the class. But the British had not provided all the talent: the Matra technicians had proved to be remarkable constructors of monocoque chassis, as their results in Formula 2 and 3 had already indicated.

A work of art

On 19 December 1967 a fierce roaring disrupted the test bench workshop at Vélizy. As usual Jean-Duc Lagardère, the President of Matra, had a jovial air, but engineer Georges Martin wore an anxious frown. He was listening to the first bellowing of his particular baby, the V12 Matra.

Georges Martin explained why his choice had fallen on a V12: 'with a unitary capacity of only 250 cc you can get a stroke-bore ratio that is very useful from the dynamic point of view. The short stroke allows very high revolutions and the large bore permits the use of big valves to assure good filling.' Outside Formula 1, Matra foresaw possibilities for using their engine in grand touring cars and sports prototypes.

The block was intended to be cast in magnesium but for the time being it was machined from aluminium alloy to simplify development work. The cylinder head was made from the same AS 9 KG alloy. The pistons in forged aluminium alloy and the titanium alloy connecting rods completed this display of alchemy, or at any rate the arcane science that contains the key to durability.

Twin camshafts, driven by a cascade of twelve pinions, turned the distributor, fuel pump and alternator. The only unadventurous feature was the single ignition.

Matra's own engine was not designed to act as a stressed chassis member like the Ford Cosworth, and so it was necessary to modify the monocoque of the MS 10. It became the MS 11 and put on a lot of weight – more than 60 kg. The tub was extended into two box-section members that ran along each side of the engine. That

The MS 11 at the end of the season with ailerons and enlarged tanks

A brilliant second place for Jean-Pierre Beltoise and the Matra MS 11 in the 1968 Dutch Grand Prix

the length, but it was in Holland that Beltoise achieved his most brilliant performance. For the whole of the Grand Prix he clung on behind Stewart's wheels, and he finished second in a deluge of rain, despite several spectacular spins.

The rest of the season was less glorious for the Matra MS 11, which rarely reached the finish, with the exception of a good fifth place for Beltoise in Italy. At the end of the season the MS 11 was given fuel tanks of greater capacity, which swelled its flanks. Then it became a mobile test bench.

Its first task was to test a hydraulic transmission system for four-wheel drive that engineer Caussin was developing. The principle of this system was as follows: a supplementary pinion in the final drive operated a gear-type pump called the transmitter. This sent high-pressure oil to two small hydraulic motors, called the receivers, mounted within the front wheels. It was thus that the drive to the front wheels was obtained when the rear wheels began to lose traction.

Built in haste between 15 April and 18 May, this prototype was never raced. For the system to become viable it would have been essential to mount the receivers inboard, to reduce unsprung weight. Another job for the MS 11 was when Jean-Pierre Beltoise used it in a hillclimb in 1969; on that occasion it was fitted with a pre-production MS 12 engine, destined for the future MS 120.

Let us not anticipate. At the time under consideration, in 1968, the MS 9 engine suffered from a chronic malady: excessive overheating. It was basically sound but to make it really competitive it needed a new approach altogether to the design of the cylinder block and head, with completely remade castings. Georges Martin's team were put to work and they spent the whole of the 1969 season working on the new MS 12 version of the Matra engine.

amounted to a lot of superfluous kilos, to which must be added the heavier engine, buried under a clutter of accessories.

The Matra MS 11, that is to say the hundred-per-cent French Matra, was brought out on 22 March 1968. Naturally, its driver was also from the appropriate side of the channel – Jean-Pierre Beltoise. The car first raced at Monaco with a shortened nose to aid cooling and reduce

MATRA AND THEIR RIVALS					
MATRA MS9	V 8	2993 cc	(85.7 × 64.8 mm)	415 bhp at 9000 rpm	540 kg
MATRA MS10	V 8	2993 cc	(85.7 × 64.8 mm)	415 bhp at 9000 rpm	560 kg
MATRA MS11	V 12	2993 cc	(79.7 × 50 mm)	390 bhp at 10 500 rpm	610 kg
BRABHAM BT26	V 8	2986 cc	(89 × 60 mm)	375 bhp at 9000 rpm	530 kg
BRM P-126 and P-133	V 12	2997 cc	(74.6 × 57.2 mm)	380 bhp at 10 000 rpm	520 kg
COOPER T-86 B	V 12	2997 cc	(74.6 × 57.2 mm)	380 bhp at 10 000 rpm	560 kg
EAGLE 104	V 12	2997 cc	(72.8 × 60 mm)	400 bhp at 10 500 rpm	540 kg
FERRARI 312 F1	V 12	2989 cc	(77 × 53.5 mm)	410 bhp at 11 000 rpm	510 kg
HONDA RA301	V 12	2993 cc	(78 × 52.2 mm)	430 bhp at 11 000 rpm	580 kg
HONDA RA302	V 8	2987 cc	(88 × 61.4 mm)	390 bhp at 10 500 rpm	500 kg
LOTUS Mk49 B	V 8	2993 cc	(85.7 × 64.8 mm)	415 bhp at 9000 rpm	515 kg
McLAREN M7 A	V 8	2993 cc	(85.7 × 64.8 mm)	415 bhp at 9000 rpm	520 kg

WORLD CHAMPION

1969

After the death of Jim Clark at Hockenheim in April 1968, Jackie Stewart, also a Scotsman, was quick to step forward as his successor. To prove his right to this position, he took the winning place in the first Grand Prix of 1969, that of South Africa.

His Matra MS 10 carried two ailerons: the usual large wing on the rear suspension, and a small supplementary aileron on the front end. There was also a new car, that had been seen in practice, but had stayed behind the stands during the race: it was the MS 80.

The pot-bellied Matra

The MS 80 showed a great number of modifications compared with the MS 10, keeping practically nothing except the Ford Cosworth engine. The work had been channelled in two directions: weight distribution, and refinement of the suspension. To combat the tendency to amplify movements, and thus in order to achieve better handling, the polar moment of inertia was reduced by curtailing overhanging weight. The oil tank, formerly in the nosecone, was placed behind the driver's seat, along with the battery that used to be right at the back. The fuel tanks were placed within the lateral bulges of the monocoque, which explained the pot-bellied appearance of the MS 80.

The basic principle of the monocoque remained unaltered: it was riveted up from two types of light-alloy sheet, AG5 weldable and AU 4G non-weldable. The tubular frame, to locate the rear suspension during an

Jackie Stewart winning a last victory for the Matra MS 10 at the 1969 South African Grand Prix

1969							
SOUTH AFRICA 1/3	**SPAIN** 4/5	**MONACO** 18/5	**NETHERLANDS** 21/6	**FRANCE** 6/7	**BRITAIN** 19/7	**GERMANY** 3/8	**ITALY** 7/9
1 MATRA Stewart	MATRA Stewart	LOTUS Hill	MATRA Stewart	MATRA Stewart	MATRA Stewart	BRABHAM Ickx	MATRA Stewart
2 LOTUS Hill	McLAREN McLaren	BRABHAM Courage	LOTUS Siffert	MATRA Beltoise	BRABHAM Ickx	MATRA Stewart	LOTUS Rindt
3 McLAREN Hulme	MATRA Beltoise	LOTUS Siffert	FERRARI Amon	BRABHAM Ickx	McLAREN McLaren	McLAREN McLaren	MATRA Beltoise
4 LOTUS Siffert	McLAREN Hulme	LOTUS Attwood	McLAREN Hulme	McLAREN McLaren	LOTUS Rindt	LOTUS Hill	McLAREN McLaren
5 McLAREN McLaren	BRM Surtees	McLAREN McLaren	BRABHAM Ickx	McLAREN Elford	BRABHAM Courage	MATRA Pescarolo	BRABHAM Courage

In the middle of the 1969 season, the Matra MS 80 was fitted with a higher aileron

The Matra-Ford MS 80, here seen at Charade, carried Jackie Stewart to his title of World Champion in 1969

ANADA 20/9	USA 5/10	MEXICO 19/10
ABHAM Ickx	LOTUS Rindt	McLAREN Hulme
ABHAM abham	BRABHAM Courage	BRABHAM Ickx
OTUS Rindt	BRM Surtees	BRABHAM Brabham
ATRA eltoise	BRABHAM Brabham	MATRA Stewart
LAREN cLaren	FERRARI Rodriguez	MATRA Beltoise

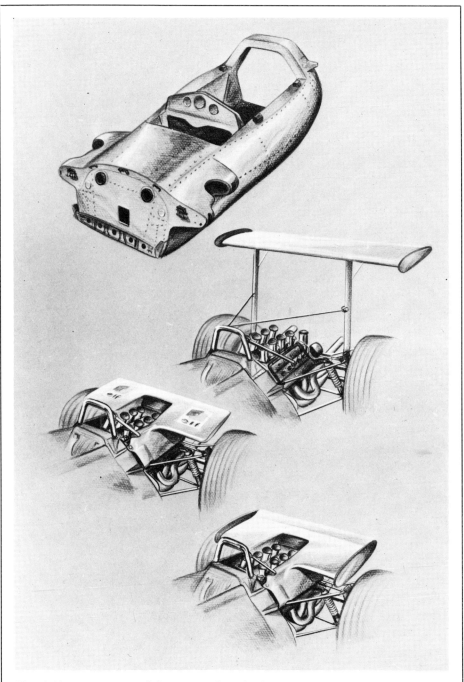

engine change, had disappeared from the MS 80 in the interest of weight-saving. The petrol tanks, packed with anti-explosive foam, extended ahead of the tub as far as the steering rack. The spring-damper units were placed outside the body to keep them cool. To reduce unsprung weight, 13 in front wheels replaced the previous 15 in size and the brake discs were henceforth slotted for cooling, thus permitting their diameter to be decreased. At the rear, they were mounted on the gearbox instead of within the wheels.

The new layout for the suspension was dictated by the wider wheel rims and consequently reduced width available for the linkages. At the rear, two parallel links were used in place of the reversed wishbone, and a double anti-roll bar was adopted. Finally, the stronger Hewland DG 400 gearbox superseded the FG 300.

Throughout the season the aerodynamic system was evolving. At first the MS 80 had a high wing mounted on the hub-carriers as on the MS 10, but after the Dutch Grand Prix a new engine bonnet was fitted, which extended into a flat, inclined surface.

So here was the first invincible French Formula 1 car since the 1927 Delage. With six victories in the nine races of the 1969 Championship, Jackie Stewart had brought Matra to the pinnacle of motor sport. It is a fair enough comment that the engine and gearbox were both of Anglo-Saxon origin. But this in no way detracts from the remarkable achievement by the Matra technicians and in particular Bernard Boyer, the chassis specialist. The MS 80 had proved to be well-balanced, effective and pleasant to drive. And after all this was only the first step.

In 1970 Matra came back with their rebuilt V12 and a new chassis. The MS 80 chassis had been constructed with a series of partitions, and it was not possible to fit into it the

The rigid monocoque and the constantly revised aerodynamics were the basis of the Matra MS 80's success

161

Inside the Matra MS 84: tubular chassis, reversed engine, Ferguson transmission

The outside of the Matra MS 84 resembled that of the MS 80 but its chassis was totally different

rubber bag-type fuel tanks that were compulsory in 1970. In the course of the year Matra had also conducted some very interesting research apart from the chassis development, as we shall now discover.

Four-wheel drive

It seemed more and more dangerous to apply the prodigious power of Formula 1 engines to only two driven wheels. Lotus, McLaren, Cosworth and Matra therefore each built, in their own style, a four-wheel drive single-seater.

The Matra MS 84 looked very like the MS 80, but from the exterior only, for its structure was tubular and not monocoque. The transmission was the work of Derek Gardner from Ferguson, the engineer who would later design the Tyrrells of 1970–6. Compared with the MS 80, the engine-gearbox unit was turned right round, the gearbox being in front. The transfer box was on the output end of the gearbox, two propeller shafts going from there to the front and rear. The torque division was 25 per cent front and 75 per cent rear, each pair of wheels having its own differential.

The advantage of driving all wheels can at once be felt on slippery surfaces. Acceleration and roadholding on corners are infinitely superior, because the driver can use all his power from a far lower speed than with a normal transmission. That advantage is counterbalanced by an excess of weight and too much power absorbed by friction.

Never having raced in the wet, the Matra MS 84 was unable to demonstrate its good points, but it was evident that four-wheel drive is not a panacea for all power transmission problems. In this area, the progress accomplished by the tyre manufacturers is now so great that four-wheel drive can be consigned to oblivion – for the time being at any rate.

MATRA AND THEIR RIVALS					
MATRA MS80	V 8	2993 cc	(85.7 × 64.8 mm)	430 bhp at 9500 rpm	550 kg
MATRA MS84	V 8	2993 cc	(85.7 × 64.8 mm)	430 bhp at 9500 rpm	600 kg
BRABHAM BT26 A	V 8	2993 cc	(85.7 × 64.8 mm)	430 bhp at 9500 rpm	
BRM P-138 and P-139	V 12	2997 cc	(74.6 × 57.2 mm)	420 bhp at 10 500 rpm	
COSWORTH	V 8	2993 cc	(85.7 × 64.8 mm)	430 bhp at 9500 rpm	
FERRARI 312 F1	V 12	2989 cc	(77 × 53.5 mm)	436 bhp at 11 000 rpm	530 kg
LOTUS Mk49 B	V 8	2993 cc	(85.7 × 64.8 mm)	430 bhp at 9500 rpm	530 kg
LOTUS Mk63	V 8	2993 cc	(85.7 × 64.8 mm)	430 bhp at 9500 rpm	550 kg
McLAREN M7B and M7C	V 8	2993 cc	(85.7 × 64.8 mm)	430 bhp at 9500 rpm	560 kg
McLAREN M9	V 8	2993 cc	(85.7 × 64.8 mm)	430 bhp at 9500 rpm	590 kg

SELF-DEPENDENCE

1970

Paradoxically for Matra, a French enterprise, the World Championship of 1969 left an after-taste of frustration. The British were too closely involved. The object of Matra was to race a car that was one hundred per cent French.

For Ken Tyrrell and Jackie Stewart, there could be no question of giving up the Ford Cosworth engine which remained the most competitive in their eyes, but Jean-Luc Lagardère was inflexible. So, Matra had to form an all-French team with Jean-Pierre Beltoise and Henri Pescarolo as drivers. The name of Matra was joined to that of Simca, with which firm there had been a commercial and technical tie-up since December 1969.

Formula 1 had become a powerful publicity medium. Lotus had set the tone in 1969 by decorating their cars in the colours of Gold Leaf cigarettes. It was the only chance of survival for a type of racing that was becoming more and more expensive.

And now a modern engine

The Matra engine was technologically old-fashioned before it was born, with its valves forming an angle of 56° when the Cosworth's were at 32°.

So Georges Martin had been at work on the problem. The included angle between the valves was closed up to 33.4° which allowed lighter pistons to be used because they were nearly flat. This brought the camshafts closer together and the cylinder heads were narrower. The inlet ports, which formerly passed between the valves, no longer had sufficient room there and were regrouped in the middle of the engine at the centre of the V.

In 1970 Matra gave up the Ford Cosworth engine in favour of their own V12 in a new version, type MS 12. The inlet ports were at the centre of the V and the included angle between the valves was reduced

						1970	
	SOUTH AFRICA 7/3	**SPAIN** 19/4	**MONACO** 10/5	**BELGIUM** 7/6	**NETHERLANDS** 21/6	**FRANCE** 5/7	**BRITAIN** 19/7	**DENMAR** 2/8
1	BRABHAM Brabham	MARCH Stewart	LOTUS Rindt	BRM Rodriguez	LOTUS Rindt	LOTUS Rindt	LOTUS Rindt	LOTUS Rindt
2	McLAREN Hulme	McLAREN McLaren	BRABHAM Brabham	MARCH Amon	MARCH Stewart	MARCH Amon	BRABHAM Brabham	FERRAR Ickx
3	MARCH Stewart	MARCH Andretti	MATRA Pescarolo	MATRA Beltoise	FERRARI Ickx	BRABHAM Brabham	McLAREN Hulme	McLARE Hulme
4	MATRA Beltoise	LOTUS Hill	McLAREN Hulme	FERRARI Giunti	FERRARI Regazzoni	McLAREN Hulme	FERRARI Regazzoni	LOTUS Fittipald
5	LOTUS Miles	MARCH Servoz	LOTUS Hill	BRABHAM Stommelen	MATRA Beltoise	MATRA Pescarolo	MARCH Amon	BRABHA Stommel

The Matra MS 120 had an angular monocoque that was entirely new. Henri Pescarolo in the German Grand Prix

Jean-Pierre Beltoise driving the Matra MS 120

The bottom end – crankshaft and connecting rods – was unchanged, but the new type MS 12 engine was clearly better proportioned for sustained high performance. Furthermore, it had undergone a structural modification, so that it could be used as a stressed chassis member, the rear suspension being directly bolted to the gearbox. A Boulogne firm called Moteur Moderne carried out the development work on an experimental single-cylinder rig.

Bernard Boyer had to design another monocoque, because that of the MS 80 was divided by bulkheads that prevented the obligatory flexible fuel tanks from being installed. The complete opposite of the pot-bellied MS 80, the MS 120 was flat and angular. Its sides formed surfaces with a negative angle of incidence, which helped to press the car onto the road at high speeds. Wider track and longer wheelbase improved stability under braking and the roadholding on fast curves. The suspension geometry followed that of the MS 80, except for narrower front bottom wishbones. Power-assisted steering of the Citroën type, with powered self-centring, was tried but not adopted.

However, it was clear from the start that the new Matra was not expected to cause any great surprise. Its V12 engine would never be able to out-distance its rivals, with a power output just about comparable with that of the Ford Cosworth V8, but the MS 120 did show great reliability. Matra reached the finish of all the Grands Prix except two. Jean-Pierre Beltoise, in Belgium and Italy, and Pescarolo, at Monaco, had the satisfaction of finishing third. Beltoise, indeed, nearly tasted victory in the Grand Prix of France on the Charade circuit. On the 15th lap he took the lead, arousing considerable

GERMANY 16/8	ITALY 6/9	CANADA 20/9	USA 4/10	MEXICO 25/10
FERRARI Ickx	FERRARI Regazzoni	FERRARI Ickx	LOTUS Fittipaldi	FERRARI Ickx
FERRARI Regazzoni	MARCH Stewart	FERRARI Regazzoni	BRM Rodriguez	FERRARI Regazzoni
BRABHAM Stommelen	MATRA Beltoise	MARCH Amon	LOTUS Wisell	McLAREN Hulme
BRM Rodriguez	McLAREN Hulme	BRM Rodriguez	FERRARI Ickx	MARCH Amon
BRM Oliver	BRABHAM Stommelen	SURTEES Surtees	MARCH Amon	MATRA Beltoise

The MS 12 engine was first tried in an MS 11 chassis: President Georges Pompidou unveiling it at the Paris Motor Show

excitement amongst the spectators, until a puncture and then shortage of fuel dashed his hopes.

Apart from that race, the performance of the Matras tended to go almost unnoticed, all attention being turned to the struggle between Lotus and Ferrari. Both of them had radically new models. Lotus won the title thanks to their surprising 72 and thanks to Jochen Rindt, who then lost his life before the end of the season and was crowned World Champion posthumously.

Ferrari returned to the front rank by virtue of a new flat 12 engine, although of course this did not impede the progress of the V8 Ford Cosworth, nor of the V12 Matra either.

MATRA AND THEIR RIVALS					
MATRA MS 120	V 12	2993 cc	(79.7 × 50 mm)	435 bhp at 11 000 rpm	560 kg
BELLASI F1-1-70	V 8	2993 cc	(85.7 × 64.8 mm)	430 bhp at 9500 rpm	560 kg
BRABHAM BT33	V 8	2993 cc	(85.7 × 64.8 mm)	435 bhp at 10 000 rpm	540 kg
BRM P-153	V 12	3000 cc	(74.6 × 57.2 mm)	440 bhp at 11 000 rpm	545 kg
DE TOMASO 505	V 8	2993 cc	(85.7 × 64.8 mm)	430 bhp at 9000 rpm	580 kg
FERRARI 312 B	flat 12	2991 cc	(78.5 × 51.5 mm)	455 bhp at 11 500 rpm	530 kg
LOTUS Mk72	V 8	2993 cc	(85.7 × 64.8 mm)	435 bhp at 10 000 rpm	530 kg
MARCH 701	V 8	2993 cc	(85.7 × 64.8 mm)	435 bhp at 10 000 rpm	570 kg
McLAREN M14 A	V 8	2993 cc	(85.7 × 64.8 mm)	435 bhp at 10 000 rpm	550 kg
McLAREN M14 D	V 8	2993 cc	(86 × 64.4 mm)	430 bhp at 10 000 rpm	560 kg
SURTEES TS7	V 8	2993 cc	(85.7 × 64.8 mm)	435 bhp at 10 000 rpm	580 kg
TYRRELL 001	V 8	2993 cc	(85.7 × 64.8 mm)	435 bhp at 10 000 rpm	560 kg

LOSING GROUND

1971

In this season Matra advanced very slowly. It must be said that their preoccupation with the Le Mans 24 Hours Race, always the major priority, prevented them from throwing all their resources into Formula 1. They had the formidable task of representing all aspects of French industry single-handed, now that Alpine-Renault were concentrating on rallying.

It rarely pays to do too many things at once, even for the manufacturers best placed to do so, like Ferrari. Matra found that out with the MS 120 Bs, entrusted to Jean-Pierre Beltoise and the New Zealander, Chris Amon. A straightforward adaptation of the 1970 model, the new MS 120 B was a better balanced car.

'The MS 120 B has incomparably lighter steering, so much so that I surprised myself by controlling the car with my left arm in coming out of the chicane, something I had not been able to do since my accident at Rheims in 1964.' These enthusiastic words were from Beltoise.

On the aerodynamic side, there was some small but real progress: the side-walls of the body were modified, a new and larger bonnet that was tried at Kyalami was definitely adopted, and a dynamic air intake was placed above the engine. The chassis was reinforced around the cockpit to obtain greater torsional rigidity.

But the main bugbear was still the engine. The new oil circulation system had overcome the loss of oil pressure in corners, which had been the problem in 1970; but the V12 remained miserly in its power output.

From the end of July, steel connecting rods of a new design replaced those of titanium, which were too subject to fatigue, but the real crack of the whip came from a new and flatter cylinder head which was not available until September. This MS 71 version of the engine was safe at higher maximum revs. It was too late, for the Matra had already lost a lot of ground. Chris Amon had managed to finish third in the Spanish Grand Prix, at the beginning of the year, but the second, less successful part of the season seemed to go on for ever.

Happy were those like Jackie Stewart and Ken Tyrrell, the World Champions, who continued to place their confidence in the Ford Cosworth engine.

							1971	
	SOUTH AFRICA 6/3	**SPAIN** 18/4	**MONACO** 23/5	**NETHERLANDS** 20/6	**FRANCE** 4/7	**BRITAIN** 17/7	**GERMANY** 29/7	**AUSTRIA** 15/8
1	FERRARI Andretti	TYRRELL Stewart	TYRRELL Stewart	FERRARI Ickx	TYRRELL Stewart	TYRRELL Stewart	TYRRELL Stewart	BRM Siffert
2	TYRRELL Stewart	FERRARI Ickx	MARCH Peterson	BRM Rodriguez	TYRRELL Cevert	MARCH Peterson	TYRRELL Cevert	LOTUS Fittipaldi
3	FERRARI Regazzoni	MATRA Amon	FERRARI Ickx	FERRARI Regazzoni	LOTUS Fittipaldi	LOTUS Fittipaldi	FERRARI Regazzoni	BRABHAM Stommelen
4	LOTUS Wisell	BRM Rodriguez	McLAREN Hulme	MARCH Peterson	BRM Siffert	MARCH Pescarolo	FERRARI Andretti	LOTUS Wisell
5	MATRA Amon	McLAREN Hulme	LOTUS Fittipaldi	SURTEES Surtees	MATRA Amon	SURTEES Stommelen	MARCH Peterson	BRABHAM Hill

ITALY 5/9	CANADA 19/9	USA 3/10
BRM Gethin	TYRRELL Stewart	TYRRELL Cevert
MARCH Peterson	MARCH Peterson	BRM Siffert
TYRRELL Cevert	McLAREN Donohue	MARCH Peterson
SURTEES Hailwood	McLAREN Hulme	BRM Ganley
BRM Ganley	LOTUS Wisell	TYRRELL Stewart

At the South African Grand Prix, the monocoque of the Matra MS 120 B no. 4 was similar to the 1970 model but the nose section was of a new design

Chris Amon in the Matra MS 120 B, chassis no. 6, with the wide nose and raised rear panel of the monocoque

The Matra MS 120 B, chassis no. 5, differed from the 1970 model by the inclined sides of the monocoque and the air intake for the engine. Jean-Pierre Beltoise at the Spanish Grand Prix

MATRA AND ITS RIVALS					
MATRA MS 120 B	V 12	2993 cc	(79.7 × 50 mm)	440 bhp at 11 000 rpm	560 kg
BRABHAM BT34	V 8	2993 cc	(85.7 × 64.8 mm)	440 bhp at 10 500 rpm	565 kg
BRM P-160	V 12	2997 cc	(74.6 × 57.2 mm)	440 bhp at 11 000 rpm	530 kg
FERRARI 312 B2	flat 12	2991 cc	(78.5 × 51.5 mm)	470 bhp at 12 500 rpm	540 kg
LOTUS Mk72 C and D	V 8	2993 cc	(85.7 × 64.8 mm)	440 bhp at 10 500 rpm	530 kg
LOTUS Mk56 B		Turbine		500 bhp	650 kg
MARCH 711 Ford	V 8	2993 cc	(85.7 × 64.8 mm)	440 bhp at 10 500 rpm	535 kg
MARCH 711 Alfa Romeo	V 8	2993 cc	(86 × 64.8 mm)	430 bhp at 9800 rpm	550 kg
McLAREN M19 A	V 8	2993 cc	(85.7 × 64.8 mm)	440 bhp at 10 500 rpm	570 kg
SURTEES TS9	V 8	2993 cc	(85.7 × 64.8 mm)	440 bhp at 10 500 rpm	550 kg
TYRRELL 002 and 003	V 8	2993 cc	(85.7 × 64.8 mm)	440 bhp at 10 500 rpm	560 kg

As far as structure was concerned, Bernard Boyer did not rest on the already withering laurels of the MS 80. The MS 120 B evolved into the MS 120 C. The code indicated modifications to the front suspension, which the new tyre dimensions required, and several aerodynamic retouches, notably a new bonnet shape and air intake.

All that was too little and in vain. Chris Amon, from this time on the only Matra driver in Formula 1, gained two points only, one at Monaco and the other at Spa, but from all the evidence the blue single-seater needed a more thorough overhaul.

A new monocoque

Chris Amon implored the boffins at Vélizy to bring out their new model, the MS 120D. This time the monocoque was totally new. It had lost the angular look of the previous series to return to a more rounded shape. The weight distribution was improved, the front wheels carrying a lighter load, and the fuel was moved to the space behind the driver's seat, formerly occupied by the oil tank which was re-sited below the wing. The rest of the car being unchanged, Chris Amon took little time in getting the new Matra ready to race. When it appeared at Charade, the MS 120 D proved to be very fast: Amon got onto the front row of the grid.

For 19 laps, the French public believed in miracles, exalted by the high, clear note of twelve cylinders. But in order to get the Charade circuit approved, the organizers had carried out some considerable alterations before the

BAD LUCK

1972

During the winter of 1971–2 Georges Martin mustered his strength and his men. Engineer Loze was in charge of development and René Fortin ran the engine test section. Together, they extracted 450 bhp from the latest version of the V12, the MS 71.

The Matra MS 120 C was a development of the MS 120 B. It could immediately be recognized by the air intake on top of the engine

	ARGENTINA 23/1	SOUTH AFRICA 4/3	SPAIN 1/5	MONACO 14/5	BELGIUM 4/6	FRANCE 2/7	BRITAIN 15/7	GERMANY 30/7
								1972
1	TYRRELL Stewart	McLAREN Hulme	LOTUS Fittipaldi	BRM Beltoise	LOTUS Fittipaldi	TYRRELL Stewart	LOTUS Fittipaldi	FERRARI Ickx
2	McLAREN Hulme	LOTUS Fittipaldi	FERRARI Ickx	FERRARI Ickx	TYRRELL Cevert	LOTUS Fittipaldi	TYRRELL Stewart	FERRARI Regazzoni
3	FERRARI Ickx	McLAREN Revson	FERRARI Regazzoni	LOTUS Fittipaldi	McLAREN Hulme	MATRA Amon	McLAREN Revson	MARCH Peterson
4	FERRARI Regazzoni	FERRARI Andretti	SURTEES de Adamich	TYRRELL Stewart	SURTEES Hailwood	TYRRELL Cevert	MATRA Amon	BRM Ganley
5	SURTEES Schenken	MARCH Peterson	McLAREN Revson	McLAREN Redman	MARCH Pace	MARCH Peterson	McLAREN Hulme	McLAREN Redman

A	ITALY 10/9	CANADA 24/9	USA 8/10
	LOTUS Fittipaldi	TYRRELL Stewart	TYRRELL Stewart
	SURTEES Hailwood	McLAREN Revson	TYRRELL Cevert
	McLAREN Hulme	McLAREN Hulme	McLAREN Hulme
	McLAREN Revson	BRABHAM Reutemann	MARCH Peterson
	BRABHAM Hill	FERRARI Regazzoni	FERRARI Ickx

The MS 120 D driven by Chris Amon. The more rounded monocoque was also more effective. Unfortunately it came too late

race and these had left their mark. The outer edges of the road were strewn with sharp little pieces of rock. One by one the competitors were slowed by punctures. Chris Amon was one of these and just when he was leading the race he had to drop back to third place. It was his many similar misfortunes that gave Chris Amon the reputation of being an unlucky driver.

At the Le Mans 24 Hours Race, on the other hand, things went better for Matra, whose drivers Pescarolo/Graham Hill and Cevert/Ganley gained first and second places. The publicity value of a Le Mans victory is very great in France, and therefore Matra began to prefer the idea of concentrating on and repeating its past successes, without attempting two different programmes at once. So they gave up Formula 1 at the end of the 1972 season.

After the success of the Matra-Ford in 1969 and the contrasting performances of the Matra-Matra, it is fair enough to question the value of V12 engines, and of the French one in particular.

The twelve-cylinder gives more power than an eight-cylinder engine, because it is capable of higher revolution speeds through the lower inertia of the reciprocating parts. If its mechanical efficiency deteriorates as a function of speed (friction losses), its thermal efficiency improves on the contrary.

The chief disadvantages, on the other hand, are that it produces less torque for acceleration, and that it consumes more fuel.

From 1973 to 1975 the battle between the eight-cylinder Ford Cosworth and the 12-cylinder Ferrari was fierce but indecisive. Would the return of the V12 Matra, in 1976, settle the matter by a casting vote?

MATRA AND ITS RIVALS					
MATRA MS 120 C	V 12	2993 cc	(79.7 × 50 mm)	450 bhp at 11 500 rpm	560 kg
MATRA MS 120 D	V 12	2993 cc	(79.7 × 50 MM)	480 bhp at 11 800 rpm	550 kg
BRABHAM BT37	V 8	2993 cc	(85.7 × 64.8 mm)	450 bhp at 10 000 rpm	
BRM P-160 B and C	V 12	2997 cc	(74.6 × 57.2 mm)	435 bhp at 11 000 rpm	
BRM P-180	V 12	2997 cc	(74.6 × 57.2 mm)	435 bhp at 11 000 rpm	550 kg
CONNEW PC 1	V 8	2993 cc	(85.7 × 64.8 mm)	440 bhp at 10 500 rpm	570 kg
EIFELLAND Type 21	V 8	2993 cc	(85.7 × 64.8 mm)	440 bhp at 10 500 rpm	560 kg
FERRARI 312 B2	flat 12	2992 cc	(80 × 49.6 mm)	485 bhp at 12 600 rpm	560 kg
LOTUS Mk72 D	V 8	2993 cc	(85.7 × 64.8 mm)	450 bhp at 10 000 rpm	550 kg
MARCH 721	V 8	2993 cc	(85.7 × 64.8 mm)	450 bhp at 10 000 rpm	560 kg
MARCH 721 G	V 8	2993 cc	(85.7 × 64.8 mm)	450 bhp at 10 000 rpm	550 kg
MARCH 721 X	V 8	2993 cc	(85.7 × 64.8 mm)	450 bhp at 10 000 rpm	550 kg
McLAREN M19 C	V 8	2993 cc	(85.7 × 64.8 mm)	450 bhp at 10 000 rpm	560 kg
POLITOYS FX3	V 8	2993 cc	(85.7 × 64.8 mm)	440 bhp at 10 500 rpm	570 kg
SURTEES TS9 B	V 8	2993 cc	(85.7 × 64.8 mm)	450 bhp at 10 000 rpm	560 kg
TECHNO PA123	flat 12	2968 cc	(81 × 48 mm)	440 bhp at 11 000 rpm	580 kg
TYRRELL 005	V 8	2993 cc	(85.7 × 64.8 mm)	450 bhp at 10 000 rpm	550 kg

THE TWO EXTREMES OF INDUSTRIAL LIFE

1976

When, in February 1975, M. Pierre Mazeaud, Secretary of State for Youth and Sports, declared that it was necessary 'to concentrate every effort towards a French Formula 1 car', it sounded like the usual political flannel, comforting but vain. But not this time.

Some big changes really were being prepared in French motor sport: two Formula 1 cars were secretly taking shape on the drawing boards. Two diametrically opposite philosophies were competing to fulfill the official decree.

On one side there was Guy Ligier, an enthusiast, impelled by his passion for speed, and on the other the Régie Renault, a giant enterprise governed by reason; the two poles of industrial life. In both cases the financial backing was national and enormous: the Elf Oil colossus supported Renault, while SEITA (the French tobacco concern) was backing Ligier.

An enthusiast's dream comes true

Guy Ligier signed his agreement with SEITA in December 1974 and started work on his single-seater right away. Born on 12 July 1927, Ligier is a fighter, as his massive silhouette shows! All his life, he has thrown himself into new adventures and taken risks. By turns, he got to the top in many sports, in rowing, in rugby and in motorcycling. In 1960, he discovered the automobile, first as a racing driver and then, from 1969, as a manufacturer.

For SEITA too, motoring competition was no novelty since Gitanes cigarettes were associated with Matra and its success at Le Mans.

Matra was the third member of the Ligier conspiracy. Matra made available to Guy Ligier the human ingredient for his project. This was Gérard Ducarouge, who took the title of director of design and operations, which meant that he controlled the whole Ligier-Gitanes team in the workshops and out on the circuits.

Michel Beaujou was already working for Ligier. He found himself catapulted, at the age of 26, to the position of master technician in charge of Formula 1 design. He is a specialist in stress calculations of materials. At his side was Paul Carillo, also from Matra, who was the project draughtsman.

1976

	BRAZIL 25/1	SOUTH AFRICA 6/3	USA-WEST 28/3	SPAIN 2/5	BELGIUM 16/5	MONACO 30/5	SWEDEN 13/6	FRANCE 4/7
1	FERRARI Lauda	FERRARI Lauda	FERRARI Regazzoni	McLAREN Hunt	FERRARI Lauda	FERRARI Lauda	TYRRELL Scheckter	McLAREN Hunt
2	TYRRELL Depailler	McLAREN Hunt	FERRARI Lauda	FERRARI Lauda	FERRARI Regazzoni	TYRRELL Scheckter	TYRRELL Depailler	TYRRELL Depailler
3	SHADOW Pryce	McLAREN Mass	TYRRELL Depailler	LOTUS Nilsson	LIGIER Laffite	TYRRELL Depailler	FERRARI Lauda	PENSKE Watson
4	MARCH Stück	TYRRELL Scheckter	LIGIER Laffite	BRABHAM Reutemann	TYRRELL Scheckter	MARCH Stück	LIGIER Laffite	BRABHAM Pace
5	TYRRELL Scheckter	PENSKE Watson	McLAREN Mass	ENSIGN Amon	SURTEES Jones	McLAREN Mass	McLAREN Hunt	LOTUS Andretti

Under the watchful eye of Georges Martin, Jean-Pierre Jarier testing the Shadow DN 7, with its Matra V12 engine, in July 1975

BRITAIN 18/7	GERMANY 1/8	AUSTRIA 15/8	NETHERLANDS 29/8	ITALY 12/9	CANADA 3/10	USA 10/10	JAPAN 24/10
FERRARI Lauda	McLAREN Hunt	PENSKE Watson	McLAREN Hunt	MARCH Peterson	McLAREN Hunt	McLAREN Hunt	LOTUS Andretti
TYRRELL Scheckter	TYRRELL Scheckter	LIGIER Laffite	FERRARI Regazzoni	FERRARI Regazzoni	TYRRELL Depailler	TYRRELL Scheckter	TYRRELL Depailler
PENSKE Watson	McLAREN Mass	LOTUS Nilsson	LOTUS Andretti	LIGIER Laffite	LOTUS Andretti	FERRARI Lauda	McLAREN Hunt
SHADOW Pryce	BRABHAM Pace	McLAREN Hunt	SHADOW Pryce	FERRARI Lauda	TYRRELL Scheckter	McLAREN Mass	SURTEES Jones
SURTEES Jones	LOTUS Nilsson	LOTUS Andretti	TYRRELL Scheckter	TYRRELL Scheckter	McLAREN Mass	MARCH Stück	FERRARI Regazzoni

Robert Choulet was an aerodynamicist from SERA (Societe d'Etudes et de la Réalisation Automobile), directed by Charles Deutsch. He had been the creator of the unusual bodies of the CD Peugeot and the Matra 640.

Matra did not only contribute the grey matter. In May 1975 discussions with Ligier resulted in the supply of the V12 engine. The Ligier was to be 100 per cent French.

It took shape. It received the type number JS 5 (Ligier gives these initials to all his cars as a tribute to his friend Jo Schlesser, who was killed at Rouen in 1968). In general design the Ligier JS 5 was conventional: soft suspension with long travel, which means wide track and long wheelbase to limit weight transfer and reduce roll (68 per cent of the weight was on the rear wheels). The suspension was classic in the best sense of the term: at the front, the springs were placed inside the body and operated by two large rockers, and at the rear the scheme was even simpler. The very rigid monocoque was sub-contracted at Vélizy by the aircraft specialist, Hurel-Dubois.

First appearance of the Ligier-Gitanes JS 5 at the Paul Ricard circuit, November 1975

Since their retirement from Formula 1, Matra had not lost contact with racing. Georges Martin's team and Jean-François Robin had continued developing the V12. In July 1975 the Matra engine had again been on the track, in a car made for the UOP Shadow team in the United States. Tony Southgate had designed a model called the Shadow DN 7 which carried the French V12. Jean-Pierre Jarier drove this car in Austria and in Italy, but it was disappointing. Designed too hastily, the DN 7 was over weight and badly balanced. Collaboration between Matra and Shadow came to an end in October 1975.

● *29 October 1975, Paris* The Ligier-Gitanes was unveiled at the headquarters of SEITA. It had a surprising shape, born in SERA's wind-tunnel at Eiffel: the sides curved elegantly, its nose was concave; and above all, covering the induction system of the engine it had an enormous airbox that was shaped rather like the liberty cap of the French Revolution.

● *5 November 1975, Le Castellet* The Ligier JS 5 entered the lists for the first time on the Paul Ricard circuit. Two drivers had their helmets on, ready to drive the car. Jean-Pierre Beltoise symbolized French motor sport in the eyes of the public and above all in the eyes of SEITA, who wished to see him at the wheel of the car. But he had not driven for a year. Jacques Laffite, on the other hand, was one of the young hopes. In 1976 he had become the European Champion in Formula 2, and he had driven for Frank Williams in Formula 1.

The two men took turns to lap the circuit. Guy Ligier closed his mind to everything except the stopwatch. Laffite was the fastest, so he was made the official driver for Ligier-Gitanes in 1976. The departure of Beltoise stirred up some ripples, but fortune had taken a new turn and no-one could alter that.

● *25 January 1976, Interlagos* The Ligier JS 5 made its first Grand Prix appearance, without much success.

● *28 March 1976, Long Beach* Third event of the season, the US Grand Prix took place in the Californian town in the shadows of the palm trees and of the Queen Mary. Laffite finished fourth and thus scored his first World Championship points.

● *2 May 1976, Madrid* New regulations on external dimensions came into force at the Spanish Grand Prix. Ligier had to review the aerodynamics of his car: the air intake had to be scaled down and the rear wing moved forward.

● *16 May 1976, Zolder* The fifth race of the year, the Belgian Grand Prix, went well for Laffite and he finished third behind two Ferrari 312 T2s.

After the Spanish Grand Prix the Ligier JS 5 received a new air intake, closer to the top of the engine

Below: *The Matra engine breathed through this muff hidden under the air box, which was shaped like a Phrygian bonnet*

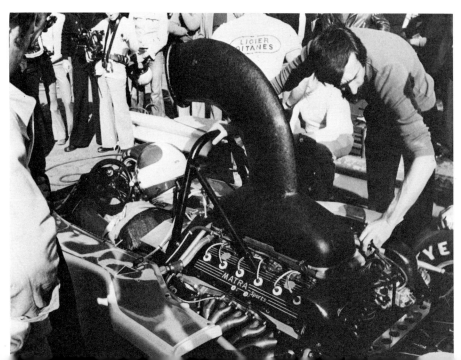

175

● *15 August 1976, Zeltweg* Laffite was using the second JS 5, which thus made its first public appearance here. It could be distinguished from the first one by its straight sides. Laffite finished second in the Austrian Grand Prix, his best result of the season.

● *12 September 1976, Monza* Laffite was on pole position at the start and finished third.

Jacques Laffite was quite satisfied to be in seventh place among the drivers in the World Championship; and the Ligier team was fifth in the Constructors' Cup. This result was encouraging for a first season in Formula 1,

above all if one takes Ligier's finances into account, for they could not compare with those of the two leading teams, Marlboro-McLaren (James Hunt) and Ferrari (Niki Lauda).

Renault goes into operation

While the Ligier team were showing their mettle on the circuits, Renault's activities were confined to the background. They were preoccupied with organizing their back-up services, developing their engine and preparing to implement the new regulations for the Formula 1 programme.

The Ligier JS 5, chassis no. 2, had a flat-sided body. Jacques Laffite finishing third in the 1976 Italian Grand Prix

Alpine-Renault A-500 unveiled at Jarama, May 1976

As in the case of Ligier-Matra, the Renault engine began its life before the car. The two-litre V6 came out in January 1973 to equip an Alpine 'Barquette' for Le Mans. In 1974 Bernard Dudot added a turbocharger. From that, the opportunity to create a 1500 cc turbocharged engine for Formula 1 was obvious. The engine men of Renault-Gordini took up their slide-rules in February 1975, with the hope at the back of their minds of getting into Formula 1. For the moment it was all in the imagination. The first stage consisted in the creation of a 'laboratory car' with which to test the engine, chassis and of course, the men.

At the end of eight months of testing, the turbocharged Renault 'Laboratoire' looked like this in December 1976

Pierre Boudy were machining the V6 cylinder block to bring it to its new dimensions (two blocks were tried, 80 × 49.4 mm and 82 × 42.8 mm).

The laboratory car, type A 500, ran on 21 May 1976 on Michelin's private track at Clermont-Ferrand. The French tyre makers had really decided to overturn Goodyear's monopoly in Formula 1. The Renault was fitted with tyres of radial ply, an innovation that would be studied closely. During the whole of the 1976 summer Jean-Pierre Jabouille tested the car. It was a methodical and laborious task, but he had to convince the directors of the Régie that the project was viable. He succeeded: in July 1976 the management of the Régie gave the green light for the Formula 1 programme. And so the first hurdle was taken.

In April 1976 the Renault organization had been re-grouped. Alpine became an industrial subsidiary, and all racing activities were handled by a new subsidiary, Renault-Sport. It was at Dieppe and, headed by Gérard Larrousse, it combined the old racing services of Renault and Alpine. Another subsidiary, Renault-Gordini, housed in workshops at Viry-Chatillon just outside Paris, assembled the Formula 1 car and developed its engine.

And so the name of Amédée Gordini reappeared in the Grand Prix world. Amédée of course was an old hand, even if he might have become a little blasé by now. But Renault? For a straight industrial firm this really was something of a gamble. The stakes were high, but the risk was calculated.

At the Alpine factory, André de Cortanze was designing a monocoque chassis and Marcel Hubert was drawing a body according to his own principles. In the Renault-Gordini workshop, François Castaing and Jean-

FRENCH CARS AND THEIR RIVALS

ALPINE RENAULT A-500	V 6	1490 cc	(80 × 49.5 mm)	500 bhp at 11 000 rpm	620 kg
LIGIER GITANES JS5	V 12	2993 cc	(79.7 × 50 mm)	500 bhp at 11 600 rpm	575 kg
BORO 001	V 8	2993 cc	(85.7 × 64.8 mm)	465 bhp at 10 500 rpm	
BRABHAM BT45	flat 12	2995 cc	(77 × 53.6 mm)	500 bhp at 11 000 rpm	585 kg
BRM P-201 C	V 12	2997 cc	(74.6 × 57.2 mm)	470 bhp at 11 500 rpm	
ENSIGN N176	V 8	2993 cc	(85.7 × 64.8 mm)	470 bhp at 10 000 rpm	
FERRARI 312 T2	flat 12	2992 cc	(80 × 49.6 mm)	500 bhp at 12 200 rpm	575 kg
FITTIPALDI FD-04	V 8	2993 cc	(85.7 × 64.8 mm)	470 bhp at 10 500 rpm	615 kg
HESKETH 308 D	V 8	2993 cc	(85.7 × 64.8 mm)	465 bhp at 10 500 rpm	
HILL GH-2	V 8	2993 cc	(85.7 × 64.8 mm)	470 bhp at 10 500 rpm	
KOJIMA KE-007	V 8	2993 cc	(85.7 × 64.8 mm)	470 bhp at 10 500 rpm	580 kg
LOTUS Mk77	V 8	2993 cc	(85.7 × 64.8 mm)	475 bhp at 10 500 rpm	
MARCH 761	V 8	2993 cc	(85.7 × 64.8 mm)	470 bhp at 10 500 rpm	610 kg
McLAREN M23	V 8	2993 cc	(85.7 × 64.8 mm)	475 bhp at 10 500 rpm	585 kg
PARNELLI VPJ-4B	V 8	2993 cc	(85.7 × 64.8 mm)	470 bhp at 10 500 rpm	
PENSKE PC-3	V 8	2993 cc	(85.7 × 64.8 mm)	470 bhp at 10 500 rpm	610 kg
PENSKE PC-4	V 8	2993 cc	(85.7 × 64.8 mm)	470 bhp at 10 500 rpm	
SHADOW DN-5 B	V 8	2993 cc	(85.7 × 64.8 mm)	470 bhp at 10 500 rpm	590 kg
SHADOW DN-8	V 8	2993 cc	(85.7 × 64.8 mm)	470 bhp at 10 500 rpm	580 kg
SURTEES TS 19	V 8	2993 cc	(85.7 × 64.8 mm)	470 bhp at 10 500 rpm	
TYRRELL P-34	V 8	2993 cc	(85.7 × 64.8 mm)	475 bhp at 10 500 rpm	600 kg
WILLIAMS FW5	V 8	2993 cc	(85.7 × 64.8 mm)	470 bhp at 10 500 rpm	

POKER HAND

1977

The technology of racing cars had reached such a rate of progress that, from one year to the next, they were out of date. Guy Ligier understood this and simply worked fast and furiously. In December 1976 his new JS 7 single-seater took part in its first tests on the Paul Ricard circuit.

The Ligier-Gitanes JS 7 had a totally new body for 1977

The aerodynamic studies started from scratch, not because the JS 5 had been unsatisfactory, but because the new characteristics of the Matra engine required a complete rearrangement of the weight distribution.

The new V12 type MS 76 lost 27 mm of height between the crankshaft centre-line and the bottom of the sump. A trifle, one might think, but it was enough to move the centre of gravity of the car, the lower-mounted engine taking with it the pivot points for the suspension. Apart from this, the oil radiators had been repositioned behind the front wheels.

The bodywork of the Ligier emerged from the Eiffel wind tunnel more rounded and portly and endowed with an adjustable front aileron like that of the Ferrari. The suspension linkages and the monocoque remained unchanged.

On the financial side, the toy manufacturer, Norev, came to the rescue. This support allowed a second JS 7 to be put in hand and it was ready for the South African Grand Prix. Laffite thus had the use of two cars which could be set up differently, and so he could choose between long or short wheelbases and five- or six-speed gearboxes.

At the beginning of the season the Ligier JS 7 ran into some problems with its new MS 76 engine, which seemed to suffer from ailments that were rather difficult to diagnose. The wrinkles on Guy Ligier's forehead increased in proportion to his disillusion. On 19 June the

	ARGENTINA 9/1	BRAZIL 23/1	SOUTH AFRICA 5/3	USA-WEST 13/4	SPAIN 8/5	BELGIUM 5/6	MONACO 22/5	SWEDE 19/6
1	WOLF Scheckter	FERRARI Reutemann	FERRARI Lauda	LOTUS Andretti	LOTUS Andretti	LOTUS Nilsson	WOLF Scheckter	LIGIER Laffite
2	BRABHAM Pace	McLAREN Hunt	WOLF Scheckter	FERRARI Lauda	FERRARI Reutemann	FERRARI Lauda	FERRARI Lauda	McLARE Mass
3	FERRARI Reutemann	FERRARI Lauda	TYRRELL Depailler	WOLF Scheckter	WOLF Scheckter	TYRRELL Peterson	FERRARI Reutemann	FERRAR Reutema
4	FITTIPALDI Fittipaldi	FITTIPALDI Fittipaldi	McLAREN Hunt	TYRRELL Depailler	McLAREN Mass	SURTEES Brambilla	McLAREN Mass	TYRREL Depaille
5	LOTUS Andretti	LOTUS Nilsson	McLAREN Mass	FITTIPALDI Fittipaldi	LOTUS Nilsson	SHADOW Jones	LOTUS Andretti	BRABHA Watso

The Matra MS 76 engine (left) not quite as tall as its predecessor, the MS 73 (right)

Right: *Official presentation of the Renault-Elf RS 01 on 10 May 1977*

Ligier-Gitanes team went without him to Anderstorp for the Swedish Grand Prix.

Laffite started from the fourth row of the grid. Calmly and intelligently he overtook the other competitors one by one, which brought him, on the 42nd lap, up to the rear wheels of Andretti's Lotus. Laffite felt sure of second place by that time, but then in the last lap he saw his mechanics making frenzied gestures. He realized that he was in the lead for the black Lotus had run short of fuel out on the circuit!

And yet the Marseillaise was not played; the Swedes had clearly not thought it possible that there could be a one hundred per cent French victory. Not even Guy Ligier believed it, and he heard of it by chance on the radio. The whole of the press greeted this Ligier-Gitanes victory: 'at last', they all said, and that was the significant phrase.

A third JS 7 was completed for the German Grand Prix. Its wheel track had been reduced by 20 cm, and with the resulting smaller frontal area, maximum speed was increased by 10 km/h.

Sadly, the Ligier team could not keep up their position. It may be that Jacques Laffite lacked self-confidence. Perhaps that is why he only finished second in the Dutch Grand Prix, not having dared to attack Niki Lauda. At every race in the season there were uncertainties about the car's state of preparation. For the whole length of the year, the absence of a real engineer to take charge at the circuits was cruelly apparent, and the new engine was slow to fulfill its promise.

The courage of great men

In unveiling their programme in December 1976, Renault made it a point of honour to participate on all fronts: Formula Renault, rallies, Le Mans, Formula 2, and now Formula 1. The Formula 1 car did not appear until May 1977.

FRANCE 3/7	BRITAIN 16/7	GERMANY 31/7	AUSTRIA 14/8	NETHERLANDS 28/8	ITALY 11/9	USA 2/10	CANADA 9/10	JAPAN 23/10
LOTUS Andretti	McLAREN Hunt	FERRARI Lauda	SHADOW Jones	FERRARI Lauda	LOTUS Andretti	McLAREN Hunt	WOLF Scheckter	McLAREN Hunt
BRABHAM Watson	FERRARI Lauda	WOLF Scheckter	FERRARI Lauda	LIGIER Laffite	FERRARI Lauda	LOTUS Andretti	TYRRELL Depailler	FERRARI Reutemann
McLAREN Hunt	LOTUS Nilsson	BRABHAM Stück	BRABHAM Stück	WOLF Scheckter	SHADOW Jones	WOLF Scheckter	McLAREN Mass	TYRRELL Depailler
LOTUS Nilsson	McLAREN Mass	FERRARI Reutemann	FERRARI Reutemann	FITTIPALDI Fittipaldi	McLAREN Mass	FERRARI Lauda	SHADOW Jones	SHADOW Jones
FERRARI Lauda	BRABHAM Stück	SURTEES Brambilla	TYRRELL Peterson	ENSIGN Tambay	ENSIGN Regazzoni	ENSIGN Regazzoni	ENSIGN Tambay	LIGIER Laffite

181

Swedish Grand Prix, 1977: at last a victory for Ligier-Gitanes, for Jacques Laffite, for the Matra engine and for France

It was presented in its yellow Renault-Sport Livery; and standing round it were François Castaing, the designer, Gérard Larousse, head of Renault-Sport, Jean Sage, sports director, and a thousand other workers, known or unknown.

The Renault RS 01 was small, both simple and ingenious at the same time, and completely built around an engine.

The V6 Renault-Gordini had a cast-iron cylinder block with wet liners and a dry sump. The crankshaft and connecting rods were of steel, with aluminium alloy cylinder heads and pistons. The Renault engine had no need of sophisticated materials and its originality lay elsewhere. It lay in the overhead camshafts driven by toothed belts, in the arrangement of the Kugelfischer fuel injection, and of course in the Garrett system turbo-supercharger.

After a minor collision in the Italian Grand Prix Jean-Pierre Jabouille had a damaged aileron on the Renault RS 01

The 1500 cc turbocharged V6 engine determined the character of the Renault RS 01

The principle is as follows, in the words of François Castaing: 'an internal combustion engine delivers exhaust gases at a sufficiently high temperature for part of their expansion to be used in a gas turbine. This in turn drives a centrifugal supercharger, which compresses the air before it is fed to the engine.'

The only problem is this: the chief defect of the turbo is that there is a time lag between the moment when the driver accelerates on leaving a corner and the instant when full power is delivered. This is the stumbling-block of the turbo-compressor.

As for the chassis, numerous changes had been made since the laboratory car. Marcel Hubert remodelled the body and had it tested in the wind tunnel at St.-Cyr. The monocoque of the RS 01 was not built like the other Formula 1 tubs, that were based on a large number of light alloy sheets riveted together. It consisted of two large folded plates, tensioned by steel couplings, a technique which assured greater rigidity and durability.

At Silverstone on 16 July 1977 the Renault RS 01 had its baptism of fire. Starting from 21st position, Jabouille had to stop after 12 laps: it was losing turbo pressure because a crack had developed in the induction system. The turbo was clearly vulnerable to thermal distortion, which occurred at the drop in temperature at the time of the pit stop.

Exactly the same happened at Zandvoort, Monza, and Watkins Glen. In achieving a competitive performance level, the Renault technicians had neglected reliability. But one thing had been proved: the turbo has its place in Formula 1.

FRENCH CARS AND THEIR RIVALS					
LIGIER-GITANES JS7	V 12	2993 cc	(79.7 × 50 mm)	500 bhp at 12 000 rpm	575 k
RENAULT RS01	V 6	1492 cc	(86 × 42.8 mm)	500 bhp at 11 000 rpm	600 k
BRABHAM BT45 B	flat 12	2995 cc	(77 × 53.6 mm)	510 bhp at 12 000 rpm	615 k
BRM P-207	V 12	2997 cc	(74.6 × 57.2 mm)	488 bhp at 11 500 rpm	
ENSIGN N177	V 8	2993 cc	(85.7 × 64.8 mm)	490 bhp at 11 000 rpm	
FERRARI 312 T2	flat 12	2992 cc	(80 × 49.6 mm)	505 bhp at 12 400 rpm	
FITTIPALDI F-5	V 8	2993 cc	(85.7 × 64.8 mm)	490 bhp at 11 000 rpm	595 k
HESKETH 308E	V 8	2993 cc	(85.7 × 64.8 mm)	490 bhp at 11 000 rpm	
KOJIMA KE-009	V 8	2993 cc	(85.7 × 64.8 mm)	490 bhp at 11 000 rpm	
LEC CRP1	V 8	2993 cc	(85.7 × 64.8 mm)	490 bhp at 11 000 rpm	
LOTUS Mk78	V 8	2993 cc	(85.7 × 64.8 mm)	495 bhp at 11 000 rpm	
MARCH 761B	V 8	2993 cc	(85.7 × 64.8 mm)	490 bhp at 11 000 rpm	620 k
MARCH 771	V 8	2993 cc	(85.7 × 64.8 mm)	490 bhp at 11 000 rpm	575 k
MARCH 240	V 8	2993 cc	(85.7 × 64.8 mm)	490 bhp at 11 000 rpm	670 k
McLAREN M26	V 8	2993 cc	(85.7 × 64.8 mm)	495 bhp at 11 000 rpm	585 k
PENSKE PC-4	V 8	2993 cc	(85.7 × 64.8 mm)	490 bhp at 11 000 rpm	
SHADOW DN-8	V 8	2993 cc	(85.7 × 64.8 mm)	490 bhp at 11 000 rpm	
SURTEES TS 19 B	V 8	2993 cc	(85.7 × 64.8 mm)	490 bhp at 11 000 rpm	
TYRRELL P-34	V 8	2993 cc	(85.7 × 64.8 mm)	495 bhp at 11 000 rpm	630 k
WOLF WR-1	V 8	2993 cc	(85.7 × 64.8 mm)	495 bhp at 11 000 rpm	575 k

THE BEGINNING OF THE FUTURE

1978

Between the 1977 and 1978 seasons France had raised herself to the level of the most important nations represented in Grands Prix. A 'Club-France' was formed, sponsored by the Secretary of State for Youth and Sports. It consisted of the seven French drivers taking part in the World Championship.

The Martini Mk 23: classic design, but extremely well built

Patrick Depailler, Didier Pironi, Jean-Pierre Jarier, Patrick Tambay, Jacques Laffite, René Arnoux and Jean-Pierre Jabouille were driving for France in 1978. Better still for the Francophile, the three last named were all driving French cars!

The third man

On 10 January 1978 Tico Martini joined the exclusive club of Formula 1 constructors with Renault and Ligier. Of Italian origin but British demeanour and with a rather friendly nature, he had been producing racing cars since 1968. Keeping up progress in his logical and prudent manner, Tico Martini used his Formula 2 experience in creating his Mk 23 for Formula 1.

The Martini combined the usual qualities of Tico's productions: classic design, functional construction, exemplary finish. There was one concession to modern Formula 1 concepts, which was inboard front suspension. For the rest, the MK 23 was quite conventional in aerodynamics and mechanics. It was therefore propelled by the eternal English Ford Cosworth engine, which had more than 100 victories to its credit since it was launched in 1967. Under these conditions, Martini was sheltered from unpleasant surprises: he had built a sensible car that was free from any deep-seated problems.

As for the personnel, his main support was from Hugues de Chaunac, the dynamic sports director, and René Arnoux, the driver, full of promise since gaining the title of European Champion in Formula 2 in 1977. The financial backing came from RMO (Entreprise Grenobloise de Travail Temporaire), Elf and Silver Match.

Long-term or short-term?

For the Ligier team, their third Grand Prix season was strewn with question marks. Their optimism was toned down a little. SEITA had taken a long time to sign a new three-year contract, delaying it until late in December 1977. This was because of new anti-tobacco laws which did not encourage cigarette advertising, even where motor sport was the medium!

There were also uncertainties about Matra, where there was a possibility of stopping development of the V12 engine for at least the short term. This did not exactly have a stimulating effect on development of the JS 9, which was the real 1978 Ligier and had a very original aerodynamic system with long stabilizing fins at the rear. For the time being therefore the JS 7 was uprated; it was given a modified rear end, incorporating the Hewland FGA six-speed gearbox that was lighter and had an easier change than the TL 200 which was previously fitted.

As for Renault-Sport, this year they were hiding behind the pretext of an experimental season, giving full priority to the Le Mans 24 Hours Race. The RS 01 continued to be evolved. Gérard Larrousse's team were making some progress with this revolutionary machine, both as regards the reliability of the turbocharged engine and the aerodynamic efficiency of the body.

In any case, there were no tyre problems. Michelin, who supplied Renault and later Ferrari, had immediately been successful with their radial ply tyres. In equipping two great teams in 1978, Michelin had upset the Goodyear monopoly; they had dealt quite a body-blow in beating their American rival at the Brazilian Grand Prix in January 1978 (Carlos Reutemann in the Ferrari 312 T2).

The future of Formula 1

This story ends as it began: with Renault and Michelin. In the past, motor racing, and especially Formula 1, was the test bench for advanced techniques and opened the way to improvements of specific qualities of production cars, such as roadholding and braking.

But little by little the use of the motor car has come to be governed very largely by artificial driving conditions arising out of compulsory speed limits and the need for fuel economy. The manufacturers have to give priority to safety, comfort and economy. These requirements have had a parallel effect on the development of motor racing.

Formula 1 has become an important means of publicizing the name of a firm internationally and asserting its world-wide reputation, just as it was the standard-bearer of the rampant nationalism of the 1930s.

In these circumstances France has come to occupy a position of some importance. In recent years the work of the Fédération Française du Sport Automobile, led by Jean-Marie Balestre, has encouraged a new generation of world-standard drivers. At the same time the big industrial companies in France – inside and outside the motor industry – have involved themselves in what had once been only an amateur sport. With their powerful resources they have pushed French motor sport into the top class of technical achievement. To all these people, in whose veins the 'blue blood' runs: thank you, and good luck.

During the winter of 1977–8 the Renault RS 01 had its body re-shaped with flat sides

187

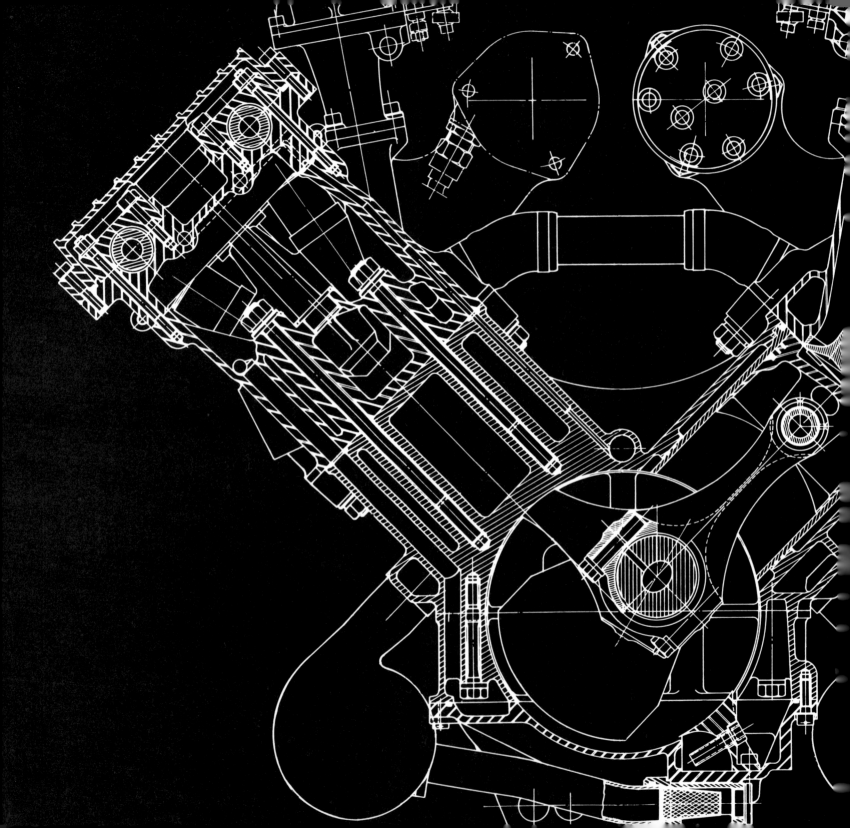

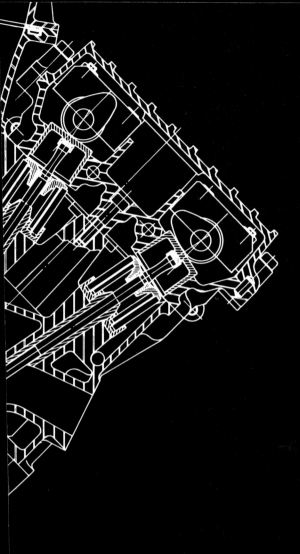

SPECIFICATIONS

 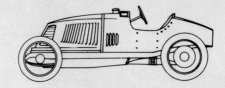 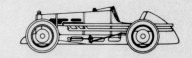

	ALCYON	ALDA	ALPHI
MAKE			
Type			
Year	1912	1914	1929
Maker	Automobiles Alcyon (Courbevoie)	Charron Ltd (Courbevoie)	
ENGINE	ALCYON	ALDA	CIME
Cylinders	4 separate cyl in line	4 cyl in line	6 cyl in line
Capacity	2994 cc	4439 cc	1485 cc
Bore × stroke	85 × 132 mm	94 × 160 mm	62 × 82 mm
Max power		95 bhp at 2800 rpm	70 bhp at 4700 rpm
Comp ratio		5 to 1	
Valve gear	2 side camshafts	1 overhead camshaft	side camshaft
	4 horizontal valves per cyl	4 vertical valves per cyl	side valves
Carburation	single carburettor	single Claudel carburettor	
			Cozette supercharger
Crankshaft			
Cooling	water	water	water
TRANSMISSION			
Type	shaft drive to rear wheels	shaft drive to rear wheels	shaft drive to rear wheels
Gearbox	4 speeds	4 speeds	
Clutch	multi-plate	cone	
CHASSIS			
Construction	channel section steel	channel section steel	channel section steel
Front suspension	rigid axle	rigid axle	rigid axle
	semi-elliptic springs	semi-elliptic springs	semi-elliptic springs
	friction shock-absorbers	Haudaille shock absorbers	friction shock absorbers
Rear suspension	live axle	live axle	live axle
	semi-elliptic springs	cantilever springs	semi-elliptic springs
	friction shock absorbers	Haudaille shock absorbers	friction shock absorbers
Front brakes			drums mechanical operation (Perrot)
Rear brakes	drums mechanical operation	drums mechanical operation	drums mechanical operation (Perrot)
Steering	worm	worm	worm
DIMENSIONS			
Wheelbase		270 cm	250 cm
Front track		135 cm	120 cm
Rear track		135 cm	120 cm
Weight	1000 kg	1000 kg	
Front tyres		Pirelli 810 × 90	
Rear tyres	Pirelli 815 × 105		
Max speed			160 km/h
PRODUCTION	3 built	3 built	1 built
Where to see			Musée du Gérier

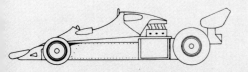 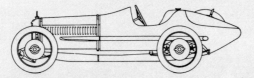 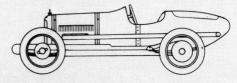

ALPINE-RENAULT A 500 1976 S.A. des Automobiles Alpine (Dieppe)	BALLOT 3 litres 1921 Automobiles Ballot (Paris)	BALLOT 2 LS 1921 Automobiles Ballot (Paris)	MAKE Type Year Maker
RENAULT-GORDINI EF1 6 cyl in 90°V 1490 cc or 1492 cc 80 × 49.4 mm or 82 × 42.8 mm 500 bhp at 11 000 rpm 7 to 1 4 overhead camshafts 4 valves per cyl at 21° 30 port injection Garrett turbocharger 4 bearings water	BALLOT 8 cyl in line 2973 cc 65 × 112 mm 107 bhp at 3800 rpm 2 overhead camshafts 4 valves per cyl at 60° 2 Claudel carburettors 5 rollers water	BALLOT 8 cyl in line 1995 cc 69.9 × 130 mm 88 bhp at 5000 rpm 2 overhead camshafts 4 valves per cyl 1 Claudel carburettor 3 bearings water	ENGINE Cylinders Capacity Bore × stroke Max power Comp ratio Valve gear Carburation Crankshaft Cooling
rear drive, central engine 5 speeds Hewland TL 200 twin plate Borg and Beck	shaft drive to rear wheels 4 speeds cone	shaft drive to rear wheels 4 speeds cone	TRANSMISSION Type Gearbox Clutch
monocoque independent suspension double wishbones, coil springs Koni telescopic dampers independent suspension upper and lower links, coil springs Koni telescopic dampers hydraulic, Lockheed discs hydraulic, Lockheed discs rack and pinion	channel section steel rigid axle semi-elliptic springs Hartford friction shock absorbers live axle semi-elliptic springs Hartford friction shock absorbers drums, mechanical servo drums, mechanical servo worm and wheel	channel section steel rigid axle semi-elliptic springs friction shock absorbers live axle semi-elliptic springs friction shock absorbers drums mechanical operation drums mechanical operation worm and wheel	CHASSIS Construction Front suspension Rear suspension Front brakes Rear brakes Steering
248 cm 136 cm 142 cm 620 kg Michelin 10 × 13 rim Michelin 18 × 13 rim 280 km/h	265 cm 133.5 cm 133.5 cm 780 kg 820 × 120 835 × 135 180 km/h	265 cm 130 cm 130 cm 780 kg 820 × 120 820 × 120 160 km/h	DIMENSIONS Wheelbase Front track Rear track Weight Front tyres Rear tyres Max speed
1 built Régie Renault	3 built Fondation Schlumpf		PRODUCTION Where to see

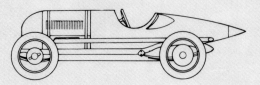 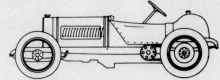 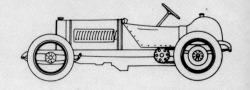

	BALLOT	BRASIER	BRASIER
MAKE	**BALLOT**	**BRASIER**	**BRASIER**
Type	2 LS		
Year	1922	1906	1907
Maker	Automobiles Ballot (Paris)	Sté des Automobiles Brasier (Ivry)	Sté des Automobiles Brasier (Ivry)
ENGINE	BALLOT	BRASIER	BRASIER
Cylinders	4 cyl in line	4 cyl in line, 2 blocks	4 cyl in line, 2 blocks
Capacity	1995 cc	12 829 cc	11 968
Bore × stroke	69.9 × 130 mm	165 × 150 mm	165 × 140 mm
Max power	90 bhp at 5000 rpm	105 bhp at 1200 rpm	110 bhp
Comp ratio			
Valve gear	twin overhead camshafts	side camshaft	side camshaft
	4 valves per cyl	side valves	side valves
Carburation	single Zenith carburettor	single Brasier carburettor	single carburettor
Crankshaft	3 bearings		
Cooling	water	water	water
TRANSMISSION			
Type	shaft drive to rear wheels	chain drive to rear wheels	chain drive to rear wheels
Gearbox	4 speeds	3 speeds	3 speeds
Clutch	cone	cone	cone
CHASSIS			
Construction	channel section steel	channel section steel	channel section steel
Front suspension	rigid axle	rigid axle	rigid axle
	semi-elliptic springs	semi-elliptic springs	semi-elliptic springs
	friction shock absorbers	Truffaut friction shock absorbers	friction shock absorbers
Rear suspension	live axle	dead axle	dead axle
	semi-elliptic springs	semi-elliptic springs	semi-elliptic springs
	friction shock absorbers	Truffaut friction shock absorbers	friction shock absorbers
Front brakes	drums, mechanical operation		
Rear brakes	drums, mechanical operation	drums, mechanical operation	drums, mechanical operation
Steering	worm and wheel	worm	worm
DIMENSIONS			
Wheelbase	280 cm	275 cm	265 cm
Front track	130 cm	135 cm	125 cm
Rear track	130 cm	135 cm	125 cm
Weight	830 kg	1000 kg	1050 kg
Front tyres	Michelin	Michelin 870 × 90	815 × 105
Rear tyres	Michelin	Michelin 880 × 120	895 × 135
Max speed	170 km/h	150 km/h	150 km/h
PRODUCTION	3 built	3 built	
Where to see			

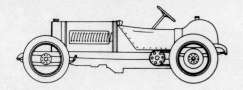 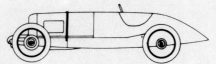 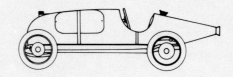

BRASIER	BUC	BUGATTI	MAKE
1908	AB6	T-30	Type
Sté des Automobiles Brasier (Ivry)	1927	1922	Year
	Bucciali Frères (Courbevoie)	Automobiles Bugatti (Molsheim)	Maker
BRASIER		BUGATTI T-30	**ENGINE**
4 cyl in line, 2 blocks	6 cyl in line	8 cyl in line	Cylinders
12 824 cc	1490 cc	1991 cc	Capacity
155 × 170 mm	61 × 85 mm	60 × 88 mm	Bore × stroke
120 bhp	70 bhp at 5000 rpm	86 bhp at 4000 rpm	Max power
			Comp ratio
side camshaft	single overhead camshaft	single overhead camshaft	Valve gear
side valves	overhead valves	3 valves per cyl	
single carburettor	twin Solex carburettors	twin horizontal Zeniths	Carburation
	7 bearings	3 ballraces	Crankshaft
water	water	water	Cooling
chain drive to rear wheels	shaft drive to rear wheels	shaft drive to rear wheels	**TRANSMISSION** Type
3 speeds	4 speeds	4 speeds	Gearbox
cone		multi-disc in oil	Clutch
channel section steel	channel section steel	channel section steel	**CHASSIS** Construction
rigid axle	rigid axle	rigid axle	Front suspension
semi-elliptic springs	semi-elliptic springs	semi-elliptic springs	
friction shock absorbers	friction shock absorbers	Bugatti friction shock absorbers	
dead axle	live axle	live axle	Rear suspension
semi-elliptic springs	semi-elliptic springs	quarter elliptic springs	
friction shock absorbers	friction shock absorbers	Bugatti friction shock absorbers	
	drums, mechanical operation	drums, mechanical operation	Front brakes
drums, mechanical operation	drums, mechanical operation	drums, mechanical operation	Rear brakes
worm	worm	worm and wheel	Steering
275 cm	245 cm	240 cm	**DIMENSIONS** Wheelbase
135 cm	120 cm	122 cm	Front track
135 cm	120 cm	122 cm	Rear track
	800 kg	730 kg	Weight
870 × 90			Front tyres
880 × 120			Rear tyres
160 km/h	170 km/h	160 km/h (165 with cowled radiator)	Max speed
		4 built	**PRODUCTION** Where to see

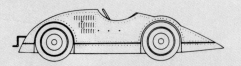 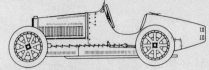 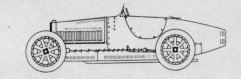

	BUGATTI	BUGATTI	BUGATTI
MAKE			
Type	T-30 Tank	T-35	T-35
Year	1923	1924	1925
Maker	Automobiles Bugatti (Molsheim)	Automobiles Bugatti (Molsheim)	Automobiles Bugatti (Molsheim)
ENGINE	BUGATTI T-30	BUGATTI T-35	BUGATTI T-35
Cylinders	8 cyl in line	8 cyl in line	8 cyl in line
Capacity	1991 cc	1991 cc	1991 cc 1495 cc
Bore × stroke	60 × 88 mm	60 × 88 mm	60 × 88 mm 52 × 88 mm
Max power	100 bhp	90 bhp at 5000 rpm	105 bhp at 5000 rpm 105 bhp at 5000 rpm
Comp ratio			
Valve gear	single overhead camshaft	single overhead camshaft	single overhead camshaft
	3 valves per cyl	3 valves per cyl	3 valves per cyl
Carburation	twin horizontal Zenith carburettors	twin horizontal Solex carburettors	twin horizontal Solex carburettors
Crankshaft	3 ballraces	3 ball, 2 roller bearings	3 ball, 2 roller bearings
Cooling	water	water	water
TRANSMISSION			
Type	shaft drive to rear wheels	shaft drive to rear wheels	shaft drive to rear wheels
Gearbox	4 speeds	4 speeds	4 speeds
Clutch	multi-disc in oil	multi-disc in oil	multi-disc in oil
CHASSIS			
Construction	steel platform, integral body	channel section steel	channel section steel
Front suspension	rigid axle	rigid axle	rigid axle
	semi-elliptic springs	semi-elliptic springs	semi-elliptic springs
	Bugatti friction shock absorbers	Bugatti friction shock absorbers	friction shock absorbers
Rear suspension	live axle	live axle	live axle
	quarter-elliptic springs	quarter-elliptic springs	quarter-elliptic springs
	Bugatti friction shock absorbers	Bugatti friction shock absorbers	friction shock absorbers
Front brakes	drums, hydraulic operation	drums, mechanical operation	drums, mechanical operation
Rear brakes	drums, mechanical operation	drums, mechanical operation	drums, mechanical operation
Steering	worm and wheel	worm and wheel	worm and wheel
DIMENSIONS			
Wheelbase	200 cm	240 cm	240 cm
Front track	100 cm	120 cm	120 cm
Rear track	100 cm	120 cm	120 cm
Weight	750 kg	655 kg	655 kg
Front tyres		Dunlop 710 × 90	710 × 90
Rear tyres		Dunlop 710 × 90	710 × 90
Max speed	185 km/h	170 km/h	175 km/h
PRODUCTION	4 built	6 built	
Where to see	Fondation Schlumpf	Musée Raffaeli (Le Castellet)	
		Hamish Moffatt Collection	
		Marc Nicolosi Collection	

 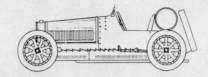 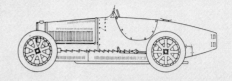

BUGATTI T-35B 1928–30 Automobiles Bugatti (Molsheim)	**BUGATTI** T-35C 1928–30 Automobiles Bugatti (Molsheim)	**BUGATTI** T-39A 1926 Automobiles Bugatti (Molsheim)	**MAKE** Type Year Maker
BUGATTI T-35B 8 cyl in line 2262 cc 60 × 100 mm 140 bhp at 5000 rpm single overhead camshaft 3 valves per cyl single Zenith updraught carb Roots supercharger 3 ball, 2 roller bearings water	BUGATTI T-35C 8 cyl in line 1991 cc 60 × 88 mm 125 bhp at 5500 rpm single overhead camshaft 3 valves per cyl single updraught carb Roots supercharger 3 ball, 2 roller bearings water	BUGATTI T-39A 8 cyl in line 1495 cc 1493 cc 52 × 88 mm 60 × 66 mm 110 bhp single overhead camshaft 3 valves per cyl single updraught carb Roots supercharger 3 ball. 2 roller bearings water	**ENGINE** Cylinders Capacity Bore × stroke Max power Comp ratio Valve gear Carburation Crankshaft Cooling
shaft drive to rear wheels 4 speeds multi-disc in oil	shaft drive to rear wheels 4 speeds multi-disc in oil	shaft drive to rear wheels 4 speeds multi-disc in oil	**TRANSMISSION** Type Gearbox Clutch
channel section steel rigid axle semi-elliptic springs friction shock absorbers live axle quarter-elliptic springs friction shock absorbers drums, mechanical operation drums, mechanical operation worm and wheel	channel section steel rigid axle semi-elliptic springs friction shock absorbers live axle quarter-elliptic springs friction shock absorbers drums, mechanical operation drums, mechanical operation worm and wheel	channel section steel rigid axle semi-elliptic springs friction shock absorbers live axle quarter-elliptic springs friction shock absorbers drums, mechanical operation drums, mechanical operation worm and wheel	**CHASSIS** Construction Front suspension Rear suspension Front brakes Rear brakes Steering
240 cm 120 cm 120 cm 750 kg 4.75 × 29 4.75 × 29 210 km/h	240 cm 120 cm 120 cm 750 kg 4.75 × 29 4.75 × 29 200 km/h	240 cm 120 cm 120 cm 750 kg 4.75 × 29 4.75 × 29 185 km/h	**DIMENSIONS** Wheelbase Front track Rear track Weight Front tyres Rear tyres Max speed
Briggs Cunningham Automotive Museum, Costa Mesa, Calif., USA (chassis 37371) Neil Corner Collection (chassis 4965)	André Binda Collection		**PRODUCTION** Where to see

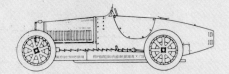 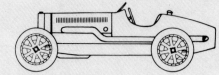 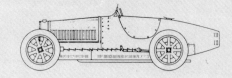

	BUGATTI	BUGATTI	BUGATTI
MAKE	**BUGATTI**	**BUGATTI**	**BUGATTI**
Type	T-39A	T-45	T-51
Year	1927	1930	1931–33
Maker	Automobiles Bugatti (Molsheim)	Automobiles Bugatti (Molsheim)	Automobiles Bugatti (Molsheim)
ENGINE	BUGATTI T-39A	BUGATTI T-45	BUGATTI T-51
Cylinders	8 cyl in line	2 × 8 cyl in line parallel	8 cyl in line
Capacity	1493 cc	3800 cc	2262 cc
Bore × stroke	60 × 66 mm	60 × 84 mm	60 × 100 mm
Max power	120 bhp at 5500 rpm	250 bhp at 5000 rpm	180 bhp at 5500 rpm
Comp ratio			
Valve gear	single overhead camshaft	2 × 1 overhead camshaft	twin overhead camshafts
	3 valves per cyl	3 valves per cyl	2 valves per cyl
Carburation	single updraught carburettor	2 horizontal Zeniths	single updraught Zenith
	Roots supercharger	2 Roots superchargers	Roots supercharger
Crankshaft	3 ball, 2 roller bearings	16 roller, 2 plain bearings	3 ball, 2 roller bearings
Cooling	water	water	water
TRANSMISSION			
Type	shaft drive to rear wheels	shaft drive to rear wheels	shaft drive to rear wheels
Gearbox	4 speeds	4 speeds	4 speeds
Clutch	multi-disc in oil	multi-disc in oil	multi-disc in oil
CHASSIS			
Construction	channel section steel	channel section steel	channel section steel
Front suspension	rigid axle	rigid axle	rigid axle
	semi-elliptic springs	semi-elliptic springs	semi-elliptic springs
	friction shock absorbers	friction shock absorbers	friction shock absorbers
Rear suspension	live axle	live axle	live axle
	quarter-elliptic springs	quarter-elliptic springs	quarter-elliptic springs
	friction shock absorbers	friction shock absorbers	friction shock absorbers
Front brakes	drums, mechanical operation	drums, mechanical operation	drums, mechanical operation
Rear brakes	drums, mechanical operation	drums, mechanical operation	drums, mechanical operation
Steering	worm and wheel	worm and wheel	worm and wheel
DIMENSIONS			
Wheelbase	240 cm	260 cm	240 cm
Front track	120 cm	125 cm	120 cm
Rear track	120 cm	125 cm	120 cm
Weight	750 kg	1000 kg	750 kg
Front tyres	4.75 × 29		5.00 × 19
Rear tyres	4.75 × 29		5.00 × 19
Max speed	185 km/h	250 km/h	230 km/h
PRODUCTION		3 built	40 built
Where to see		Fondation Schlumpf	Donington Collection

196

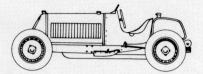 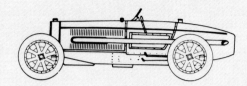 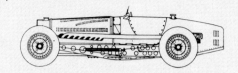

BUGATTI T-53 1932 Automobiles Bugatti (Molsheim)	BUGATTI T-54 1931–33 Automobiles Bugatti (Molsheim)	BUGATTI T-59 1933 Automobiles Bugatti (Molsheim)	MAKE Type Year Maker
BUGATTI T-50 8 cyl in line 4972 cc 86 × 107 mm 300 bhp at 4400 rpm twin overhead camshafts 2 valves per cyl 2 updraught Zenith carbs Roots supercharger 9 plain bearings water	BUGATTI T-50 8 cyl in line 4972 cc 86 × 107 mm 300 bhp at 4400 rpm twin overhead camshafts 2 valves per cyl 2 updraught Zenith carbs Roots supercharger 9 plain bearings water	BUGATTI T-59 8 cyl in line 2820 cc 67 × 100 mm 240 bhp at 5400 rpm twin overhead camshafts 2 valves per cyl 2 updraught Zenith carbs Roots supercharger 6 plain bearings water	ENGINE Cylinders Capacity Bore × stroke Max power Comp ratio Valve gear Carburation Crankshaft Cooling
shaft drive to all four wheels 4 speeds multi-disc	shaft drive to rear wheels 3 speeds multi-disc	shaft drive to rear wheels 4 speeds dry multi-disc	TRANSMISSION Type Gearbox Clutch
channel section steel independent suspension transverse springs friction shock absorbers live axle quarter-elliptic springs friction shock absorbers drums, mechanical operation drums, mechanical operation worm and wheel	channel section steel rigid axle semi-elliptic springs friction shock absorbers live axle quarter-elliptic springs friction shock absorbers drums, mechanical operation drums, mechanical operation worm and wheel	channel section steel rigid axle semi-elliptic springs friction shock absorbers live axle quarter-elliptic springs friction shock absorbers drums, mechanical operation drums, mechanical operation worm and wheel	CHASSIS Construction Front suspension Rear suspension Front brakes Rear brakes Steering
250 cm 125 cm 125 cm 940 kg 5.00 × 28 5.00 × 28 240 km/h	275 cm 140 cm 140 cm 940 kg 6.00 × 19 6.00 × 19 250 km/h	260 cm 125 cm 125 cm 750 kg 5.50 × 19 5.50 × 19 250 km/h	DIMENSIONS Wheelbase Front track Rear track Weight Front tyres Rear tyres Max speed
2 built Fondation Schlumpf	4 built Musée de Nettelsteedt	2 built	PRODUCTION Where to see

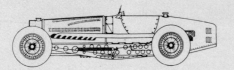 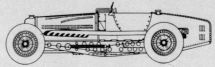 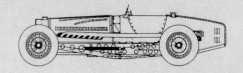

	BUGATTI	BUGATTI	BUGATTI
MAKE	**BUGATTI**	**BUGATTI**	**BUGATTI**
Type	T-59	T-59	T-59
Year	1934	1935	1936
Maker	Automobiles Bugatti (Molsheim)	Automobiles Bugatti (Molsheim)	Automobiles Bugatti (Molsheim)
ENGINE	BUGATTI T-59	BUGATTI T-50B	BUGATTI T-50B
Cylinders	8 cyl in line	8 cyl in line	8 cyl in line
Capacity	3257 cc	4744 cc	3984 cc
Bore × stroke	72 × 100 mm	84 × 107 mm	77 × 107 mm
Max power	250 bhp at 5750 rpm	320 bhp	
Comp ratio			
Valve gear	twin overhead camshafts	twin overhead camshafts	twin overhead camshafts
	2 valves per cyl	2 valves per cyl	2 valves per cyl
Carburation	2 updraught Zenith carbs	2 carburettors	2 carburettors
	Roots supercharger	Roots supercharger	Roots supercharger
Crankshaft	6 bearings	9 bearings	9 bearings
Cooling	water	water	water
TRANSMISSION			
Type	shaft drive to rear wheels	shaft drive to rear wheels	shaft drive to rear wheels
Gearbox	4 speeds	4 speeds	4 speeds
Clutch	dry multi-disc	dry twin-plate	dry multi-disc
CHASSIS			
Construction	channel section steel	channel section steel	channel section steel
Front suspension	rigid axle	rigid axle	rigid axle
	semi-elliptic springs	semi-elliptic springs	semi-elliptic springs
	de Ram shock absorbers	de Ram shock absorbers	de Ram shock absorbers
Rear suspension	live axle	live axle	live axle
	quarter-elliptic springs	quarter-elliptic springs	quarter-elliptic springs
	de Ram shock absorbers	de Ram shock absorbers	de Ram shock absorbers
Front brakes	drums, mechanical operation	drums, mechanical operation	drums, mechanical operation
Rear brakes	drums, mechanical operation	drums, mechanical operation	drums, mechanical operation
Steering	worm and wheel	worm and wheel	worm and wheel
DIMENSIONS			
Wheelbase	260 cm	265 cm	260 cm
Front track	125 cm	125 cm	125 cm
Rear track	125 cm	125 cm	125 cm
Weight	750 kg	750 kg	
Front tyres	Dunlop 5.50 × 19	5.50 × 19	5.50 × 19
Rear tyres	Dunlop 5.50 × 19	5.50 × 19	5.50 × 19
Max speed	250 km/h	260 km/h	
PRODUCTION	4 built	4 built	
Where to see	Neil Corner Collection		

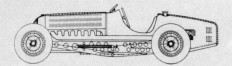 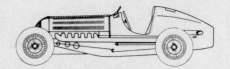 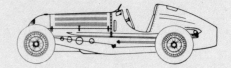

			MAKE
BUGATTI 4.7 litre Single-seater 1936 Automobiles Bugatti (Molsheim)	**BUGATTI** 4.5 litre Single-seater 1937 Automobiles Bugatti (Molsheim)	**BUGATTI** 3 litre Single-seater 1938 Automobiles Bugatti (Molsheim)	**Type** **Year** **Maker**
BUGATTI T-50B 8 cyl in line 4744 cc 84 × 107 mm 370 bhp at 5700 rpm twin overhead camshafts 2 valves per cyl 2 carburettors Roots supercharger 9 bearings water	BUGATTI T-50B 8 cyl in line 4431 cc 84 × 100 mm twin overhead camshafts 2 valves per cyl 1 carburettor 9 bearings water	BUGATTI T-50B 111 8 cyl in line 2982 cc 78 × 78 mm 270 bhp at 6000 rpm twin overhead camshafts 2 valves per cyl 2 carburettors Roots supercharger 9 bearings water	**Engine** **Cylinders** **Capacity** **Bore × Stroke** **Max Power** **Comp ratio** **Valve gear** **Carburation** **Crankshaft** **Cooling**
shaft drive to rear wheels 4 speeds dry multi-disc	shaft drive to rear wheels 4 speeds dry multi-disc	shaft drive to rear wheels 4 speeds dry multi-disc	**TRANSMISSION** **Type** **Gearbox** **Clutch**
channel section steel rigid axle semi-elliptic springs de Ram shock absorbers live axle quarter-elliptic springs de Ram shock absorbers drums, mechanical operation drums, mechanical operation worm and wheel	channel section steel rigid axle semi-elliptic springs de Ram shock absorbers live axle quarter-elliptic springs de Ram shock absorbers drums, mechanical operation drums, mechanical operation worm and wheel	channel section steel rigid axle semi-elliptic springs de Ram shock absorbers live axle quarter-elliptic springs de Ram shock absorbers drums, mechanical operation drums, mechanical operation worm and wheel	**CHASSIS** **Construction** **Front suspension** **Rear suspension** **Front brakes** **Rear brakes** **Steering**
260 cm 125 cm 125 cm 750 kg 5.50 × 19 5.50 × 19 270 km/h	260 cm 125 cm 125 cm	260 cm 125 cm 125 cm 280 km/h	**DIMENSIONS** **Wheelbase** **Front track** **Rear track** **Weight** **Front tyres** **Rear tyres** **Max speed**
1 built (by modifying 1935 model)	1 built (by rebuilding 1936 model)	1 built (by modifying 1937 model)	**PRODUCTION** **Where to see**

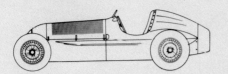 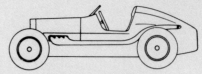 

MAKE	BUGATTI	BUGATTI	BUGATTI
Type	4.7 litre Single-seater	T-73C	T-251/2
Year	1939–45	1948	1956
Maker	Automobiles Bugatti (Molsheim)	Automobiles Bugatti (Molsheim)	Automobiles Bugatti (Molsheim)
ENGINE	BUGATTI T-50B	BUGATTI T-73C	BUGATTI
Cylinders	8 cyl in line	8 cyl in line	8 cyl in line
Capacity	4744 cc	1451 cc	2431 cc
Bore × stroke	84 × 107 mm	76 × 82 mm	75 × 68.8 mm
Max power		230 bhp	230 bhp at 7500 rpm
Comp ratio			7.5 to 1
Valve gear	twin overhead camshafts	twin overhead camshafts	twin overhead camshafts
	2 valves per cyl	2 valves per cyl	2 valves per cyl
Carburation	twin carburettors	1 Solex carburettor	4 twin-choke Webers, 42 mm
		Roots supercharger	
Crankshaft	9 bearings	5 bearings	10 bearings
Cooling	water	water	water
TRANSMISSION			
Type	shaft drive to rear wheels	shaft drive to rear wheels	central engine rear drive
Gearbox	4 speeds	4 speeds	5 speeds, Porsche synchro
Clutch	dry multi-disc	single dry plate	dry multi-disc
CHASSIS			
Construction	channel section steel	channel section steel	multi-tubular
Front suspension	rigid axle	rigid axle	rigid axle
	semi-elliptic springs	semi-elliptic springs	inboard inclined coil springs
	de Ram shock absorbers	de Ram shock absorbers	telescopic dampers
Rear suspension	live axle	live axle	de Dion axle
	quarter-elliptic springs	quarter-elliptic springs	inboard inclined coil springs
	de Ram shock absorbers	de Ram shock absorbers	telescopic dampers
Front brakes	drums, hydraulic operation	drums, hydraulic operation	drums, hydraulic operation
Rear brakes	drums, hydraulic operation	drums, hydraulic operation	drums, hydraulic operation
Steering	worm and wheel	worm and wheel	worm and sector
DIMENSIONS			
Wheelbase	260 cm	240 cm	220 cm
Front track	125 cm	125 cm	130 cm
Rear track	125 cm	125 cm	128 cm
Weight	850 kg	800 kg	750 kg
Front tyres		5.50 × 19	Pirelli 6.00 × 17
Rear tyres		5.50 × 19	Pirelli 6.00 × 17
Max speed	300 km/h	230 km/h	260 km/h
PRODUCTION	1 built	2 built	1 built
Where to see	Fondation Schlumpf	Fondation Schlumpf (bare chassis)	Fondation Schlumpf

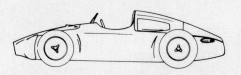 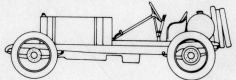 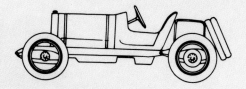

BUGATTI	CLÉMENT BAYARD	CLÉMENT BAYARD	MAKE
T-251/2			Type
1956	1906–7	1908	Year
Automobiles Bugatti (Molsheim)	Bayard Clément	Bayard Clément	Maker
BUGATTI			**ENGINE**
8 cyl in line	4 separate cyl in line	4 cyl in line, 2 blocks	Cylinders
2431 cc	12 861 cc	13 963 cc	Capacity
75 × 68.8 mm	160 × 160 mm	155 × 185	Bore × stroke
265 bhp at 7500 rpm	125 bhp at 1350 rpm	135 bhp	Max power
12.5 to 1			Comp ratio
twin overhead camshafts	side camshaft	single overhead camshaft	Valve gear
2 valves per cyl	side valves	2 valves per cyl at 45°	
4 twin-choke Webers, 42 mm	1 carburettor	1 carburettor	Carburation
10 bearings			Crankshaft
water	water	water	Cooling
central engine, rear drive	shaft drive to rear wheels	shaft drive to rear wheels	**TRANSMISSION** Type
5 speeds, Porsche synchro	4 speeds	4 speeds	Gearbox
dry multi-disc	Hele-Shaw	multi-disc	Clutch
multi-tubular	channel section steel	channel section steel	**CHASSIS** Construction
rigid axle	rigid axle	rigid axle	Front suspension
external coil springs	semi-elliptic springs	semi-elliptic springs	
telescopic dampers	friction shock absorbers	friction shock absorbers	
de Dion axle	live axle	live axle	Rear suspension
external coil springs	semi-elliptic springs	semi-elliptic springs	
telescopic dampers	friction shock absorbers	friction shock absorbers	
drums, hydraulic operation			Front brakes
drums, hydraulic operation	drums, mechanical operation	drums, mechanical operation	Rear brakes
worm and sector	worm	worm	Steering
230 cm	290 cm	275 cm	**DIMENSIONS** Wheelbase
130 cm	135 cm	130 cm	Front track
128 cm	135 cm	130 cm	Rear track
750 kg	1000 kg		Weight
Pirelli 6.00 × 17		870 × 90	Front tyres
Pirelli 6.00 × 17		880 × 120	Rear tyres
265 km/h	160 km/h	170 km/h	Max speed
1 built	3 built in 1906		**PRODUCTION**
Fondation Schlumpf			Where to see

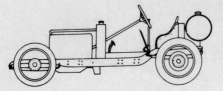 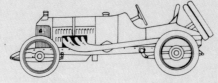 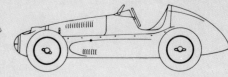

	CORRE	CÔTE	CTA-ARSENAL
MAKE			
Type			
Year	1907	1912	1947
Maker	Sté des Autos Corre (Levallois)	Sté des Autos et Motos Côte (Pantin)	C d'Ét Tech de l'Auto et du Cycle
Engine		CÔTE	CTA ARSENAL
Cylinders	4 cyl in line, 2 blocks	4 cyl in line, 2 blocks	90° V8
Capacity	10 603 cc	2984 cc	1482 cc
Bore × stroke	150 × 150 mm	89 × 120 mm	60 × 65.6 mm
Max power		70 bhp at 1800 rpm	266 bhp at 7500 rpm (theoretical)
Comp ratio			7 to 1
Valve gear	side camshaft	two-stroke	4 overhead camshafts
			2 valves per cyl
Carburation		1 Zenith carburettor	2 twin-choke Solex
			2 Roots superchargers
Crankshaft			
Cooling	water	water	water
TRANSMISSION			
Type	shaft drive to rear wheels	shaft drive to rear wheels	gearbox with differential
Gearbox	3 speeds	4 speeds	4 speeds
Clutch	cone	cone	dry multi-disc
CHASSIS			
Construction	channel section steel	channel section steel	ladder frame
Front suspension	rigid axle	rigid axle	independent suspension
	semi-elliptic springs	semi-elliptic springs	longitudinal torsion bars
	friction shock absorbers	friction shock absorbers	de Ram shock absorbers
Rear suspension	live axle	live axle	independent suspension
	semi-elliptic springs	semi-elliptic springs	transverse torsion bars
	friction shock absorbers	friction shock absorbers	de Ram shock absorbers
Front brakes			drums, hydraulic operation
Rear brakes	drums, mechanical operation	drums, mechanical operation	drums, hydraulic operation
Steering	worm	worm	
DIMENSIONS			
Wheelbase	280 cm	260 cm	246 cm
Front track	140 cm	135 cm	
Rear track	140 cm	135 cm	
Weight	850 kg	850 kg	
Front tyres	Michelin	815 × 105	Englebert 5.00 × 17
Rear tyres	Michelin	815 × 105	Englebert 7.00 × 16
Max speed		125 km/h	240 km/h
PRODUCTION			
Where to see			

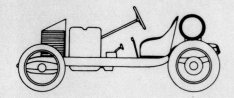  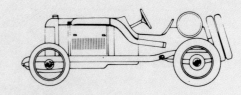

DARRACQ	DB-PANHARD	DELAGE	MAKE
	Supercharged	Type Y Special	**Type**
1906–7	1955	1913	**Year**
Soc A. Darracq, Usines Perfecta (Suresnes)	Deutsch et Bonnet (Champigny)	Delage et Cie (Courbevoie)	**Maker**
DARRACQ	PANHARD	DELAGE	**ENGINE**
4 cyl in line, 2 blocks	flat-twin	4 cyl in line	**Cylinders**
12 711 cc (06) 15 268 cc (07)	746 cc	7032 cc	**Capacity**
170 × 140 mm 180 × 150 mm	79.6 × 75 mm	110 × 185 mm	**Bore × stroke**
125 bhp at 1200 rpm (07)	85 bhp at 6000 rpm	105 bhjp at 2300 rpm	**Max power**
	6.5 to 1		**Comp ratio**
side camshaft, pushrods	central camshaft, pushrods	2 side camshafts, pushrods	**Valve gear**
2 overhead valves per cyl	2 overhead valves per cyl	4 horizontal valves per cyl	
1 carburettor	1 Solex downdraught carb	1 carburettor	**Carburation**
	Mag supercharger		
	2 bearings		**Crankshaft**
water	air	water	**Cooling**
shaft drive to rear wheels	front-wheel drive	shaft drive to rear wheels	**TRANSMISSION** **Type**
3 speeds	4 speeds	5 speeds	**Gearbox**
cone	single dry plate	multi-disc	**Clutch**
channel section steel	steel frame	channel section steel	**CHASSIS** **Construction**
rigid axle	independent suspension	rigid axle	**Front suspension**
semi-elliptic springs	2 transverse springs	semi-elliptic springs	
friction shock absorbers	telescopic dampers	friction shock absorbers	
live axle	independent suspension	live axle	**Rear suspension**
semi-elliptic springs	transverse torsion bars	semi-elliptic springs	
friction shock absorbers	telescopic dampers	friction shock absorbers	
	Messier discs, hydraulic operation		**Front brakes**
drums, mechanical operation	drums, hydraulic operation	drums, mechanical operation	**Rear brakes**
worm	rack and pinion	worm	**Steering**
285 cm	203 cm	275 cm	**DIMENSIONS** **Wheelbase**
135 cm	122 cm	140 cm	**Front track**
135 cm	115 cm	130 cm	**Rear track**
860 kg	350 kg	950 kg	**Weight**
	Dunlop 15 in		**Front tyres**
	Dunlop 15 in		**Rear tyres**
165 km/h	180 km/h		**Max speed**
3 built in 1906	2 built	3 built	**PRODUCTION** **Where to see**
		Indianapolis Motor Speedway Museum (Edgar L. Roy Collection)	

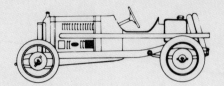 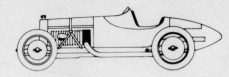 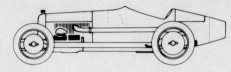

	DELAGE	DELAGE	DELAGE
MAKE			
Type	Type S	2 LCV	2 LCV
Year	1914	1923	1924
Maker	Delage et Cie (Courbevoie)	Automobiles Delage (Courbevoie)	Automobiles Delage (Courbevoie)
ENGINE	DELAGE	DELAGE	DELAGE
Cylinders	4 cyl in line	60° V12	60° V12
Capacity	4439 cc	1984 cc	1984 cc
Bore × stroke	94 × 160 mm	51.3 × 80 mm	51.3 × 80 mm
Max power		105 bhp at 6200 rpm	116 bhp at 8000 rpm
Comp ratio		6.2 to 1	7 to 1
Valve gear	twin camshafts, desmodromic	4 overhead camshafts	4 overhead camshafts
	4 valves per cyl	2 valves per cyl	2 valves per cyl
Carburation	1 Claudel carb	2 Zenith updraught carbs	2 Zenith updraught carbs
Crankshaft		7 roller bearings	7 roller bearings
Cooling	water	water	water
TRANSMISSION			
Type	shaft drive to rear wheels	shaft drive to rear wheels	shaft drive to rear wheels
Gearbox	5 speeds	4 speeds	4 speeds
Clutch	multi-disc	dry multi-disc	dry multi-disc
CHASSIS			
Construction	channel section steel	channel section steel	channel section steel
Front suspension	rigid axle	rigid axle	rigid axle
	semi-elliptic springs	semi-elliptic springs	semi-elliptic springs
	friction shock absorbers	Hartford-Repusseau dampers	Hartford-Repusseau dampers
Rear suspension	live axle	live axle	live axle
	semi-elliptic springs	semi-elliptic springs	semi-elliptic springs
	friction shock absorbers	Hartford-Repusseau dampers	Hartford-Repusseau dampers
Front brakes	drums, Perrot mech operation	drums, mech servo	drums, mech servo
Rear brakes	drums, Perrot mech operation	drums, mech servo	drums, mech servo
Steering	worm	worm and sector	worm and sector
DIMENSIONS			
Wheelbase	273 cm	260 cm	260 cm
Front track	135 cm	125 cm	130 cm
Rear track	135 cm	125 cm	130 cm
Weight		690 kg	680 kg
Front tyres		795 × 105	765 × 105
Rear tyres		795 × 105	765 × 105
Max speed		180 km/h	185 km/h
PRODUCTION	3 built	1 built	4 built
Where to see			

  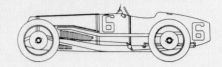

DELAGE	DELAGE	DELAGE	MAKE
2 LCV	15-S-8	15-S-8	Type
1925	1926	1927	Year
Automobiles Delage (Courbevoie)	Automobiles Delage (Courbevoie)	Automobiles Delage (Courbevoie)	Maker
DELAGE	DELAGE	DELAGE	**ENGINE**
60° V12	8 cyls in line	8 cyls in line	Cylinders
1984 cc	1487 cc	1487 cc	Capacity
51.3 × 80 mm	55.8 × 76 mm	55.8 × 76 mm	Bore × stroke
205 bhp at 6500 rpm	170 bhp at 8000 rpm	177 bhp at 8000 rpm	Max power
	5 to 1	5 to 1	Comp ratio
4 overhead camshafts	twin overhead camshafts	twin overhead camshafts	Valve gear
2 valves per cyl	2 valves per cyl	2 valves per cyl	
2 Zenith carburettors	1 Cozette horizontal carb	2 Zenith carburettors	Carburation
2 Roots superchargers	Roots supercharger	2 Roots superchargers	
7 roller bearings	9 roller bearings	9 roller bearings	Crankshaft
water	water	water	Cooling
shaft drive to rear wheels	shaft drive to rear wheels	shaft drive to rear wheels	**TRANSMISSION** Type
5 speeds	5 speeds	5 speeds	Gearbox
dry multi-disc	dry multi-disc	dry multi-disc	Clutch
channel section steel	channel section steel	channel section steel	**CHASSIS** Construction
rigid axle	rigid axle	rigid axle	Front suspension
semi-elliptic springs	semi-elliptic springs	semi-elliptic springs	
Hartford-Repusseau dampers	Hartford friction dampers	Hartford friction dampers	
live axle	live axle	live axle	Rear suspension
semi-elliptic springs	semi-elliptic springs	semi-elliptic springs	
Hartford-Repusseau dampers	Hartford friction dampers	Hartford friction dampers	
drums, mech servo	drums, mech servo	drums, mech servo	Front brakes
drums, mech servo	drums, mech servo	drums, mech servo	Rear brakes
worm and sector	worm and sector	worm and sector	Steering
260 cm	246 cm	246 cm	**DIMENSIONS** Wheelbase
130 cm	130 cm	130 cm	Front track
130 cm	130 cm	130 cm	Rear track
720 kg	750 kg	760 kg	Weight
	Michelin 765 × 120	Michelin 765 × 120	Front tyres
	Michelin 765 × 120	Michelin 765 × 120	Rear tyres
215 km/h	200 km/h	205 km/h	Max speed
4 built (by rebuilding 1924 models) John Rowley Collection	3 built	4 built Briggs Cunningham Automotive Museum, Costa Mesa, Calif., U.S.A.	**PRODUCTION** Where to see

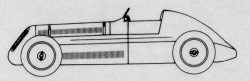 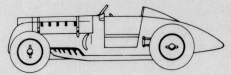 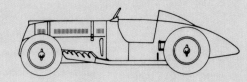

	DELAGE	DELAHAYE	DELAHAYE
MAKE	**DELAGE**	**DELAHAYE**	**DELAHAYE**
Type	D6 écurie Walter-Watney	145 two-seater	145 two-seater
Year	1947	1937–8	1939
Maker	Automobiles Delahaye-GFA (Paris)	Sté des Autos Delahaye (Paris)	Sté des Autos Delahaye (Paris)
ENGINE	DELAGE D6–70	DELAHAYE 145	DELAHAYE 145
Cylinders	6 cyl in line	60° V12	60° V12
Capacity	2988 cc	4490 cc	4490 cc
Bore × stroke	83.7 × 90.5 mm	75 × 84.7 mm	75 × 84.7 mm
Max power	142 bhp at 5300 rpm	225 bhp at 5500 rpm	235 bhp at 5000 rpm
Comp ratio			8.5 to 1
Valve gear	side camshaft, pushrods	1 central, 2 side camshafts	1 central, 2 side camshafts
	2 valves per cyl	2 valves per cyl	2 valves per cyl
Carburation	3 carburettors	3 twin-choke Strombergs	3 twin-choke Strombergs
Crankshaft	4 bearings	7 bearings	7 bearings
Cooling	water	water	water
TRANSMISSION			
Type	shaft drive to rear wheels	shaft drive to rear wheels	shaft drive to rear wheels
Gearbox	4 speeds Cotal electromagnetic	4 speeds Cotal electromagnetic	4 speeds Cotal electromagnetic
Clutch	single dry plate	dry multi-disc	dry multi-disc
CHASSIS			
Construction	steel chassis frame	steel chassis frame	steel chassis frame
Front suspension	independent suspension	independent suspension	independent suspension
	transverse spring	transverse spring	transverse spring
	friction shock absorbers	Rax friction dampers	Rax friction dampers
Rear suspension	live axle	live axle	live axle
	semi-elliptic springs	semi-elliptic springs	semi-elliptic springs
	friction dampers	Rax friction dampers	Rax friction dampers
Front brakes	drums, mechanical operation	drums, mechanical operation	drums, mechanical operation (Bendix)
Rear brakes	drums, mechanical operation	drums, mechanical operation	drums, mechanical operation (Bendix)
Steering	worm and nut	worm and nut	worm and nut
DIMENSIONS			
Wheelbase	315 cm	270 cm	270 cm
Front track	146 cm	135 cm	138 cm
Rear track	146 cm	136.5 cm	136 cm
Weight		1060 kg	1060 kg
Front tyres	5.50 × 17	6.00 × 18	6.00 × 18
Rear tyres	5.50 × 17	6.50 × 18	6.50 × 18
Max speed	180 km/h	225 km/h (230 version Tripoli)	230 km/h
PRODUCTION	5 built	4 built	1937 and 1938 models
Where to see		Musée de Villiers-en-Lieu	
		Musée du Gérier	

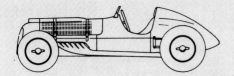 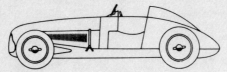 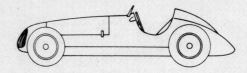

DELAHAYE 155 1938 Sté des Autos Delahaye (Paris)	DELAHAYE 135 MS 1946–7 Sté des Autos Delahaye (Paris)	DELAHAYE 175 1948 Sté des Autos Delahaye (Paris)	**MAKE** Type Year Maker
DELAHAYE 145 60° V12 4490 cc 75 × 84.7 mm 235 bhp at 5000 rpm 8.5 to 1 1 central, 2 side camshafts 2 valves per cyl 3 twin-choke Strombergs 7 bearings water	DELAHAYE 135 6 cyls in line 3557 cc 84 × 107 mm 152 bhp at 4300 rpm 1 side camshaft 2 valves per cyl 3 twin-choke Solex 4 bearings water	DELAHAYE 175 6 cyls in line 4455 cc 94 × 107 mm 200 bhp at 4350 rpm 1 side camshaft 2 valves per cyl 3 twin-choke Solex 4 bearings water	**ENGINE** Cylinders Capacity Bore × stroke Max power Comp ratio Valve gear Carburation Crankshaft Cooling
shaft drive to rear wheels 4 speeds Cotal electromagnetic dry multi-disc	shaft drive to rear wheels 4 speeds Cotal electromagnetic single dry plate	shaft drive to rear wheels 4 speeds Cotal electromagnetic twin dry plate	**TRANSMISSION** Type Gearbox Clutch
steel chassis frame independent suspension transverse spring Rax friction dampers de Dion axle transverse spring Rax friction dampers drums, mechanical operation drums, mechanical operation worm and nut	steel chassis frame independent suspension transverse spring dampers live axle semi-elliptic springs dampers drums, mechanical operation drums, mechanical operation worm and nut	steel chassis frame independent suspension transverse spring Haudaille hydraulic dampers live axle semi-elliptic springs Haudaille hydraulic dampers drums, hydraulic operation drums, hydraulic operation worm and nut	**CHASSIS** Construction Front suspension Rear suspension Front brakes Rear brakes Steering
270 cm 138 cm 136 cm 860 kg 250 km/h	270 cm 134.5 cm 137 cm 900 kg 6.00 × 17 6.00 × 17 185 km/h	270 cm 195 km/h	**DIMENSIONS** Wheelbase Front track Rear track Weight Front tyres Rear tyres Max speed
1 built	20 built (in 1936–9)	1 built	**PRODUCTION** Where to see

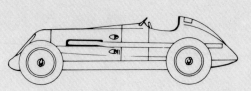 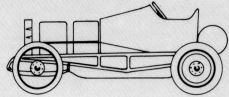 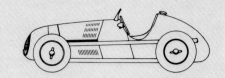

	DOMMARTIN	GOBRON-BRILLIÉ	GORDINI
MAKE	**DOMMARTIN**	**GOBRON-BRILLIÉ**	**GORDINI**
Type	EP 88		
Year	1948	1906–7	1952
Maker	Compagnie des Moteurs Dommartin	Sté Gobron-Brillié (Boulogne s/Seine)	Automobiles Gordini (Paris)
ENGINE	DOMMARTIN	GOBRON-BRILLIÉ	GORDINI
Cylinders	2 × 4 cyls in line	4 paired cyls in line	6 cyls in line
Capacity	3619 cc	13 546 cc	1988 cc
Bore × stroke	80 × 90 mm	140 × 220 mm	75 × 75 mm
Max power	200 bhp at 6500 rpm	110 bhp at 1200 rpm	155 bhp at 6000 rpm
Comp ratio			
Valve gear	4 overhead camshafts	1 side camshaft	twin overhead camshafts
	2 valves, semi-desmo	side valves	2 valves per cyl
Carburation		1 carburettor	3 twin-choke Webers, 38 mm
Crankshaft			
Cooling	water	water	water
TRANSMISSION			
Type	shaft drive to rear wheels	chain drive to rear wheels	shaft drive to rear wheels
Gearbox	4 speeds Cotal electromagnetic	4 speeds	5 speeds
Clutch	dry multi-disc	Hérisson segments	single dry plate
CHASSIS			
Construction	steel chassis frame	tubular section steel	tubular ladder frame
Front suspension	independent suspension	rigid axle	independent suspension
	coil springs	semi-elliptic springs	torsion bars
	hydraulic dampers	friction shock absorbers	hydraulic dampers
Rear suspension	live axle	dead axle	live axle
	coil springs	semi-elliptic springs	torsion bars
	hydraulic dampers	friction shock absorbers	hydraulic dampers
Front brakes	drums, hydraulic operation		drums, hydraulic operation
Rear brakes	drums, hydraulic operation	drums, mechanical operation	drums, hydraulic operation
Steering	worm and sector	worm	worm and finger
DIMENSIONS			
Wheelbase	275 cm	300 cm	230 cm
Front track	140 cm	140 cm	140 cm
Rear track	126 cm	140 cm	140 cm
Weight	920 kg	1000 kg	450 kg
Front tyres			Englebert 5.50 × 15
Rear tyres			Englebert 6.00 × 15
Max speed	220 km/h	160 km/h	250 km/h
PRODUCTION	1 built	1 built	3 built
Where to see	Musée de Chatellerault		Fondation Schlumpf

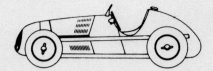 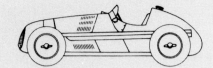 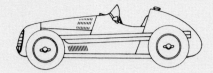

GORDINI	GORDINI	GORDINI	MAKE
1953	1954	1955–6	Type / Year
Automobiles Gordini (Paris)	Automobiles Gordini (Paris)	Automobiles Gordini (Paris)	Maker
GORDINI 6 cyls in line 1988 cc 75 × 75 mm 160 bhp twin overhead camshafts 2 valves per cyl 3 twin-choke Webers water	GORDINI 6 cyls in line 2473 cc 80 × 82 mm 220 bhp at 6000 rpm twin overhead camshafts 2 valves per cyl 3 carburettors water	GORDINI 6 cyls in line 2473 cc 80 × 82 mm 230 bhp at 6500 rpm twin overhead camshafts 2 valves per cyl 3 carburettors water	ENGINE Cylinders Capacity Bore × stroke Max power Comp ratio Valve gear Carburation Crankshaft Cooling
shaft drive to rear wheels 5 speeds single dry plate	shaft drive to rear wheels 4 or 5 speeds single dry plate	shaft drive to rear wheels 4 speeds single dry plate	TRANSMISSION Type Gearbox Clutch
tubular ladder frame independent suspension torsion bars hydraulic dampers live axle torsion bars hydraulic dampers drums, hydraulic operation drums, hydraulic operation worm and finger	tubular ladder frame independent suspension torsion bars Messier hydraulic dampers live axle torsion bars Messier hydraulic dampers drums, hydraulic operation drums, hydraulic operation worm and finger	tubular ladder frame independent suspension torsion bars Messier hydraulic dampers live axle torsion bars Messier hydraulic dampers Messier discs Messier discs worm and finger	CHASSIS Construction Front suspension Rear suspension Front brakes Rear brakes Steering
230 cm 140 cm 140 cm 450 kg Englebert 5.50 × 15 Englebert 6.00 × 15 250 km/h	230 cm 140 cm 140 cm 560 kg Englebert 260 km/h	230 cm 140 cm 140 cm 560 kg Englebert 260 km/h	DIMENSIONS Wheelbase Front track Rear track Weight Front tyres Rear tyres Max speed
	Musée Henri Malartre (La Rochetaillée) Fondation Schlumpf		PRODUCTION Where to see

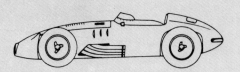

MAKE	GORDINI	GORDINI	GRÉGOIRE
Type	Type 32	Type 32	
Year	1955	1956	1906
Maker	Automobiles Gordini (Paris)	Automobiles Gordini (Paris)	Grégoire et Cie (Poissy)
ENGINE	GORDINI	GORDINI	GRÉGOIRE
Cylinders	8 cyls in line	8 cyls in line	4 paired cyls in line
Capacity	2474 cc	2474 cc	7433 cc
Bore × stroke	75 × 70 mm	75 × 70 mm	130 × 140 mm
Max power	256 bhp at 7300 rpm (230 actual)		70 bhp at 1200 rpm
Comp ratio	12.5 to 1		
Valve gear	twin overhead camshafts	twin overhead camshafts	1 side camshaft
	2 valves per cyl	2 valves per cyl	2 OHV per cyl
Carburation	4 twin-choke Webers	4 twin-choke Webers	1 Grégoire carburettor
Crankshaft			
Cooling	water	water	water
TRANSMISSION			
Type	shaft drive to rear wheels	shaft drive to rear wheels	shaft drive to rear wheels
Gearbox	5 speeds	5 speeds	3 speeds
Clutch			cone
CHASSIS			
Construction	tubular ladder frame	tubular ladder frame	channel section steel
Front suspension	independent suspension	independent suspension	rigid axle
	torsion bars	torsion bars	semi-elliptic springs
	Messier hydraulic dampers	Messier hydraulic dampers	friction shock absorbers
Rear suspension	independent suspension	independent suspension	live axle
	torsion bars	torsion bars	semi-elliptic springs
	Messier hydraulic dampers	Messier hydraulic dampers	friction shock absorbers
Front brakes	Messier discs	Messier discs	
Rear brakes	Messier discs	Messier discs	drums, mechanical operation
Steering			worm
DIMENSIONS			
Wheelbase	230 cm	230 cm	225 cm
Front track	126 cm	126 cm	120 cm
Rear track	121.6 cm	121.6 cm	120 cm
Weight	650 kg	650 kg	750 kg
Front tyres	Englebert 5.50 × 16	Englebert 5.50 × 16	810 × 90
Rear tyres	Englebert 7.00 × 16	Englebert 7.00 × 16	880 × 120
Max speed	270 km/h	270 km/h	140 km/h
PRODUCTION	1 built	1 built	2 built
Where to see	Fondation Schlumpf (chassis no. 41)	Fondation Schlumpf (chassis no. 42)	

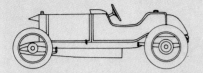 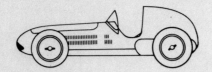 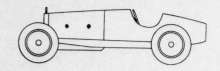

GRÉGOIRE	GUÉRIN	GUYOT SPÉCIALE	MAKE
1912	De Coucy	GS 25	Type
Grégoire et Cie (Poissy)	1946	1925	Year
	Automobiles Guérin	Albert Guyot (Levallois-Perret)	Maker
GRÉGOIRE	**DE COUCY**	**BURT McCOLLUM**	**ENGINE**
4 paired cyls in line	8 cyls in line	6 cyls in line	Cylinders
2980 cc or 2995 cc	1487 cc	1986 cc	Capacity
78 × 156 mm 80 × 149 mm	59 × 68 mm	70 × 86 mm	Bore × stroke
	255 bhp at 8200 rpm	125 bhp at 5500 rpm	Max power
			Comp ratio
2 or 1 side camshafts	twin overhead camshafts	single sleeve valves	Valve gear
4 horizontal or 2 OHV	2 valves per cyl		
1 Zenith carburettor	1 carburettor	1 Cozette carburettor	Carburation
	2 stage supercharging	Cozette supercharger	
		7 bearings	Crankshaft
water	water	water	Cooling
shaft drive to rear wheels	shaft drive to rear wheels	shaft drive to rear wheels	**TRANSMISSION** Type
6 speeds	5 speeds	4 speeds	Gearbox
cone		multi-disc	Clutch
channel section steel		channel section steel	**CHASSIS** Construction
rigid axle	independent suspension	rigid axle	Front suspension
semi-elliptic springs		semi-elliptic springs	
friction shock absorbers		friction shock absorbers	
Live axle	independent suspension	live axle	Rear suspension
semi-elliptic springs		semi-elliptic springs	
friction shock absorbers		friction shock absorbers	
	drums, hydraulic operation	drums, mechanical servo	Front brakes
drums, mechanical operation	drums, hydraulic operation	drums, mechanical operation	Rear brakes
worm			Steering
		250 cm	**DIMENSIONS** Wheelbase
		120 cm	Front track
		120 cm	Rear track
		700 kg	Weight
875 × 105	Dunlop 5.25 × 17	4.75 × 28	Front tyres
875 × 105	Dunlop 6.50 × 16	4.75 × 28	Rear tyres
		180 km/h	Max speed
4 built	1 built		**PRODUCTION** Where to see

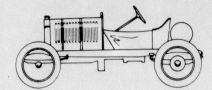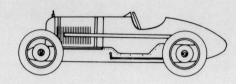

MAKE Type Year Maker	HISPANO-SUIZA 1912 Hispano-Suiza SA (Levallois)	HOTCHKISS HH 1906 Ets Hotchkiss (Saint-Denis)	JEAN GRAF Special 1925–6 Jean Graf
ENGINE Cylinders Capacity Bore × stroke Max power Comp ratio Valve gear Carburation Crankshaft Cooling	HISPANO-SUIZA 4 cyls in line 2996 cc 85 × 132 mm 100 bhp approx 1 overhead camshaft 2 valves per cyl 1 Hispano carburettor experimental supercharger water	HOTCHKISS 4 paired cyls in line 16 277 cc 180 × 160 mm 125 bhp at 1150 rpm 1 side camshaft side valves 1 carburettor 5 ball bearings water	LA PERLE 6 cyls in line 1493 cc 60 × 88 mm 65 bhp at 4300 rpm 1 overhead camshaft 2 valves per cyl 2 Solex carburettors 4 bearings water
TRANSMISSION Type Gearbox Clutch	shaft drive to rear wheels multi-disc	shaft drive to rear wheels 4 speeds cone	shaft drive to rear wheels
CHASSIS Construction Front suspension Rear suspension Front brakes Rear brakes Steering	channel section steel rigid axle semi-elliptic springs friction shock absorbers live axle semi-elliptic springs friction shock absorbers drums, mechanical operation worm	channel section steel rigid axle semi-elliptic springs friction shock absorbers live axle semi-elliptic springs friction shock absorbers drums, mechanical operation worm	channel section steel rigid axle semi-elliptic springs friction shock absorbers live axle semi-elliptic springs friction shock absorbers drums, mechanical operation drums, mechanical operation
DIMENSIONS Wheelbase Front track Rear track Weight Front tyres Rear tyres Max speed		265 cm 145 cm 145 cm 1000 kg 160 km/h	265 cm 125 cm 125 cm 150 km/h
PRODUCTION Where to see		3 built	1 built

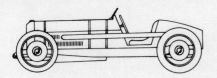

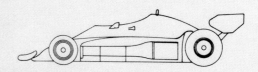

LA PERLE	LIGIER-GITANES	LIGIER-GITANES	MAKE
Six	JS 5	JS 7	Type
1930	1976	1977–8	Year
La Perle (Boulogne sur Seine)	Automobiles Ligier (Vichy)	Automobiles Ligier (Vichy)	Maker
LA PERLE	MATRA MS 73	MATRA MS 76	**ENGINE**
6 cyls in line	60° V12	60° V12	Cylinders
1493 cc	2993 cc	2993 cc	Capacity
60 × 80 mm	79.7 × 50 mm	79.7 × 50 mm	Bore × stroke
85 bhp at 4500 rpm	500 bhp at 11 600 rpm	500 bhp at 12 000 rpm	Max power
	11 to 1	11 to 1	Comp ratio
1 overhead camshaft	4 overhead camshafts	4 overhead camshafts	Valve gear
2 valves per cyl	4 valves per cyl	4 valves per cyl	
2 Solex carburettors	Lucas port injection	Lucas port injection	Carburation
Cozette supercharger			
4 bearings	7 bearings	7 bearings	Crankshaft
water	water	water	Cooling
shaft drive to rear wheels	central engine, rear drive	central engine, rear drive	**TRANSMISSION** Type
	5 speeds Hewland TL2-200	5 speeds TL2-200, 6 speeds FGA	Gearbox
	Borg and Beck twin dry plate	Borg and Beck twin dry plate	Clutch
channel section steel	monocoque	monocoque	**CHASSIS** Construction
rigid axle	independent suspension	independent suspension	Front suspension
semi-elliptic springs	inboard coil springs	inboard coil springs	
friction shock absorbers	telescopic dampers	telescopic dampers	
live axle	independent suspension	independent suspension	Rear suspension
semi-elliptic springs	outboard coil springs	outboard coil springs	
friction shock absorbers	telescopic dampers	telescopic dampers	
drums, mechanical operation	Girling discs	Girling discs	Front brakes
drums, mechanical operation	Girling discs	Girling discs	Rear brakes
	rack and pinion	rack and pinion	Steering
265 cm	260.8 cm	260.8 cm or 280 cm	**DIMENSIONS** Wheelbase
120 cm	153.6 cm	153.6 cm or 138 cm	Front track
120 cm	160 cm	160 or 140 cm	Rear track
645 kg	575 kg	575 kg	Weight
	Goodyear, 13 × 10 wheels	Goodyear, 13 × 10 wheels	Front tyres
	Goodyear, 13 × 18 or 19 wheels	Goodyear, 13 × 18 or 19 wheels	Rear tyres
170 km/h	300 km/h	300 km/h	Max speed
1 built	2 built (chassis 01, 02)	3 built (chassis 01, 02, 03)	**PRODUCTION** Where to see

 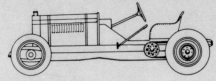 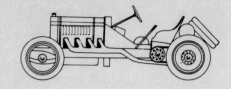

	LION PEUGEOT	LORRAINE-DIETRICH	LORRAINE-DIETRICH
MAKE	**LION PEUGEOT**	**LORRAINE-DIETRICH**	**LORRAINE-DIETRICH**
Type	L3		
Year	1912	1906–7	1908
Maker	Les Fils de Peugeot Frères (Beaulieu)	Anc. Etab. de Dietrich et Cie	Anc. Etab. de Dietrich et Cie
ENGINE	PEUGEOT	LORRAINE-DIETRICH	LORRAINE-DIETRICH
Cylinders	4 cyls in line	4 cyls in line, 2 blocks	4 cyls in line, 2 blocks
Capacity	2980 cc	18146 cc (06) 17304 cc (07)	13586 cc
Bore × stroke	78 × 156 mm	190 × 160 mm 180 × 170 mm	155 × 180 mm
Max power	90 bhp at 2800 rpm	130 bhp at 1100 rpm (07)	115 bhp at 1100 rpm
Comp ratio			
Valve gear	twin overhead camshafts	1 side camshaft	1 side camshaft
	4 valves per cyl	side valves	2 OHV per cyl
Carburation	1 Claudel carburettor	1 carburettor	1 carburettor
Crankshaft	3 bearings		
Cooling	water	water	water
TRANSMISSION			
Type	shaft drive to rear wheels	chain drive to rear wheels	chain drive to rear wheels
Gearbox	4 speeds	4 speeds	4 speeds
Clutch	cone	cone (06), segments (07)	segments
CHASSIS			
Construction	channel section steel	channel section steel	channel section steel
Front suspension	rigid axle	rigid axle	rigid axle
	semi-elliptic springs	semi-elliptic springs	semi-elliptic springs
	friction shock absorbers	friction shock absorbers	friction shock absorbers
Rear suspension	live axle	dead axle	dead axle
	semi-elliptic springs	semi-elliptic springs	semi-elliptic springs
	friction shock absorbers	friction shock absorbers	friction shock absorbers
Front brakes			
Rear brakes	drums, mechanical operation	drums, mechanical operation	drums, mechanical operation
Steering	worm	worm	worm
DIMENSIONS			
Wheelbase	285 cm	295 cm	271 cm
Front track	140 cm	140 cm	137 cm
Rear track	140 cm	140 cm	137 cm
Weight	810 kg	950 kg	1100 kg
Front tyres	810 × 90	Michelin	Michelin 875 × 105
Rear tyres	820 × 120		Michelin 935 × 135
Max speed	150 km/h	170 km/h	165 km/h
PRODUCTION	1 built	3 built	3 built
Where to see			

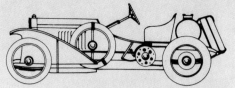
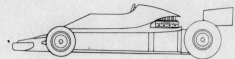
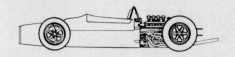

LORRAINE-DIETRICH	MARTINI	MATRA	MAKE
1912 Anc. Etab. de Dietrich et Cie	MK 23 1978 Automobiles Martini (Magny Cours)	MS 9 1968 S.A. Engins Matra (Vélizy)	Type Year Maker
LORRAINE-DIETRICH 4 cyls in line, 2 blocks 15 095 cc 155 × 200 mm 160 bhp 1 side camshaft 2 OHV per cyl 1 carburettor water	FORD COSWORTH DFV 90° V8 2993 cc 85.6 × 64.8 mm 490 bhp at 11 000 rpm 4 overhead camshafts 4 valves per cyl at 32° port injection 5 bearings water	FORD COSWORTH DFV 90° V8 2993 cc 85.6 × 64.8 mm 415 bhp at 9000 rpm 11 to 1 4 overhead camshafts 4 valves per cyl at 32° Lucas port injection 5 bearings water	ENGINE Cylinders Capacity Bore × stroke Max power Comp ratio Valve gear Carburation Crankshaft Cooling
chain drive to rear wheels 4 speeds cone	central engine, rear drive 5 or 6 speeds, Hewland FGA Borg & Beck twin plate	central engine, rear drive 5 speeds Hewland DG 300 Borg & Beck twin plate	TRANSMISSION Type Gearbox Clutch
channel section steel rigid axle semi-elliptic springs friction shock absorbers dead axle semi-elliptic springs friction shock absorbers drums, mechanical operation worm	monocoque independent suspension inboard coil springs Koni telescopic dampers independent suspension outboard coil springs Koni telescopic dampers Lockheed discs Lockheed discs rack and pinion	monocoque independent suspension inboard coil springs telescopic dampers independent suspension outboard coil springs telescopic dampers Girling discs Girling discs rack and pinion	CHASSIS Construction Front suspension Rear suspension Front brakes Rear brakes Steering
875 × 105 880 × 120	267 cm 154 cm 150 cm 600 kg Goodyear 9.5/20 × 13 Goodyear 16.2/26.0 × 13 300 km/h	242 cm 142 cm 148 cm 540 kg Dunlop, 15 × 9 wheels Dunlop, 15 × 11 wheels 270 km/h	DIMENSIONS Wheelbase Front track Rear track Weight Front tyres Rear tyres Max speed
		1 built Musée Raffaëlli (Le Castellet)	PRODUCTION Where to see

MAKE Type Year Maker	**MATRA** MS 10 1968 S.A. Engins Matra (Vélizy)	**MATRA** MS 11 1968 S.A. Engins Matra (Vélizy)	**MATRA** MS 80 1969 S.A. Engins Matra (Vélizy)
ENGINE Cylinders Capacity Bore × stroke Max power Comp ratio Valve gear Carburation Crankshaft Cooling	FORD COSWORTH DFV 90° V8 2993 cc 85.6 × 64.8 mm 415 bhp at 9000 rpm 11 to 1 4 overhead camshafts 4 valves per cyl at 32° Lucas port injection 5 bearings water	MATRA MS 9 60° V12 2993 cc 79.7 × 50 mm 390 bhp at 10 500 rpm 11 to 1 4 overhead camshafts 4 valves per cyl at 55.6° Lucas port injection 7 bearings water	FORD COSWORTH DFV 90° V8 2993 cc 85.6 × 64.8 mm 430 bhp at 9500 rpm 11 to 1 4 overhead camshafts 4 valves per cyl at 32° Lucas port injection 5 bearings water
TRANSMISSION Type Gearbox Clutch	central engine, rear drive 5 speeds Hewland FG 400 Borg and Beck twin plate	central engine, rear drive 5 speeds Hewland DG 300 Borg and Beck twin plate	central engine, rear drive 5 speeds Hewland DG 300 Borg and Beck twin plate
CHASSIS Construction Front suspension Rear suspension Front brakes Rear brakes Steering	monocoque independent suspension inboard coil springs telescopic dampers independent suspension outboard coil springs telescopic dampers Girling discs Girling discs rack and pinion	monocoque independent suspension inboard coil springs telescopic dampers independent suspension outboard coil springs telescopic dampers Girling discs Girling discs rack and pinion	monocoque independent suspension external coil springs, wishbones telescopic dampers independent suspension outboard coil springs telescopic dampers Girling discs Girling discs rack and pinion
DIMENSIONS Wheelbase Front track Rear track Weight Front tyres Rear tyres Max speed	242 cm 143 cm 148 cm 560 kg Dunlop 450/1 160 × 15 Dunlop 550/1 360 × 15 280 km/h	242 cm 143 cm 148 cm 610 kg Dunlop, 15 × 9 or 10 wheels Dunlop, 15 × 11, 12, or 13 wheels 280 km/h	240 cm 160 cm 160 cm 550 kg Dunlop, 13 × 9, 10, or 11 wheels Dunlop, 15 × 11, 15 or 17 wheels 285 km/h
PRODUCTION Where to see	2 built (chassis 01, 02) Musée Raffaëlli (Le Castellet)	3 built (chassis 01, 02, 03) Musée Raffaëlli (Le Castellet)	2 built (01, 02 + spare) Musée Raffaëlli (Le Castellet) Collection Matra

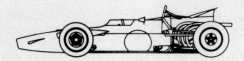 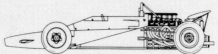 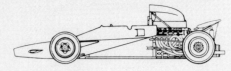

MATRA MS 84 1969 S.A. Engins Matra (Vélizy)	MATRA-SIMCA MS 120 1970 S.A. Engins Matra (Vélizy)	MATRA-SIMCA MS 120 B 1971 S.A. Engins Matra (Vélizy)	MAKE Type Year Maker
FORD COSWORTH DFV 90° V8 2993 cc 85.6 × 64.8 mm 430 bhp at 9500 rpm 11 to 1 4 overhead camshafts 4 valves per cyl at 32° Lucas port injection 5 bearings water	MATRA MS 12 60° V12 2993 cc 79.7 × 50 mm 435 bhp at 11 000 rpm 11 to 1 4 overhead camshafts 4 valves per cyl at 33.3° Lucas port injection 7 bearings water	MATRA MS 12 (MS 71 after Sept) 60° V12 2993 cc 79.7 × 50 mm 440 bhp at 11 000 rpm 4 overhead camshafts 4 valves per cyl at 33.3° Lucas port injection 7 bearings water	ENGINE Cylinders Capacity Bore × stroke Max power Comp ratio Valve gear Carburation Crankshaft Cooling
4 wheel drive (Ferguson) 5 speeds Hewland DG 300 dry twin-plate	central engine, rear drive 5 speeds Hewland FG 400 dry twin-plate	central engine, rear drive 5 speeds dry twin-plate	TRANSMISSION Type Gearbox Clutch
multi-tubular independent suspension coil springs, wishbones telescopic dampers independent suspension outboard coil springs telescopic dampers Girling discs Girling discs rack and pinion	monocoque independent suspension coil springs, wishbones telescopic dampers independent suspension outboard coil springs telescopic dampers Girling discs Girling discs rack and pinion	monocoque independent suspension coil springs, wishbones telescopic dampers independent suspension outboard coil springs telescopic dampers Girling discs Girling discs rack and pinion	CHASSIS Construction Front suspension Rear suspension Front brakes Rear brakes Steering
248 cm 160 cm 164 cm 600 kg Dunlop, 15 × 9, 11, or 12 wheels Dunlop, 15 × 11, 15, or 17 wheels 285 km/h	250 cm 164 cm 160 cm or 170 cm 560 kg Goodyear, 13 × 9, 10, or 11 wheels Goodyear, 13 or 15 × 13, 15, 16, or 17 wheels	250 cm 164 cm 160 cm or 170 cm 560 kg Goodyear Goodyear 285 km/h	DIMENSIONS Wheelbase Front track Rear track Weight Front tyres Rear tyres Max speed
1 built (dismantled)	3 built (chassis 01, 02, 03) Collection Jean-Pierre Beltoise	3 built (chassis 04, 05, 06) Musée Raffaëlli	PRODUCTION Where to see

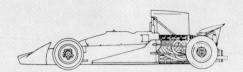 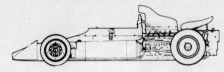 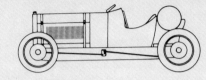

	MATRA-SIMCA	MATRA-SIMCA	MONTIER
MAKE			
Type	MS 120 C	MS 120 D	
Year	1972	1972	1930
Maker	S.A. Engins Matra (Vélizy)	S.A. Engins Matra (Vélizy)	Charles Montier et Cie (Levallois-Perret)
ENGINE	MATRA MS 71	MATRA MS 72	FORD MODEL A
Cylinders	60° V12	60° V12	4 cyl in line
Capacity	2993 cc	2993 cc	3282 cc
Bore × stroke	79.9 × 50 mm	79.7 × 50 mm	98.4 × 107.9 mm
Max power	450 bhp at 11 500 rpm	480 bhp at 11 800 rpm	
Comp ratio	11 to 1		
Valve gear	4 overhead camshafts	4 overhead camshafts	1 side camshaft
	4 valves per cyl at 31.2°	4 valves per cyl at 31.2°	side valves
Carburation	Lucas port injection	Lucas port injection	1 carburettor 36 mm
Crankshaft	7 bearings	7 bearings	3 bearings
Cooling	water	water	water
TRANSMISSION			
Type	central engine, rear drive	central engine, rear drive	shaft drive to rear wheels
Gearbox	5 speeds Hewland FG 400	5 speeds Hewland FG 400	3 speeds
Clutch	Borg & Beck twin-plate	Borg & Beck twin-plate	single dry plate
CHASSIS			
Construction	monocoque	monocoque	channel section steel
Front suspension	independent suspension	independent suspension	rigid axle
	outboard coil springs, wishbones	outboard coil springs, wishbones	transverse spring
	telescopic dampers	telescopic dampers	hydraulic dampers
Rear suspension	independent suspension	independent suspension	live axle
	outboard coil springs	outboard coil springs	transverse spring
	telescopic dampers	telescopic dampers	hydraulic dampers
Front brakes	Girling discs	discs, hydraulic operation	drums, mechanical operation
Rear brakes	Girling discs	discs, hydraulic operation	drums, mechanical operation
Steering	rack and pinion	rack and pinion	worm and sector
DIMENSIONS			
Wheelbase	250 cm	250 cm	263 cm
Front track	164 cm	164 cm	142 cm
Rear track	160 cm or 170 cm	160 cm or 170 cm	142 cm
Weight	560 kg	560 kg	
Front tyres	Goodyear, 13 × 9, 10, or 11 wheels	Goodyear, 13 × 10 or 11 wheels	4.75 × 19
Rear tyres	Goodyear, 13 or 15 × 13, 15, 16, or 17 wheels	Goodyear, 13 × 15 or 17 wheels	4.75 × 19
Max speed	285 km/h	290 km/h	
PRODUCTION	2 (chassis 120 B 05, 06 rebuilt)	1 built (chassis 07)	2 built
Where to see	Musée Rafaëlli (05, 06)	Collection Matra	

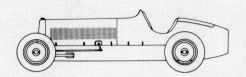 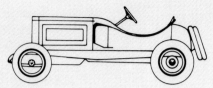 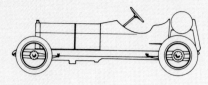

MONTIER	MORS	MOTOBLOC	MAKE
			Type
1933	1908	1907	Year
Charles Montier et Cie (Levallois-Perret)	Soc. des Automobiles Mors (Paris)	Automobile Motobloc (Bordeaux)	Maker
FORD	MORS	MOTOBLOC	**ENGINE**
2 × 4 cyl in line	4 cyl in line, 2 blocks	4 cyl in line, 2 blocks	Cylinders
4072 cc	12 824 cc	11 974 cc	Capacity
77.5 × 107.9 mm	155 × 170 mm	180 × 150 mm	Bore × stroke
	120 bhp at 1400 rpm		Max power
			Comp ratio
2 × 1 side camshaft	1 side camshaft		Valve gear
side valves	2 OHV per cyl		
2 carburettors	1 carburettor	1 carburettor	Carburation
2 × 3 bearings			Crankshaft
water	water	water	Cooling
shaft drive to rear wheels	chain drive to rear wheels	chain drive to rear wheels	**TRANSMISSION** Type
3 speeds	3 speeds	4 speeds	Gearbox
single dry plate	cone	segments	Clutch
channel section steel	channel section steel	channel section steel	**CHASSIS** Construction
rigid axle	rigid axle	rigid axle	Front suspension
transverse spring	semi-elliptic springs	semi-elliptic springs	
hydraulic dampers	friction shock absorbers	friction shock absorbers	
live axle	dead axle	dead axle	Rear suspension
transverse spring	semi-elliptic springs	semi-elliptic springs	
hydraulic dampers	friction shock absorbers	friction shock absorbers	
drums, mechanical operation			Front brakes
drums, mechanical operation	drums, mechanical operation	drums, mechanical operation	Rear brakes
worm and sector	worm	worm	Steering
	263 cm	278 cm	**DIMENSIONS** Wheelbase
	126 cm	130 cm	Front track
	126 cm	130 cm	Rear track
	1100 kg	1000 kg	Weight
	815 × 105		Front tyres
	895 × 135		Rear tyres
180 km/h			Max speed
1 built	3 built	3 built	**PRODUCTION** Where to see

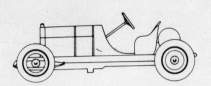
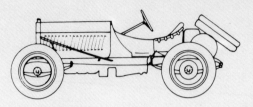
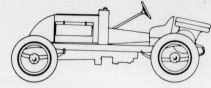

MAKE Type Year Maker	**MOTOBLOC** 1908 Automobiles Motobloc (Bordeaux)	**PANHARD & LEVASSOR** 1906 Anc. Ets. Panhard et Levassor (Paris)	**PANHARD & LEVASSOR** 1907 Anc. Ets Panhard et Levassor (Paris)
ENGINE Cylinders Capacity Bore × stroke Max power Comp ratio Valve gear Carburation Crankshaft Cooling	MOTOBLOC 4 cyl in line, 2 blocks 12 824 cc 155 × 170 mm 1 side camshaft 2 OHV per cyl 1 carburettor water	PANHARD ET LEVASSOR 4 separate cyl in line 18 269 cc 185 × 170 mm 130 bhp at 1100 rpm 2 side camshafts side valves, T heads 1 carburettor water	PANHARD ET LEVASSOR 4 separate cyl in line 15 427 cc 170 × 170 mm 110 bhp at 1100 rpm 2 side camshafts side valves, T heads 1 Krebs carburettor water
TRANSMISSION Type Gearbox Clutch	chain drive to rear wheels 4 speeds segments	shaft drive to rear wheels 4 speeds multi-disc	shaft drive to rear wheels 4 speeds multi-disc
CHASSIS Construction Front suspension Rear suspension Front brakes Rear brakes Steering	channel section steel rigid axle semi-elliptic springs friction shock absorbers dead axle semi-elliptic springs friction shock absorbers drums, mechanical operation worm	channel section steel rigid axle semi-elliptic springs friction shock absorbers live axle semi-elliptic springs friction shock absorbers drums, mechanical operation worm	channel section steel rigid axle semi-elliptic springs friction shock absorbers live axle semi-elliptic springs friction shock absorbers drums, mechanical operation worm
DIMENSIONS Wheelbase Front track Rear track Weight Front tyres Rear tyres Max speed	264 cm 130 cm 130 cm 1225 kg 870 × 90 880 × 120	285 cm 140 cm 140 cm 1005 kg	265 cm 130 cm 130 cm 1050 kg 870 × 90 880 × 120
PRODUCTION Where to see	3 built	3 built	3 built

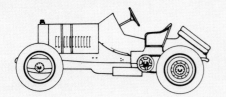 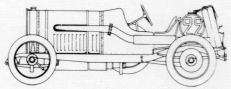 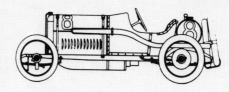

PANHARD & LEVASSOR	PEUGEOT	PEUGEOT	MAKE
1908	L 76	EX 3	Type
	1912	1913	Year
Anc. Ets Panhard et Levassor (Paris)	Auto. et Cycles Peugeot (Beaulieu)	Auto. et Cycles Peugeot (Beaulieu)	Maker
PANHARD ET LEVASSOR	PEUGEOT	PEUGEOT	**ENGINE**
4 separate cyl in line	4 cyl in line	4 cyl in line	Cylinders
12 824 cc	7598 cc	5652 cc	Capacity
155 × 170 mm	110 × 200 mm	100 × 180 mm	Bore × stroke
120 bhp at 1300 rpm	148 bhp at 2200 rpm	115 bhp at 2200 rpm	Max power
			Comp ratio
2 side camshafts	twin overhead camshafts	twin overhead camshafts	Valve gear
side-valves, T heads	4 valves per cyl	4 valves per cyl	
1 updraught Krebs carburettor	1 Claudel carburettor	1 Claudel carburettor	Carburation
5 bearings	5 bearings	5 bearings	Crankshaft
water	water	water	Cooling
chain drive to rear wheels	shaft drive to rear wheels	shaft drive to rear wheels	**TRANSMISSION** Type
4 speeds	4 speeds	4 speeds	Gearbox
multi-discs	multi-discs	multi-discs	Clutch
channel section steel	channel section steel	channel section steel	**CHASSIS** Construction
rigid axle	rigid axle	rigid axle	Front suspension
semi-elliptic springs	semi-elliptic springs	semi-elliptic springs	
friction shock absorbers	Hartford friction shock absorbers	friction shock absorbers	
dead axle	live axle	live axle	Rear suspension
semi-elliptic springs	semi-elliptic springs	semi-elliptic springs	
friction shock absorbers	Hartford friction shock absorbers	friction shock absorbers	
			Front brakes
drums, mechanical operation	drums, mechanical operation	drums, mechanical operation	Rear brakes
worm	worm	worm	Steering
265 cm	295 cm		**DIMENSIONS** Wheelbase
130 cm	135 cm		Front track
130 cm	135 cm		Rear track
1224 kg	1140 kg	1040 kg	Weight
Michelin 880 × 120	Continental 875 × 105	880 × 120	Front tyres
Michelin 895 × 135	Continental 895 × 135	895 × 135	Rear tyres
155 km/h	190 km/h	170 km/h	Max speed
3 built	3 built	3 built	**PRODUCTION**
Fondation Schlumpf			Where to see

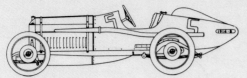 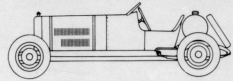 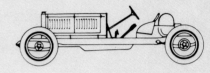

	PEUGEOT	PEUGEOT	PORTHOS
MAKE	**PEUGEOT**	**PEUGEOT**	**PORTHOS**
Type	EX 5	174 S	
Year	1914	1929–30	1907
Maker	Auto. et Cycles Peugeot (Beaulieu)	Automobiles Peugeot (Sochaux)	Automobiles Porthos (Billancourt)
ENGINE	PEUGEOT	PEUGEOT TYPE PC	PORTHOS
Cylinders	4 cyl in line	4 cyl in line	8 cyl in line, 4 blocks
Capacity	4465 cc	3990 cc	9123 cc
Bore × stroke	92 × 168 mm	97 × 135 mm	110 × 120 mm
Max power	112 bhp at 2800 rpm	110 bhp at 3000 rpm	
Comp ratio	5.4 to 1		
Valve gear	twin overhead camshafts		2 side camshafts
	4 valves per cylinder	Knight sleeve valves	side valves, T heads
Carburation	1 Zenith carburettor	1 Zenith carburettor	
Crankshaft	3 bearings	5 bearings	
Cooling	water	water	water
TRANSMISSION			
Type	shaft drive to rear wheels	shaft drive to rear wheels	shaft drive to rear wheels
Gearbox	4 speeds	4 speeds	4 speeds
Clutch	cone	single dry plate	cone
CHASSIS			
Construction	channel section steel	channel section steel	channel section steel
Front suspension	rigid axle	rigid axle	rigid axle
	semi-elliptic springs	semi-elliptic springs	semi-elliptic springs
	friction shock absorbers	friction shock absorbers	friction shock absorbers
Rear suspension	live axle	live axle	live axle
	semi-elliptic springs	semi-elliptic springs	semi-elliptic springs
	friction shock absorbers	friction shock absorbers	friction shock absorbers
Front brakes	drums, mechanical operation	drums, mechanical operation	
Rear brakes	drums, mechanical operation	drums, mechanical operation	drums, mechanical operation
Steering	worm	worm and nut	worm
DIMENSIONS			
Wheelbase	270 cm	327 cm	295 cm
Front track	137 cm	143 cm	135 cm
Rear track	137 cm	143 cm	135 cm
Weight	910 kg	930 kg	850 kg
Front tyres	875 × 105	4.40 × 27	
Rear tyres	880 × 120	4.75 × 28	
Max speed	180 km/h	175 km/h	
PRODUCTION	4 built	6 built	1 built
Where to see			

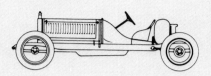 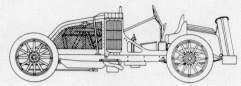 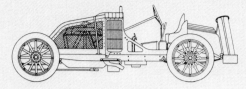

PORTHOS	RENAULT	RENAULT	MAKE
	AK	AK	Type
1908	1906	1907	Year
Automobiles Porthos (Billancourt)	Renault Frères (Billancourt)	Renault Frères (Billancourt)	Maker
PORTHOS	RENAULT	RENAULT	**ENGINE**
6 cyl in line, 3 blocks	4 cyl in line, 2 blocks	4 cyl in line, 2 blocks	Cylinders
9121 cc	12 823 cc	12 823 cc	Capacity
127 × 120 mm	165 × 150 mm	165 × 150 mm	Bore × stroke
	105 bhp at 1200 rpm	105 bhp at 1200 rpm	Max power
	4 to 1	4 to 1	Comp ratio
2 side camshafts	1 side camshaft	1 side camshaft	Valve gear
side valves, T heads	side valves	side valves	
	1 Renault carburettor	1 Renault carburettor	Carburation
			Crankshaft
water	water	water	Cooling
shaft drive to rear wheels	shaft drive to rear wheels	shaft drive to rear wheels	**TRANSMISSION** Type
3 speeds	3 speeds	3 speeds	Gearbox
cone	cone	cone	Clutch
channel section steel	channel section steel	channel section steel	**CHASSIS** Construction
rigid axle	rigid axle	rigid axle	Front suspension
semi-elliptic springs	semi-elliptic springs	semi-elliptic springs	
friction shock absorbers	Renault hydraulic dampers	Renault hydraulic dampers	
live axle	live axle	live axle	Rear suspension
semi-elliptic springs	semi-elliptic springs	semi-elliptic springs	
friction shock absorbers	Renault hydraulic dampers	Renault hydraulic dampers	
			Front brakes
drums, mechanical operation	drums, mechanical operation	drums, mechanical operation	Rear brakes
worm	worm	worm	Steering
270 cm	290 cm	290 cm	**DIMENSIONS** Wheelbase
132 cm	135 cm	135 cm	Front track
132 cm	135 cm	135 cm	Rear track
875 kg	985 kg	985 kg	Weight
875 × 105	Michelin 870 × 90	Michelin 870 × 90	Front tyres
875 × 105	Michelin 880 × 120	Michelin 880 × 120	Rear tyres
	160 km/h	160 km/h	Max speed
3 built	3 built	3 built	**PRODUCTION**
		Museum of Automobiles, Morrilton, Ark., USA	Where to see

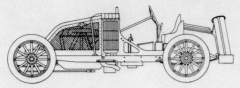  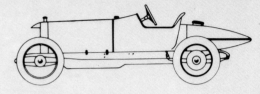

MAKE Type Year Maker	RENAULT AQ 1908 Renault Frères (Billancourt)	RENAULT RS 01 1977 Renault-Sport (Dieppe Viry-Chatillon)	ROLLAND-PILAIN 1912 Sté Rolland-Pilain (Tours)
ENGINE Cylinders Capacity Bore × stroke Max power Comp ratio Valve gear Carburation Crankshaft Cooling	RENAULT 4 cyl in line 12 070 cc 155 × 160 mm 105 bhp at 1800 rpm 1 side camshaft side valves 1 Renault carburettor water	RENAULT-GORDINI EF1 90° V6 1492 cc 86 × 42.8 mm 500 bhp at 11 000 rpm 7 to 1 4 overhead camshafts 4 valves per cylinder Kugelfischer port injection Garrett turbocharger 4 bearings water	ROLLAND-PILAIN 4 cyl in line 6269 cc 110 × 165 mm 1 overhead camshaft 4 valves per cylinder 1 Claudel carburettor water
TRANSMISSION type Gearbox Clutch	shaft drive to rear wheels 3 speeds cone	central engine, rear drive 6 speeds Hewland FGA 400 Borg and Beck twin-plate	chain drive to rear wheels 4 speeds cone
CHASSIS Construction Front suspension Rear suspension Front brakes Rear brakes Steering	channel section steel rigid axle semi-elliptic springs Renault hydraulic dampers live axle semi-elliptic springs Renault hydraulic dampers drums, mechanical operation worm	monocoque independent suspension inboard coil springs telescopic dampers independent suspension outboard coil springs telescopic dampers Lockheed discs Girling discs rack and pinion	channel section steel rigid axle semi-elliptic springs friction shock absorbers dead axle semi-elliptic springs friction shock absorbers drums, mechanical operation worm
DIMENSIONS Wheelbase Front track Rear track Weight Front tyres Rear tyres Max speed	290 cm 135 cm 135 cm 985 kg Michelin 870 × 90 Michelin 935 × 120 160 km/h	250 cm 142.5 cm 152.5 cm 600 kg Michelin, 13 × 11.5 wheels Michelin, 13 × 19.5 wheels 300 km/h	 1350 kg 815 × 105
PRODUCTION Where to see	3 built	3 built	2 built

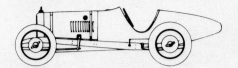
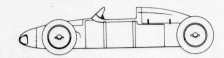

ROLLAND-PILAIN	ROLLAND-PILAIN	SACHA GORDINE	MAKE
			Type
1922	1923	1953	**Year**
Sté Rolland-Pilain (Tours)	Sté Rolland-Pilain (Tours)	Sacha Gordine	**Maker**
ROLLAND-PILAIN	ROLLAND-PILAIN	GORDINE	**ENGINE**
8 cyl in line	8 cyl in line	90° V8	**Cylinders**
1982 cc	1982 cc	1970 cc	**Capacity**
59.2 × 90 mm	59.2 × 90 mm	70 × 64 mm	**Bore × stroke**
90 bhp	100 bhp	191 bhp at 8000 rpm	**Max power**
			Comp ratio
twin overhead camshafts	twin overhead camshafts	4 overhead camshafts	**Valve gear**
2 valves per cyl	2 valves per cyl	2 valves per cyl	
2 Cozette carburettors	4 carburettors	4 twin-choke carburettors	**Carburation**
5 roller bearings	5 roller bearings	5 bearings	**Crankshaft**
water	water	water + glycol	**Cooling**
			TRANSMISSION
shaft drive to rear wheels	shaft drive to rear wheels	central engine, rear drive	**Type**
4 speeds	4 speeds	5 speeds	**Gearbox**
single-plate	multi-disc	twin-plate	**Clutch**
			CHASSIS
channel section steel	channel section steel	steel tubular frame	**Construction**
rigid axle	rigid axle	independent suspension	**Front suspension**
semi-elliptic springs	semi-elliptic springs	transverse torsion bars	
friction shock absorbers	friction shock absorbers	friction and hydraulic dampers	
live axle	live axle	de Dion axle	**Rear suspension**
semi-elliptic springs	semi-elliptic springs	longitudinal torsion bars	
friction shock absorbers	friction shock absorbers	friction and hydraulic dampers	
drums, hydraulic operation	drums, hydraulic operation	drums, hydraulic operation	**Front brakes**
drums, hydraulic operation	drums, hydraulic operation	drums, hydraulic operation	**Rear brakes**
		rack and pinion	**Steering**
			DIMENSIONS
250 cm	250 cm	254 cm	**Wheelbase**
125 cm	130 cm	133 cm	**Front track**
115 cm	130 cm	130 cm	**Rear track**
700 kg	820 kg	470 kg	**Weight**
	Pirelli 765 × 105	5.50 × 17	**Front tyres**
	Pirelli 765 × 105	6.00 × 17 or 7.50 × 18	**Rear tyres**
160 km/h	175 km/h	280 km/h (theoretical)	**Max speed**
			PRODUCTION
3 built		1 built	**Where to see**
	Musée Henri Malartre (La Rochetaillée)		

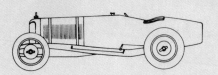
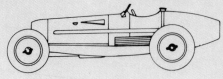
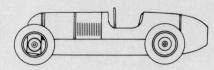

	SCHMID	SEFAC	SIMA-VIOLET
MAKE	**SCHMID**	**SEFAC**	**SIMA-VIOLET**
Type			
Year	1924	1935–9	1926
Maker	Ernest Schmid (Annecy)	Sté d'Et. et de Fab. d'Auto. de Course	Marcel Violet
ENGINE	SCHMID/SRO	SEFAC	SIMA-VIOLET
Cylinders	6 cyl in line	2 × 4 cyl in line	flat 4
Capacity	1978 cc	2771 cc	1484 cc
Bore × stroke	64.8 × 100 mm	70 × 90 mm	75 × 84 mm
Max power	100 bhp at 5000 rpm	250 bhp at 6500 rpm	100 bhp (estimated)
Comp ratio			
Valve gear		4 overhead camshafts	
	cuff valves	2 valves, semi-desmodromic	two-stroke
Carburation	2 twin-choke Zeniths	2 Solex downdraught carbs	2 Solex carburettors
		Petit supercharger	1 supercharger
Crankshaft	2 ball, 2 roller bearings		roller bearings
Cooling	water	water	water
TRANSMISSION			
Type	shaft drive to rear wheels	shaft drive to rear wheels	shaft drive to rear wheels
Gearbox	4 speeds	4 speeds Cotal electromagnetic	4 speeds with rear axle
Clutch	cone	dry multi-disc	multi-disc
CHASSIS			
Construction	channel section steel	channel section steel	central backbone, stressed body
Front suspension	rigid axle	independent suspension	rigid axle
	semi-elliptic springs	coil springs	transverse spring
	friction shock absorbers	dampers	dampers
Rear suspension	live axle	live axle	live axle
	semi-elliptic springs	coil springs	quarter-elliptic springs
	friction shock absorbers	dampers	dampers
Front brakes	drums, mechanical operation	drums, mechanical operation	drums, mechanical operation
Rear brakes	drums, mechanical operation	drums, mechanical operation	drums, mechanical operation
Steering	worm	worm and sector	worm and finger
DIMENSIONS			
Wheelbase	250 cm	270 cm	240 cm
Front track	110 cm	128 cm	130 cm
Rear track	110 cm	128 cm	130 cm
Weight	880 kg	910 kg	700 kg (with 200 kg ballast)
Front tyres		Dunlop	
Rear tyres			
Max speed	180 km/h	240 km/h	140 km/h (unsupercharged)
PRODUCTION	2 built	1 built	1 built
Where to see			

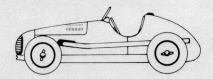 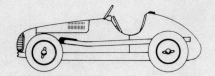 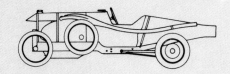

SIMCA GORDINI	SIMCA GORDINI	SIZAIRE & NAUDIN	MAKE
			Type
1950	1951	1912	Year
Automobiles Gordini (Paris)	Automobiles Gordini (Paris)	Sizaire et Naudin (Paris)	Maker
SIMCA	GORDINI	SIZAIRE ET NAUDIN	**ENGINE**
4 cyl in line	4 cyl in line	4 cyl in line	Cylinders
1430 cc	1491 cc	2980 cc	Capacity
	78 × 78 mm	78 × 156 mm	Bore × stroke
100 bhp at 7000 rpm			Max power
			Comp ratio
1 side camshaft	twin overhead camshafts	2 side camshafts	Valve gear
2 OHV per cylinder	2 valves per cyl at 90°	4 horizontal valves per cyl	
2 carburettors	2 carburettors	1 Zenith carburettor	Carburation
Wade supercharger	Wade supercharger		
3 bearings	5 bearings		Crankshaft
water	water	water	Cooling
shaft drive to rear wheels	shaft drive to rear wheels	shaft drive to rear wheels	**TRANSMISSION** Type
4 speeds	5 speeds	4 speeds with differential	Gearbox
single dry plate	single dry plate	single plate	Clutch
tubular ladder frame	tubular ladder frame	channel section steel	**CHASSIS** Construction
independent suspension	independent suspension	independent suspension	Front suspension
coil springs	coil springs	transverse spring	
hydraulic dampers	hydraulic dampers	friction shock absorbers	
live axle	live axle	live axle	Rear suspension
longitudinal torsion bars	longitudinal torsion bars	semi-elliptic springs	
telescopic dampers	telescopic dampers	friction shock absorbers	
drums, hydraulic operation	drums, hydraulic operation		Front brakes
drums, hydraulic operation	drums, hydraulic operation	drums, mechanical operation	Rear brakes
		worm	Steering
225 cm	225 cm		**DIMENSIONS** Wheelbase
112 cm	112 cm		Front track
112 cm	112 cm		Rear track
		1100 kg	Weight
		875 × 105	Front tyres
		820 × 120	Rear tyres
235 km/h	235 km/h		Max speed
		3 built	**PRODUCTION** Where to see

227

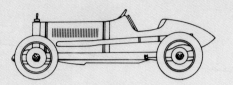 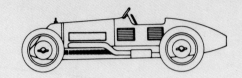 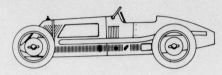

	TALBOT-DARRACQ	TALBOT	TALBOT
MAKE Type Year Maker	1921 Automobiles Talbot (Suresnes)	1926 Automobiles Talbot (Suresnes)	1927 Automobiles Talbot (Suresnes)
ENGINE Cylinders Capacity Bore × stroke Max power Comp ratio Valve gear Carburation Crankshaft Cooling	STD 8 cyl in line 2973 cc 65 × 112 mm 108 bhp at 4000 rpm twin overhead camshafts 4 valves per cyl 4 Zeniths or Claudel-Hobsons 5 plain bearings water	TALBOT 8 cyl in line 1488 cc 56 × 75.5 mm 145 bhp at 6500 rpm twin overhead camshafts 2 valves per cyl 1 Solex carburettor Roots supercharger roller bearings water	TALBOT 8 cyl in line 1488 cc 56 × 75.5 mm 150 bhp at 7000 rpm twin overhead camshafts 2 valves per cyl 1 Solex carburettor Roots supercharger roller bearings water
TRANSMISSION Type Gearbox Clutch	shaft drive to rear wheels 4 speeds multi-disc	shaft drive to rear wheels 4 speeds multi-disc in oil	shaft drive to rear wheels 4 speeds multi-disc in oil
CHASSIS Construction Front suspension Rear suspension Front brakes Rear brakes Steering	channel section steel rigid axle semi-elliptic springs Hartford friction shock absorbers live axle semi-elliptic springs Hartford friction shock absorbers drums, mechanical operation drums, mechanical operation worm	pierced channel section rigid axle semi-elliptic springs friction shock absorbers live axle semi-elliptic springs friction shock absorbers drums, mechanical operation drums, mechanical operation worm	pierced channel section rigid axle semi-elliptic springs friction shock absorbers live axle semi-elliptic springs friction shock absorbers drums, mechanical operation drums, mechanical operation worm
DIMENSIONS Wheelbase Front track Rear track Weight Front tyres Rear tyres Max speed	267 cm 1010 kg 815 × 105 815 × 105 170 km/h	262 cm 127 cm 124 cm 715 kg Dunlop 190 km/h	262 cm 127 cm 124 cm 700 kg Dunlop 200 km/h
PRODUCTION Where to see	2 built		

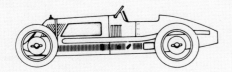 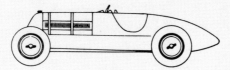 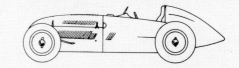

			MAKE
TALBOT 1928–30 Automobiles Talbot (Suresnes)	**TALBOT** Lago Spéciale 1938 Automobiles Talbot (Suresnes)	**TALBOT** Offset 1939 Automobiles Talbot (Suresnes)	**MAKE** Type Year Maker
TALBOT 8 cyl in line 1488 cc 1707 cc 56 × 75.5 mm 60 × 75.5 mm 155 bhp twin overhead camshafts 2 valves per cyl 1 carburettor Roots supercharger roller bearings water	TALBOT 6 cyl in line 4467 cc 92 × 112 mm 1 side camshaft 2 valves per cyl 7 bearings water	TALBOT 6 cyl in line 4434 cc 94 × 106.5 mm 1 side camshaft 2 valves per cyl 7 bearings water	**ENGINE** Cylinders Capacity Bore × stroke Max power Comp ratio Valve gear Carburation Crankshaft Cooling
shaft drive to rear wheels 4 speeds multi-disc in oil	shaft drive to rear wheels 4 speeds Wilson preselector single dry plate	shaft drive to rear wheels 5 speeds Wilson preselector	**TRANSMISSION** Type Gearbox Clutch
pierced channel section rigid axle semi-elliptic springs friction shock absorbers live axle semi-elliptic springs friction shock absorbers drums, mechanical operation drums, mechanical operation worm	steel chassis frame independent suspension transverse spring hydraulic dampers live axle semi-elliptic springs hydraulic dampers drums, mechanical operation drums, mechanical operation worm and nut	steel chassis frame independent suspension transverse spring dampers live axle semi-elliptic springs dampers drums, mechanical operation drums, mechanical operation worm	**CHASSIS** Construction Front suspension Rear suspension Front brakes Rear brakes Steering
262 cm 127 cm 124 cm 700 kg 210 km/h	265 cm 132 cm 132 cm 210 km/h	 240 km/h	**DIMENSIONS** Wheelbase Front track Rear track Weight Front tyres Rear tyres Max speed
	2 built	2 built	**PRODUCTION** Where to see

MAKE	TALBOT	TALBOT	TALBOT-LAGO
Type	single-seater	single-seater	T-26 C
Year	1939	1947	1948
Maker	Automobiles Talbot (Suresnes)	Automobiles Talbot (Suresnes)	Automobiles Talbot (Suresnes)
ENGINE	TALBOT	TALBOT	TALBOT T-26
Cylinders	6 cyl in line	6 cyl in line	6 cyl in line
Capacity	4483 cc	4483 cc	4483 cc
Bore × stroke	93 × 110 mm	93 × 110 mm	93 × 110 mm
Max power	210 bhp at 4500 rpm	220 bhp	240 bhp at 4700 rpm
Comp ratio	10.5 to 1		8 to 1
Valve gear	1 side camshaft	1 side camshaft	2 side camshafts
	2 valves per cyl	2 valves per cyl	2 valves per cyl
Carburation	3 horizontal Zenith-Strombergs	3 horizontal Zenith-Strombergs	3 downdraught Zenith-Strombergs
Crankshaft	7 bearings	7 bearings	7 bearings
Cooling	water	water	water
TRANSMISSION			
Type	shaft drive to rear wheels	shaft drive to rear wheels	shaft drive to rear wheels
Gearbox	4 speeds Wilson preselector	4 speeds Wilson preselector	4 speeds Wilson preselector
Clutch			single dry plate
CHASSIS			
Construction	steel chassis frame	steel chassis frame	steel chassis frame
Front suspension	independent suspension	independent suspension	independent suspension
	transverse spring	transverse spring	transverse spring
	friction and hydraulic dampers	friction and hydraulic dampers	hydraulic dampers
Rear suspension	live axle	live axle	live axle
	semi-elliptic springs	semi-elliptic springs	semi-elliptic springs
	friction and hydraulic dampers	friction and hydraulic dampers	hydraulic dampers
Front brakes	drums, Bendix mechanical	drums, Lockheed hydraulic	drums, Lockheed hydraulic
Rear brakes	drums, Bendix mechanical	drums, Lockheed hydraulic	drums, Lockheed hydraulic
Steering	worm	worm	worm
DIMENSIONS			
Wheelbase			250 cm
Front track			137 cm
Rear track			130 cm
Weight	850 kg	850 kg	915 kg
Front tyres			
Rear tyres			
Max speed	250 km/h	250 km/h	250 km/h
PRODUCTION	1 built	1 built (by rebuilding 1939 model)	6 built
Where			Donington Collection
			Fondation Schlumpf
			Hondayer and Clark Collection

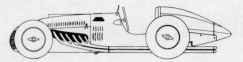  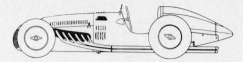

TALBOT-LAGO T-26 C 1949 Automobiles Talbot (Suresnes)	TALBOT-LAGO T-26 C 1950 Automobiles Talbot (Suresnes)	TALBOT-LAGO T-26 C 1951 Automobiles Talbot (Suresnes)	**MAKE** Type Year Maker
TALBOT T-26 6 cyl in line 4483 cc 93 × 110 mm 240 bhp at 4700 rpm 8 to 1 2 side camshafts 2 valves per cyl 3 downdraught Zenith-Strombergs 7 bearings water	TALBOT T-26 6 cyl in line 4483 cc 93 × 110 mm 280 bhp at 5000 rpm 11 to 1 2 side camshafts 2 valves per cyl 3 horizontal Zenith carbs 7 bearings water	TALBOT T-26 6 cyl in line 4483 cc 93 × 110 mm 280 bhp at 5000 rpm 11 to 1 2 side camshafts 2 valves per cyl 3 horizontal Zenith carbs 7 bearings water	**ENGINE** Cylinders Capacity Bore × stroke Max power Comp ratio Valve gear Carburation Crankshaft Cooling
shaft drive to rear wheels 4 speeds Wilson preselector single dry plate	shaft drive to rear wheels 4 speeds Wilson preselector single dry plate	shaft drive to rear wheels 4 speeds Wilson preselector single dry plate	**TRANSMISSION** Type Gearbox Clutch
steel chassis frame independent suspension transverse spring hydraulic dampers live axle semi-elliptic springs hydraulic dampers drums, Lockheed hydraulic drums, Lockheed hydraulic worm	steel chassis frame independent suspension transverse spring hydraulic dampers live axle semi-elliptic springs hydraulic dampers drums, Lockheed hydraulic drums, Lockheed hydraulic worm	steel chassis frame independent suspension transverse spring hydraulic dampers live axle semi-elliptic springs hydraulic dampers drums, Lockheed hydraulic drums, Lockheed hydraulic worm	**CHASSIS** Construction Front suspension Rear suspension Front brakes Rear brakes Steering
250 cm 137 cm 130 cm 915 kg 260 km/h	250 cm 137 cm 130 cm 910 kg 270 km/h	250 cm 137 cm 130 cm 910 kg 270 km/h	**DIMENSIONS** Wheelbase Front track Rear track Weight Front tyres Rear tyres Max speed
	Musée Henri Malartre (La Rochetaillée) Pilkington Collection (chassis 11057)	Briggs Cunningham Automotive Museum, Costa Mesa, Calif., USA (chassis 11005)	**PRODUCTION** Where to see

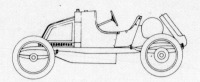 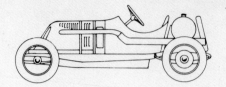 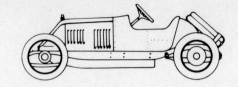

	TH. SCHNEIDER	TH. SCHNEIDER	TH. SCHNEIDER
MAKE **Type** **Year** **Maker**	1912 Théophile Schneider (Besançon)	1913 Théophile Schneider (Besançon)	1914 Théophile Schneider (Besançon)
ENGINE **Cylinders** **Capacity** **Bore × stroke** **Max power** **Comp ratio** **Valve gear** **Carburation** **Crankshaft** **Cooling**	TH. SCHNEIDER 4 cyl in line 2994 cc 2815 cc 80 × 149 mm 80 × 140 mm 1 side camshaft side valves 1 Zenith carburettor water	TH. SCHNEIDER 4 cyl in line 5501 cc 96 × 190 mm 1 side camshaft inclined side valves 1 Claudel carburettor water	TH. SCHNEIDER 4 cyl in line 4439 cc 94 × 160 mm 1 side camshaft inclined side valves 1 Claudel carburettor water
TRANSMISSION **Type** **Gearbox** **Clutch**	shaft drive to rear wheels 4 speeds cone	shaft drive to rear wheels 4 speeds cone	shaft drive to rear wheels 5 speeds cone
CHASSIS **Construction** **Front suspension** **Rear suspension** **Front brakes** **Rear brakes** **Steering**	channel section steel rigid axle semi-elliptic springs friction shock absorbers live axle semi-elliptic springs friction shock absorbers drums, mechanical operation worm	channel section steel rigid axle semi-elliptic springs hydraulic dampers live axle semi-elliptic springs hydraulic shock absorbers drums, mechanical operation worm	channel section steel rigid axle semi-elliptic springs friction shock absorbers live axle semi-elliptic springs friction shock absorbers drums, mechanical operation worm
DIMENSIONS **Wheelbase** **Front track** **Rear track** **Weight** **Front tyres** **Rear tyres** **Max speed**	280 cm 140 cm 140 cm 1150 kg 875 × 105 875 × 105		
PRODUCTION **Where to see**	2 built		

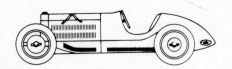 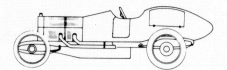 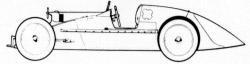

VERNANDI	VINOT-DEGUINGAND	VOISIN	MAKE
			Type
1929	1912	Laboratoire	Year
Vernandi (Garches)	Vinot et Deguingand (Puteaux)	1923	Maker
		Avions Voisin (Issy-les-Moulineaux)	
VERNANDI	VINOT-DEGUINGAND	VOISIN KNIGHT	**ENGINE**
90° V8	4 cyl in line, 2 blocks	6 cyl in line	Cylinders
1481 cc	2984 cc	1992 cc	Capacity
55.7 × 76 mm	89 × 120 mm	62 × 110 mm	Bore × stroke
		80 bhp at 4500 rpm	Max power
		7 to 1	Comp ratio
1 central camshaft	1 side camshaft		Valve gear
2 OHV per cyl	2 valves per cyl, inlet over exhaust	sleeve valves	
2 Solex carburettors	2 Zenith carburettors		Carburation
2 Zoller superchargers			
		3 bearings	Crankshaft
water	water	water	Cooling
shaft drive to rear wheels	shaft drive to rear wheels	shaft drive to rear wheels	**TRANSMISSION** Type
4 speeds	3 speeds	3 speeds	Gearbox
	cone	cone	clutch
channel section steel	channel section steel	monocoque	**CHASSIS** Construction
rigid axle	rigid axle	rigid axle	Front suspension
semi-elliptic springs	semi-elliptic springs	semi-elliptic springs	
dampers	friction shock absorbers	friction shock absorbers	
live axle	live axle	live axle	Rear suspension
semi-elliptic springs	semi-elliptic springs	semi-elliptic springs	
dampers	friction shock absorbers	friction shock absorbers	
drums, mechanical operation		drums, mechanical operation	Front brakes
drums, mechanical operation	drums, mechanical operation	drums, mechanical operation	Rear brakes
	worm		Steering
260 cm		272 cm	**DIMENSIONS** Wheelbase
130 cm		145 cm	Front track
130 cm		75 cm	Rear track
		750 kg	Weight
4.75 × 19	815 × 105		Front tyres
4.75 × 19			Rear tyres
190 km/h		170 km/h	Max speed
1 built	3 built	4 built	**PRODUCTION** Where to see

MAKE Type Year Maker	**VULPÈS** 1906 Automobiles Vulpès (Paris)
ENGINE Cylinders Capacity Bore × stroke Max power Comp ratio Valve gear Carburation Crankshaft Cooling	VULPÈS 4 cyl in line 16 277 cc 180 × 160 mm 120 bhp at 1100 rpm 1 carburettor water
TRANSMISSION Type Gearbox Clutch	 chain drive to rear wheels multi-disc
CHASSIS Construction Front suspension Rear suspension Front brakes Rear brakes Steering	 channel section steel rigid axle semi-elliptic springs friction shock absorbers dead axle semi-elliptic springs friction shock absorbers drums, mechanical operation worm
DIMENSIONS Wheelbase Front track Rear track Weight Front tyres Rear tyres Max speed	 280 cm 144 cm 144 cm over-weight, disqualified
PRODUCTION Where to see	1 built

INDEX

BIBLIOGRAPHY

Histoire mondiale de l'automobile
by Jacques Rousseau and Michel Iatca
A pictorial survey of racing cars 1919–1939
by T.A.S.O. Mathieson (Motor Racing Publications)
The Grand Prix car
by Laurence Pomeroy (Motor Racing Publications)
A history of motor racing
by Giovanni Lurani (Hamlyn)
The Grand Prix
by L. J. K. Setright (Nelson)
Le sport automobile
by Georges-Michel Fraichard (Hachette)
Bugatti, le pur-sang de Molsheim
by Pierre Dumont (Editions E.P.A.)
Motor racing Mavericks
by Doug Nye (Batsford)
A story of Formula one
by Denis Jenkinson (Grenville)
Das grosse Sport und Rennwagenbuch
by Erwin Tragatsch (Hallwag)
Bugatti
by Hugh Conway (Foulis)
Competition cars of Europe
by Anthony Pritchard (Hale)
Magazines: *Fanatique de l'Automobile,
Automobile Quarterly,
L'Auto-Journal, L'Année Automobile*

ACKNOWLEDGEMENTS

The author and publishers wish to thank all those who have
helped in the creation of this book:

René Bonnet
André Binda
Jacques Borgé
Jean-Paul Caron
Amédée Gordini
Jacques Greilsamer
Pierre Lenoir (ACF)
Henri Malartre
Marc Nicolosi
Henri Petiet
Antoine Raffaëlli
Jacques Robert (Régie Renault)

PHOTOGRAPHIC ACKNOWLEDGEMENTS

A.F.P.: 100.

Serge Bellu: 14, 149 (collection Henri Malartre/ville de Lyon, La Rochetaillée-sur-Saône).

Bernard-Cahier: 164.

Jean-Paul Caron: 146 (Briggs Cunningham collection, Costa Mesa, U.S.A.).

Historical Commission of the ACF: 20, 26, 30, 31, 44, 45, 54, 57, 71, 94, 102, 103, 106.

D.P.P.I.: 167, 173, 176, 182.

E.T.A.I.—Grâce: 152.

Fanatique de l'Automobile: 76.

Keystone: 88, 92, 117.

Alberto Martinez/L'Auto-Journal: 151.

Morelli-Berthier: 170, 174, 175.

Jean-Loup Nory: 144, 147 (collection Henri Binda).

Antoine Raffaelli: 156.

M.-L. Rosenthal: 107, 109, 112, 113, 119, 122, 123, 124, 126, 128, 129, 131, 133, 136, 138, 140, 142, 235.

Roger Viollet: 17, 22, 28, 38, 42, 43, 49, 53, 90.

All rights reserved for all other illustrations in this book.

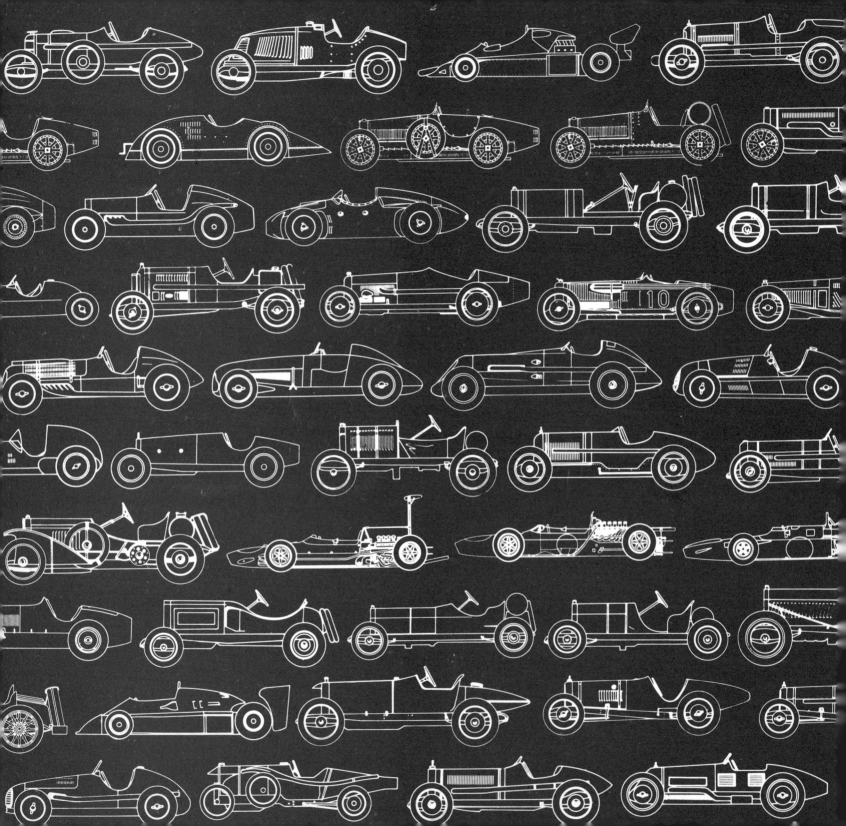